I believe I shall begin cross writing
shewd you a letter I received when
must recollect it if not Wm does —
and all acquaintances (both sexes) — Ed
Royal Ma

Nov. 12. 1802

My D. Sister,

It appears to be conceived th
pleasure I am ... the receipt of your very welcome
letter of the ... which I received this evening — I was
... I was kept in a state of anxiety for the last
three days ... if I had received yours at the
time I had to have written by this evenings post fear
something had happened with you or that it was possible
for my letter to have miscarried, however your reason
is sufficient — I put on the Red Coat for the first time
last Sunday & between Guard mounting & other duties
time has been almost taken up ever since but will
be more easy for the future as Officers are coming
in every day from leave — George Jenkins's brig sailed
before I arrived for Lisbon with Troops therefore t'was
lucky I had not brought his things round, I hope you
have apologized to his parents for my inattention — The
place is remarkably dull since the Peace company
... with the year ... a few Guard Ships, Frigates &c are all

LIEUTENANT JOHN GEORGE
ROYAL MARINES

LETTERS
1799-1808

For my grandson
MAX MASON
Lieutenant R.N.

LIEUTENANT JOHN GEORGE

ROYAL MARINES

LETTERS
1799-1808

Edited by
Dillwyn Miles

Gwasg Dinefwr Press

A CIP catalogue record for this book is
available from the British Library.

ISBN 0 9540569 7 3

Printed and published in Wales by
Gwasg Dinefwr Press Ltd.
Rawlings Road, Llandybie
Carmarthenshire
SA18 3YD

Cover illustration by courtesy of
The Royal Marines Museum.

End papers:
Front: Letter with cross-writing.
Back: John George's last letter.

Contents

Introduction

I first heard of the letters of Lieutenant John George in 1950, that they were missing, and fifty years were to pass before they were found.

The letters were discovered in 1939, in the early days of the war, by Gunner (later His Honour Judge) Charles Neville Pitchford, who was stationed at Haverfordwest with 329 Battery, 83rd Field Regiment, Royal Artillery. 'We were sent to clear a yard and warehouse in Quay Street,' he recalled, 'and on the first floor of the warehouse we found an old trunk out of which spilt some letters.' He gathered as many as he could and took them to his home in Newport, Monmouthshire, where he left them with his father, Mr J. B. Pitchford.

Mr Pitchford was president of the Newport (Monmouthshire) Naturalists' Society and, on February 2nd 1948, he presided at a meeting addressed by the naturalist R. M. Lockley, whom he entertained after the meeting. Mr Lockley recorded in his diary that, 'over a meal at his house', Mr Pitchford had given him 'a bundle of letters to read, written from 1799 to 1814 by John George, Royal Marines.' His son, 'as a soldier quartered in a warehouse at Haverford-west in the war, had picked up the letters which were "leaking" from an old trunk burst open there and saved them from being swept away with other rubbish.' Charles Pitchford was, in fact, billeted in a private house in Haverfordwest which he remembers well as the man of the house had taken him ferreting.

A month later, on March 1st, Mr Lockley recorded that he was 'at Cardiff discussing formation of a Wales Nature Reserve Society with Lord Mayor, Principal Rees and others.' Sir Frederick Rees, the Principal of the University College of Wales, Cardiff, was a native of Milford and Lockley states that he 'showed an interest in the George letters, and asked if he could read them. I agreed but he must return them to Pitchford, who had only allowed me the loan to read.' On August 15th that year, Sir Frederick wrote to Mr Lockley apologising for having 'kept the George letters so long. After the first reading at Easter I set them aside for leisure to go through them the second time,' as they were 'extremely interesting to a Pembrokeshire man.' He would like to see the letters 'in print, with introduction and notes.' In replying to a letter dated September 9th 1971 from Mr Stephen Green of Haverfordwest, enquiring about the letters, Mr Lockley stated that he had 'no record of Rees ever returning them' to him, and assumed 'that he sent them back to Pitchford. I certainly never saw them again.' Mr Green had deposited copies of 17 other letters written by George at the Pembrokeshire Record Office in 1968.

Enquiries I made at the National Library of Wales, the British Museum, the British Library, the Glamorgan Record Office, the Gwent Record Office, the Newport Library and Information Service, the Pembrokeshire Record Office, the Public Record Office, the Royal Commission on Historical Manuscripts, the National Register of Archives, the Royal Naval Museum and the National Maritime Museum brought negative replies, except for the Cardiff Library where 3 letters were found. Regrettably, I only became aware of the existence of the Royal Marines Museum in July 2000 and it was with great delight that I received a reply from the Museum's Archivist, Mr M. G. Little, stating that the letters were at his museum, having been deposited there by Lieutenant-Commander C. J. Gass, RN, in 1986.

Of the 139 letters in this collection, 127 were written by John George to members of the family – 99 to his sister, Mary, 18 to his parents, and 10 to his brother William. In addition, there are 6 letters addressed to George – one each by his brother James writing on board HMS *Lucifer* (121), D. J. McCarthy of HMS *Argo* (108), George Robbin of Haverfordwest on HMS *Canopus* (109), K. Lupton, formerly of HMS *Fisgard*, writing from Stamford (118), B. L. Taylor, on *Fisgard* off Cape Maisi, in the West Indies (121), and J Moull on *Fisgard* at Port Royal (120).

In addition to the letter that George addressed to the Rev. William Cleaveland,[1] I have included one that Lieutenant William Davies wrote on HMS *Spartiate* (112) addressed to his cousin, Mary George, as it is relevant to the correspondence. Two letters that James George had written on HMS *Lucifer*, one to his brother William, dated December 6th 1805, and the other to his father on December 10th 1806, and two letters he had sent from on HMS *Barracouta* to his sister, from the Straits of Sunda, on September 29th 1812, and from the Cape of Good Hope, on June 20th 1814, have been included as Appendix III.

Some of the letters were damaged, or otherwise made indecipherable. They are, in the main, written in a fair hand, but the later ones are less easy to read. Missing and unreadable words and phrases account for the occasional square brackets. The practice of cross-writing, that is, writing at right angles across existing as a means of getting more words on the sheet of paper, in which he and his sister indulged from November 21st 1802 to October 15th 1806, made unscrambling laborious and often impossible.

John George set out from Haverfordwest on a day in January 1799 to join the Marines. He was nineteen years of age, the eldest son of Stephen George of the Blue Boar Inn at Haverfordwest. He had two brothers, William and James, and a sister, Mary, to whom most of the letters are addressed.

When he reached London he went to the Admiralty and appeared before the Sea Lords, who approved of him and gave him 'the satisfaction to say' that he 'was immediately passed'. He was posted to Stone House Barracks at Plymouth, where he found 'it quite lonesome, in a strange place and all strangers,' and he longed for home and old friends. Letters were to be his salvation, and in his first letter to his parents, he begs them to 'write by the first post for the only thing that will give me pleasure is in hearing from you,' and this plea was repeated regularly in his letters. He confesses that his 'greatest pleasure was in writing home,' and that he would write to his family and friends by every post, were it not for the cost of postage. There was a limit to the number of letters that could be franked, and he urges his parents to write as often as they can get franks, informing them that they could 'get 2 or 3 franks or more if they are wanted.'

The letters refer to relatives of the family, such as the Georges of Hook and of Freystrop, and Uncle George in Bristol, while some of the several Mathiases mentioned could be related on the maternal side. Lieutenant William Davies, of HMS *Doris*, is referred to as a cousin. George met him accidentally on the street at Portsmouth (61) and Davies took him to his lodgings to meet his wife, 'a nice little woman & a very fine child.' Davies was about to leave the *Doris* and was waiting to join 'the *Tigress* bomb at Harwich' (64). Davies and his wife became estranged, however, and, from 1802 onward, he spent much of his time at Haverfordwest on half-pay. Mrs Davies was alleged to have been too friendly with a surgeon who stayed at the same house, but George vehemently defends her character until, one day, meeting in Plymouth, when she tried to avoid him, he began 'to suspect the rectitude of her conduct.'

George had an exceptional warmth of feeling towards his sister. 'I could not conceal my sentiments from you, the height of affection that subsists between us is so strong that I should call myself unnatural if I did,' he writes.

He frequently requests that his compliments be conveyed to a Mr Duberlin, among other gentlemen, and his 'respectful love' to young ladies, notably Miss Gould, Miss Fisher, Miss Fields and Miss Davies, sometimes wishes to be remembered 'in short to all my old friends and acquaintances.' He met the young ladies when he was home on leave, and had '*a tête-à-tête*' with them, but he does not appear to have made any further progress. When Miss Gould found another '*beau*', he was upset, and when he heard that Miss Fisher had become Mrs Evans he 'blots her out' of his mind. The reference to Miss Davies going to Ireland to be married and 'was no longer Mrs Edwardes' may hint at a little dalliance. He fancies Miss Jane of Penlan and confesses: 'Was I blessed with a good fortune, I don't know a person I would sooner tender it to than her.' But a Marine Officer, he had already realised, could hardly support himself, let alone a wife.

George was concerned about the future careers of his two brothers. Although he felt that William had 'chosen a Trade', when he learned that he was 'determined to go to sea', he sets out to give him advice and wonders, in vain, whether Lady Kensington 'could procure him a cadetship in India.' (38) William went to sea, presumably as a midshipman, on board the *Nautilus*, sailing to Tobago (64), but after that voyage he appears to have been at home endeavouring to obtain a commission in the Navy through the good offices of Lord Kensington. George maintains that William had 'very great claim over Lord K.' (85) and urges that he be reminded of his 'repeated promises' (93), as he had been informed that his lordship's 'memory required refreshing' (95), but William received nothing but disappointment, despite Lord Kensington's 'flattering promises.' He was a bad-tempered young man and George explains that he felt 'very unpleasant at thinking of the disagreeable disposition of William,' and recalled 'the several disputes they had which would have ended very serious' had he not held his tongue.

James went to sea when he was sixteen years of age, as an apprentice on the merchant navy ship *Britannia*. When he came home, his brother feared, unless he got into the Royal Navy, that he would be 'at the mercy of the Press Gangs'. (87). He returned to sea, however, and his ship passed within hailing distance of *Bellona* off Lisbon. (113) When his apprenticeship was up, his brother warns him again that if he stayed on the *Britannia*, 'pressed he will be for a certainty.' (115) This happened soon after *Britannia* returned to Plymouth, when he was 'pressed in The Downs from *Britannia* of London by the boats of the *Ariadne*.' (116) George wrote to a brother officer on *Ariadne* seeking his help but the result is not known and nothing further is known until the following December when James wrote to his brother William from HMS *Lucifer* off Southwold. In the letter he wrote on September 17th 1806, addressed to 'Lieut. John George, Royal Marines, on board HMS *Surveillante*, Deptford, River Thames (To be forwarded)', he states that he has been 'rated mate' but was desperately short of money and begs him to 'spare a trifle' until he is able to repay him. Three months later he writes to his father offering half his pay, namely, £1.16.0 (£1.80) per month, in repayment of an advance. In the letter written on HMS *Barracouta* in the Straits of Sunda, on September 29th 1812, he states that his brother-in-law, John Green, has given him 'a hint about a little Parsell' which is clearly a reference to his subsequent marriage, in Steynton church in 1815, to Elizabeth Parsell, niece of Walter Parsell of Bunkers Hill, Milford, by whom he had a daughter. He married secondly, in 1830, Anne Baillieu of Hubberston, by whom he also had issue.

He regularly expresses his concern for the family's health and welfare and is distressed to hear of his father's suffering from gout. He enquires about the use being made of the inn's chaise, and wants a report on the state of custom at the bar and of the accounts of certain customers, among them Colonel Edwardes, later the second Baron Kensington, whose bill, by this time, 'must be to a very great amount.'(9)

John George writes very well and it is evident that he had received a good education, most probably at the Haverfordwest Grammar School. The school then stood in Church Lane, adjoining St Thomas's churchyard. A new school was built in 1856 in Dew Street, and the school's biology laboratory was later erected approximately on the site of the Blue Boar, where the Registry Office now stands.

John found pleasure in reading and, soon after he had settled in the barracks, he informs his sister that he was able to borrow books from a library for a small fee, as they had done, no doubt, at Potter's Lending Library in High Street, Haverfordwest. There is no evidence that he was musical beyond his appreciative references to the performance of the regimental band, but he sends sheets of popular music to his brother, James, and promises to send a Mrs George some 'Tongues and Sounds.' He also takes the opportunity of sending Sally Mathias 'a favourite piece of musick which I hope she will make herself perfect in by the time I see her: tho' not acquainted with the Pianoforte hope she will get Miss Jane Jones or some friend to instruct her.'

He is courteous at all times and always addresses people by their proper titles, apart from his close friend John Potter, who was always John Potter, and Sally Mathias for whom he 'hated the formal Miss.' At the same time, he was anxious to preserve his dignity, as became a Marine Officer. When Mr Ellis, originally from Pembrokeshire, called to see him, he states that his 'appearance was such that it would not do for my associating with him . . . Appearances must be kept up, you know.' On the other hand, when he saw Woodcock, the hawker, in the street in Dartmouth, he went up and spoke to him, although Woodcock had not at first recognised him.

The first letter in the collection was written before George left London and is addressed to the Reverend William Cleaveland, rector of St Thomas à Becket Church at Haverfordwest, reporting his success and expressing 'thanks innumerable for the very great kindness you have done in getting the commission for me.' At the same time, he complains to his parents about the costs involved and had he known as much as he did then, he would 'not have joined the Marines, being so expensive.' He had thought, by 'Mr Powell's discourse that a mere trifle would fit one out,' but he could 'see it much now to the contrary,' having been on a shopping expedition, 'accompanied by one of the Clerks of the Admiralty.' He had purchased accoutrements, comprising a sword, plate, gorget, belt, sash, sword knot and epaulets, which had cost him £12.19.6

(£12.97), and 'the expense attending the Commission and Power of Attorney' to his agent had cost him £7. There were also items of uniform, such as a 3-cocked hat, boots, cot bed and bedding, silver cutlery,' and numerous articles too tedious to mention.' His salary was £85 per annum, less 2½% payable as his agent's fee. He had to borrow money and he was in debt from the outset. His only hope for relief lay in the capture of enemy ships for prize money. George was aware of the sacrifice that his parents had made in his upbringing and he was most anxious to impress on them that he lived frugally. He assures his sister, who had also loaned him some money, that he was not 'in the least extravagant' and that there is 'not an officer in all Barracks who lives more upright than what I does' and that he 'never entered into any vice.' (14) He also assures his parents that he will repay them and that his conduct is such that it has met the approval of his General. (15).

His stay in London had been prolonged by having to wait for the King to sign his commission which, in the end, he had to have sent on by his agent. On January 23rd he left by the evening mail for Exeter, where he had to pay an additional 17s.0d. (85p.) to the 'Heavy Coach' for Plymouth, and arrived there 'after a long and fatiguing journey.'

Lieutenant George embarked on HMS *Bellona* on April 24th 1799 on the Hamoaze, the stretch of water between Plymouth and Devonport, and, six days later, the ship received orders to join the Channel Fleet and to proceed to become a part of Admiral the Earl of St Vincent's fleet in the Mediterranean. The French fleet, comprising 25 sail-of-the-line, had recently escaped from Brest and entered the Mediterranean, followed by a Spanish fleet of 17 ships from Cadiz. Admiral Lord Keith pursued them and Nelson was ordered to despatch 10 ships to him at Minorca to assist him while he remained at Palermo to cover the approaches to Malta and Egypt. In August Keith pursued the French and Spanish fleets back through the Straits of Gibraltar, leaving Nelson in command of the Mediterranean fleet.

George kept an account of the cruise from the time they left the Hamoaze until they returned to this country the following August, under the heading 'Remarks made on Board Her Majesty's Ship *Bellona* 1799' (Appendix II). The *Bellona* had joined a squadron under Sir Alan Gardner in Cawsand Bay, in Plymouth Sound, and had reached Cape Ortegal, on the north coast of Spain by May 11th and, by the 16th, they were standing off Lisbon on their way to Gibraltar. They caught up with Lord St Vincent's fleet on June 1st off Toulon and *Îles d'Hyères*, known in Roman times for its lavender. On the 4th they were abreast of Nice and then they sailed past Villefranche-sur-Mer and San Remo, not far from which was 'a lighthouse nearly like the Eddystone,' and San Lorenzo al Mare, and on to Capo Mele.

The Admiral then made a signal to 'bear up for Minorca', off which the *Bellona* was glad to receive thirty hogsheads of wine by launch from the *St Theresa* as a prize. By the 12th they were off Mahòn, the capital of Minorca, which the British had fortified as its principal military and economic base in the Mediterranean at a cost of a million pounds, and where Nelson had a grand house above the harbour, which he occupied during his stay on the island. By the 15th there was 'a plentiful scarcity of fresh stock in the Fleet.' The price of mutton had risen 2000 per cent [*sic*] and so they had to resort to eating sheep's heads and offal. On the 19th, having left Mahòn, the Admiral signalled to give chase and the *Bellona* and *Centaur* caught up with some enemy ships: *Centaur* fired a shot at one and *Bellona* at another. *Bellona* took possession of the prize, comprising three French frigates and two brigs from Napoleon's army in Alexandria, and was employed in shifting the prisoners, including a French Admiral, on to various ships. The prisoners were demoralised and unkempt and, not having heard from home for fifteen months, knew nothing of the defeats suffered by the French. The men on *Bellona* were also low in spirit when they saw the last pig being killed. They stood off Genoa but could not land the prisoners there, as the Austrians were expected to attack the town and so they took them to Antibes. They then returned to Minorca where they were joined, on July 7th, by Sir Charles Cotton. When they heard that the French and Spanish fleets had joined forces at Cartagena, the Admiral made signal but, the wind being contrary, they were unable to proceed against the enemy. They took on water at Mahòn and endeavoured to obtain stock but found sheep and pigs, and vegetables very expensive, the prices having been raised when the natives saw them arrive. On the 14th, the fleet, comprising 31 sail-of-the-line, weighed and made sail towards the Straits of Gibraltar under Lord Keith, in place of Lord St Vincent who had resigned the command owing to ill health and, to George's delight, they took a further prize. The wind blowing strong into the Straits, they anchored in Tetuan Bay and Mazareen Bay, in Morocco, for watering. Each ship had to carry a Marine guard to go ashore and had to make a present to the natives of two cartridges before they were allowed to take water. As the plague was still raging along the coast, they were not allowed to land, but they had food and wine brought by transports from Gibraltar.

Off the coast of Spain, Lieutenant George and his colleagues had the melancholy duty of burying, 'with the Honours of War', Captain Betty of the Marines, who had died following an apoplectic fit. Having heard 'that the French fleet, with that of the Spaniards, had gone in to Brest,' they made for home and, despite stormy weather which damaged many of the British ships, they reached Torbay on August 16th. The *Bellona* had been at sea for fifteen weeks without putting into port, except to water at Mahòn and Tetuan Bay, and had suffered privation when the stocks ran low. George was pleased to report that they had captured three frigates, two brigs and nine merchant ships and felt that he was entitled to £10 prize money.

For the remainder of 1799, and the first half of 1800, George's letters were written at Torbay or Cawsand Bay, where *Bellona* awaited orders. Not infrequently, when orders came through, there was a change of wind direction and she was unable to sail, or else she had to return to port. He dined with the Captain, Sir Thomas Thompson, who stated that they expected orders to go to Spithead.

John writes to his sister on March 29th 1800 to say that he has met Davies the Jew, 'a character' that she would have known by sight 'for a long time', having seen him in Haverfordwest 'frequently with a box under his arm.' The 'poor fellow looked shabby and seemed distressed', but as George was in uniform at the time and in the company of fellow officers, he 'did not like to take him by the hand.' He would 'embrace a future opportunity of falling in with him,' when he was in private clothes but, shortly afterwards, he had 'received orders to go to sea immediately.' A month later, while *Bellona* was at anchor in Cawsand Bay, George was surprised to see Davies, with three others, in a boat 'coming alongside with slops, &c.' and asking to see him saying that he had a letter for him from his father. George knew this not to be true and had gone below leaving orders that Davies be told that he was not on board. Davies, who knew otherwise, was annoyed and he shouted abuse and, worst of all, falsely claimed, before the Captain and the ship's company, that he was related to George. Had he come alone, George would have received him, but as he had behaved in so outrageous a manner, he was 'provoked almost to blow his brains out.'

On July 1st they were off *Île d'Ouessant* (Ushant) while an inshore squadron was at anchor off Brest harbour 'in sight of the enemy's fleet' so that it was 'impossible for them to come out without being observed.' A part of the British fleet, with a number of troop ships, lay off Quiberon.

George's reference to the Belle Isle (*Belle-Île*) expedition, off Quiberon, appears to be misleading. The Austrians, having endeavoured to starve the Genoese into submission, were attacked from the rear by Napoleon, who had come through the St Bernard Pass. Napoleon's victory at Marengo had restored the French to a strong position and Britain made the mistake of dispersing her forces. Instead of reinforcing Minorca as a base for attack on the south of France, the British aimed to distract the French by small affrays. They sent 6,000 men to capture Belle Île and 5,000 to Minorca, but the two expeditions had to be brought together to go to the aid of the Austrians.

The *Bellona* returned to Plymouth before the end of August and on September

5th, George had the 'disagreeable necessity of informing' his sister that they were 'going to sea immediately', but subsequent letters report 'boisterous weather' and rumours that 'a Naval Armistice will take place between England & France' seemed to indicate that sailing was not necessary. On October 28th, he proudly informs his sister that the Commander-in-Chief, the Earl of St Vincent, intended hoisting his flag on the *Bellona*, which would be not only a great honour but also the means of keeping the ship in port throughout the winter, as St Vincent was a sick man and would not be going to sea. In his next letter he reports that the flag was on board and that the Fleet had sailed, leaving them behind. A week later, however, he was 'under the disagreeable necessity to say' that his lordship had 'shifted his flag into the *Ville de Paris*, therefore our hopes are all done away and we are going to sea with the Fleet the first wind.'

On New Year's day 1801, at Spithead, they 'expended a little powder' in firing a Royal Salute as Prince Augustus Frederick, the sixth son of King George III, embarked on HMS *Endymion* for Lisbon, and they also marked in a similar manner the Union of Great Britain and Ireland that had taken place that day.

John writes later that month stating that they were preparing for war against the Armed Neutrality of the Northern League, comprising Russia, Sweden, Denmark and Prussia, formed by Paul, Czar of Russia against Britain, fighting for survival against France. They were under orders to detain all Russian, Danish and Swedish ships and 'there was everything but a declaration of war.' (64) By the end of February they were at Spithead and under the command of Vice-Admiral Lord Nelson, who had hoisted his flag on the *St George*, and was to go to the Baltic as second-in-command to Admiral Sir Hyde Parker, (65) to force Denmark to withdraw from the Armed Neutrality and, if they resisted, their fleet was to be destroyed. George writes from Yarmouth on March 10th as part of an 'expedition that is going forward' for the Baltic with a fleet of 'about 22 sail-of-the-line, about thirty frigates, bombs & gun brigs, a very formidable fleet to salute the Danes & Swedes'.

The attack was made on Copenhagen. The Danish fleet was anchored in a defensive formation in the King's Deep, the channel in front of the city, and Nelson transferred to the 74-gun *Elephant*, Captain Thomas Foley, which had a more shallow draft. Nelson began the attack on the morning of April 2nd 1801 and when he saw some of our ships grounded, Parker gave the signal to withdraw. Nelson, placing his telescope to his blind eye, exclaimed to the *Elephant*'s captain: 'You know, Foley, I have only one eye. I do not see the signal.' He then proceeded to destroy the Danish fleet. Hyde Parker was re-called and Nelson was given his command. He paraded the fleet off Revel and

Kronstadt and in mid-June, while still off Copenhagen, he received news that he had been made a viscount and was relieved of his command.

Any letters that George may have written between that March 10th and June 4th are missing, and we may never know what account he gave of the battle of Copenhagen. Three of the British ships ran aground on the shoals outside Copenhagen harbour, but they were still able to bombard the port: *Bellona* was one of them. George purchased two copies of 'a drawing of the action' which, he complains, gave the *Bellona* 'a peaceful berth'. (68) The *Bellona* was at Revel, now Tallinn, in the latter part of May, having been cruising with a squadron off the island of Bornholm. On June 4th she was lying three miles off Danzig and, as it was the King's fortieth birthday, the yards were manned at eight that morning and saluted at one.

George makes scant reference to Captain Foley, simply stating that the *Elephant* was on a cruise and that Foley had gone home (73). He would surely be aware of his local connection, as Foley's brother had built Foley House at Haverfordwest. It is probable that he referred to Foley in some of the missing letters.

The victory at Copenhagen, the assassination of Czar Paul of Russia and the succession of his son, Alexander, had hastened the break-up of the Armed Neutrality. George was glad to hear that Alexander had invited Nelson to St Petersburg 'being anxious to see the Hero of the Nile,' hoping that this would shorten their stay in the Baltic. He rejects his sister's reference to their success 'in taking a valuable Prize,' stating that they had not taken 'a single thing' since they had left England, except at Copenhagen & that will be very trifling.' He then refers ruefully to newspaper reports that 'gave an account of a very valuable Prize which the *Bellona* captured & took into Gibraltar, which is a very great falsehood.' They had, in fact, taken 'a Spanish sloop in a prize to the Fleet but of no consequence as for Prize Money.'

They were off Cadiz at the beginning of November and George is overjoyed at having heard 'the glorious news of the Peace,' – the Peace of Amiens, of which it was said that it was 'a peace which all men are glad of but no man can be proud of.' According to its terms, England gave up all her conquests except Trinidad and Ceylon; Malta was restored to the Knights of St John, and the King gave up the title of King of France.

By December they were at Gibraltar, where George 'had the pleasure' of dining with Colonel Edwardes and his wife, whom he found 'very pleasant indeed,' but he does not say why they were there. Edwardes arranged for him to meet Captain Propert of the *Cambrian*, who had taken upon himself to bring together young men from Pembrokeshire serving in that area and George had enjoyed 'a fine round Welsh party' at which there were present several men from Haverfordwest, including Charles Phillips and George Robbin, and Howells the Pedlar's son and Dicky Harries, who lived near the Blue Boar. Whenever he went ashore, George met some of his *'Cambrian* friends', and he found that two of the ship's officers were from Pembrokeshire, Smith from Jeffreston and Lewis from somewhere near Pembroke, 'two very agreeable people.' George referred later, somewhat confusingly, to *The Cambrian*, a standing order for which he had placed at Potter's News Agency in High Street. *The Cambrian* was the first weekly newspaper to be published in Wales, having been founded in 1804 as a means of fostering the commercial growth of Swansea.

George Jenkins, from Haverfordwest, was working at the Admiral's Office and George was able to correspond with his sister through him. Jenkins also offered to have anything sent to him when he was on sea, and later, when Jenkins served on HMS *Escort*, which called at Milford on its regular trips to Ireland, he conveyed letters, and brought news from home. Small wonder that George regarded him as 'a particular friend for his kind attention.'

When Lieutenant George dined with Colonel Edwardes at Gibraltar on December 20th 1801, they were unaware that Lord Kensington had died a few days earlier and that the Colonel had already succeeded to the barony.

While they were at Gibraltar, Sir James de Saumarez received a dispatch, which indicated that they were for the West Indies and, by mid-February, they were in Jamaica, which they reached after a pleasant voyage of 26 days. Four French sail-of-the-line had left Cadiz for Santo Domingo to join the French squadron sent there from Brest 'in order to quell the Negroes'. The *Bellona*, with the *Warrior* and other ships, were under the command of Admiral Duckworth, who defeated the French squadron and was appointed Commander-in-Chief Jamaica in the following year. George was always happy to find that the *Warrior* was in his squadron as it enabled him to maintain contact with his friend Charles Phillips, who served on her.

George was pleased with Jamaica where the fruit, especially pineapple, was very reasonable but the mutton, the fowls and the turkeys and everything else were treble the price one paid at home. The 'serious thing', however, was that they had not got any Prize Money. He wrote from Port Royal and soon after they received orders to join Admiral Montagu's squadron cruising off Navassa, a small island between Jamaica and Haiti. They were back in this country by the end of June and, soon after their arrival at Spithead, George's good friend Birch, by now Surveying Master, came on board to greet him and take him to his lodgings, in Unicorn Street, Portsea. (75)

On June 29th 1802, George informs his sister that they should now be addressed 'Royal Marines'. The Marines, one of the oldest units in the British armed forces, were formed in 1664 as the Duke of York and Albany's Maritime

Regiment of Foot and were described at the time, as 'land soldiers prepared for sea service'. They became part of the naval establishment in 1755 and manned some of the ship's armament, as well as providing landing forces. They had their own mess and sleeping quarters apart from the sailors. In the same letter he states that the ship was likely to be paid off in the near future and asks her to address her letters to him at Birch's lodgings.

John George had left HMS *Bellona* by November 1802 and was stationed at the Royal Marine Barracks at Plymouth where he 'put on the Red Coat', mounting guard over the dockyard. He spent much of his leisure time with young Mr Curgenven in a 'snug little room behind his shop and a good companion in it, a cask of good Welsh Ale' which had been sent to him by Mr Barzey of Arnold's Hill. He also called on Colonel Vaughan and dined with the family. The Colonel was about to leave the Garrison and retire to live in his 'old house at Cartlett', in Haverfordwest. He and his wife would travel by road and, to save expense, the rest of the family would 'go by water.'

There are references, from time to time, to matters that remain mysterious, either by their nature as relating to the family, or by the absence or loss of intervening letters. Such is the reference to Price, who disappears from the correspondence (40), and to the 'Delf party' (41) which, at least, introduced a reference to the Blue Boar, albeit by George, as 'the principal inn' in town. George's observations on the countryside and his father's interest in crops indicate that Stephen George also had a farm. Its location is not known.

George describes Christmas 1802 at the Royal Marine Barracks, as 'only the name, no feasting or anything else,' although he had spent it with 'a brother Red Coat in the Guard Room', having a roast fowl & mince pies, with a bottle of wine after.' He had heard that there was a proposal to send a battalion of Marines to New South Wales in order to form a penal settlement 'about 1,000 miles from Botany Bay,' (81) which he doubted, probably correctly. There is no account of such a settlement being established between those built at Newcastle in 1801 and at Port Macquarie in 1821.

Early in 1803, George became worried about the effect of impressment, which gave the Crown the right to take men for the defence of the realm in manning warships. Merchant seamen were especially vulnerable and his brother James, now in the Merchant Navy, would have been at the mercy of the Press Gang. Up to 500 parties of Marines had been sent out as 'recruiting parties', though none, as yet, to Wales.

War was 'talk of the day' at Plymouth, he writes, with a large squadron gathering in Cawsand Bay. The *Escort* and the *Nemesis* had sailed with dispatches, to the West Indies it was thought. They, together with the *Spitfire* and the *Insolent*, are referred to as the Milford ships, as they sailed back and fore to Ireland, calling at Milford on their way. George had offered to exchange posts with an officer on the *Nemesis* with a view to being able to visit his home, but without success. He felt that Providence was on their side in the discovery of 'a chest of flags that floated ashore near Brighton' from a French vessel that had 'stranded with 100,000 stand of arms, supposed for Ireland: the flags were Irish united with France.' (86)

He complains that he does not have much opportunity for outdoor recreation and was surprised to find that farmers in England were unwilling to allow him to shoot on their land. He had managed a day's shooting, however, and had 'knocked down a few thrushes' which he would have liked to have presented to his sister. There was better indoor entertainment and, in April 1803, he writes excitedly to say that 'Mr Le Sugg, who displayed his abilities in Haverfordwest last summer, is here performing wonders,' and he proposes paying him a visit. 'The Players' were there all the year round and, at that season, 'some of the Covent Garden and Drury Lane folks' came down to Plymouth. This was in contrast to the Gosport Theatre, for 'such an infamous house' he never saw, 'even Haverfordwest was Drury Lane to it.' The statement implies that there was a theatre in the county town.

George endeavours to save money on his passage by catching a vessel carrying coal or limestone from south Pembrokeshire across the channel to Bideford and it was in the hope of doing so that he found himself at Tenby, scribbling a note to his sister at half past eight on a Sunday morning at the end of June 1803, to say that he has just arrived there. He had been home on leave and his brother, William, and his cousin, Tom George, had accompanied him as far as Arnold's Hill and had left him there at nine o'clock the previous evening, while he walked on through the night. He writes again, the same day, from Tenby, at 5 p.m., to say that he has just come back from Saundersfoot where the vessel had failed to float at high water and he planned to return there for the next tide, which would be at 2 o'clock in the morning. In the waiting time, he had been to Hean Castle to see Miss Roberts, formerly of Wiston, who was the housekeeper there. The vessel sailed on the night tide and 'after a tedious passage of 36 hours' he arrived at Bideford. He then set out to walk the forty miles to Tavistock, overnight, and took a coach from there to Plymouth where he arrived 'cursedly fatigued.'

On September 13th 1803, Lieutenant George embarked on HMS *Fisgard*, 'one of the most desirable ships' in the harbour, and one in which, in the event of a Spanish war, he hoped to 'make something'. He thinks that it was 'rather apropos' in him 'embarking in the ship that landed the troops in the neighbourhood of Fishguard & taking her name from it afterwards, and being on the spot at the time myself.' It was only three and a half years since the news of the invasion had reached Haverfordwest, on the evening of February 22nd 1797, and George, would, have remembered the occasion without doubt.

HMS *Fisgard* left Plymouth a week later for the Mediterranean, which George regarded as good hunting ground for prizes. In November they were at Lisbon, where he saw some 'very fine churches as well as other public buildings' but he was disgusted to find so many convents, that were 'more like gaols, with grated windows,' He and a messmate had visited the only English convent where one of the nuns 'through the grate conversed' with them and said that they were all happy and had not 'the smallest inclination' to leave. They had been to the opera twice, and to a ball, where no one wanted to know them. They were back at Spithead by December (98) and were moved down off St Helens, on the Isle of Wight, ready 'to meet the Usurper [Napoleon] and his flotilla mid-channel should he hazard an attempt to invade,' which George welcomed as it might bring a good prize.

Early in February 1804, *Fisgard* was off Falmouth for some days waiting for a fair wind, and she was back at Spithead again by mid-June, when George complained that his 'mind for some time past has been kept in a perplexed state in consequence of a Court Martial taking place between two messmates' which affected the harmony on board. He had also to give evidence.

At the beginning of July, they sailed to the Mediterranean, 'to Malta first, thence to Lord Nelson to put ourselves under his orders.' Their passage was 'very pleasant' and, 'after waiting 3 days at Gibraltar' proceeded to Toulon 'to join Lord Nelson.' Nelson, in the *Victory*, was now in command of the Mediterranean and he had the task of defending Gibraltar, Malta and Sicily and to prevent the French fleet at Toulon from escaping and joining the fleet at Brest so as to gain command of the English Channel. The danger increased when the Spanish fleet entered the war on the side of France in December 1804. The fleet at Toulon eventually succeeded in passing through the Straits of Gibraltar, but on account of contrary winds, Nelson was unable to follow them through the Straits for a month. Off Cape Trafalgar, in early May, Nelson was informed that, joined by some Spanish vessels from Cadiz, the French had headed for the West Indies. He gave chase but found that the Franco-Spanish fleet had returned and lay along the French coast, threatening an invasion of Britain. Nelson, after having some leave, returned and prepared for the battle of Cape Trafalgar.

George complained that, after having joined Nelson's fleet, they had not had a sight of him until the morning of August 16th, 'after looking out three weeks for him.' They had 10 sail-of-the-line and a great number of frigates, and the French had 'an equal force but don't seem at all inclined to face us.' By the end of November *Fisgard* was off Cape St Vincent and George is happy to say that, being by now at war with Spain, they had captured, 'about two hours ago, a valuable ship (Spanish) from Rio de la Plata' on its way to Cadiz, which might yield 'one or two hundred pounds.' They had been ordered by Nelson to cruise, but he feared that Sir John Orde, Commander-in-Chief, Cadiz, would send them back to the Mediterranean where there would be no prizes.

'After a five weeks' silence,' John writes to his sister from *Fisgard* 'off Cartagena' on December 31st 1804. He states that soon after they arrived at Lisbon, James's ship, *Britannia*, had come in, but as they were in quarantine, they were only able to approach her within a hundred yards. Yet they were within hailing distance, and George is able to say that 'James appeared very well and assured me of the welfare of the family.' *Britannia* then sailed up the Tagus. (113)

On their way to Gibraltar, *Fisgard* captured a French Letter of Marque bound for Cadiz, and when they arrived, they found the port still in quarantine because of fever. Their task now was to cruise between Gibraltar and Cartagena under Nelson's command and, George complains that there was 'nothing whatever to be picked.' Until his fellow officer, Peregrine, had written to his parents at Haverfordwest about it, he had not referred to 'a serious affray' that had taken place, when they boarded a Greek armed vessel near Cartagena, from which he escaped unhurt but his 'valuable and faithful servant' had been killed.

HMS *Fisgard* was in Madeira in June 1805, where they 'were treated in the most hospitable manner by the English merchants – a large party every day.' In a letter he received from K. Lupton, of Stamford, who was a fellow officer on *Fisgard*, dated August 13th, Lupton complains that he had not received prize money that was due to him but, following the threat of a lawyer's letter, he had obtained £180 in part payment.

On January 9th 1806, George writes to his sister from Port Royal, Jamaica, stating that he has written to her four weeks earlier from Barbados. They had been at Port Royal for six days and he complains that the mail he has received from her has been considerably delayed and advises that future letters should be sent to him at Port Royal by the Mail, that is made up in London the first Wednesday in every month, 'instead of trusting to friends.' They knew that a part of the French fleet from Brest was at sea and they were prepared 'to give them a warm reception,' leaving the following day, on a cruise lasting 10 to 12 weeks, in pursuit of them. While he was writing he hears that a French squadron had arrived at Martinique and has been blockaded by Admiral Duckworth. He and Peregrine have an unexpected visitor on board in the person of David Bevan, formerly of Marloes Court farm, Marloes. Bevan was master of the *Petherel*.

John George, for a while, held 'the honourable post of Caterer' which entailed visits to Kingston market in order to buy provisions and this gave him the pleasure of pricing the commodities and comparing the cost with that of home produce. He reminds his sister that it is 2¼ years since he left home, and that it was likely to be that length of time before he would have 'the extreme satisfaction of embracing my dear Mary.' But he was home before then, and appears to have been on leave for five months. On his way back, on April 6th 1807, he writes to his brother, William, from Swansea, where he had arrived at seven the previous evening 'after a jolting day's journey' and, while waiting for the Packet, he sees a collier going to Bideford.

George writes to Mary, on April 18th addressing her for the first time as Mrs Green, at Bridge Street, Haverfordwest, where she lived with her husband, John Green, whom she had married the previous February. Green had also acquired the adjoining property where he carried on his business as currier and maltster. Having written to his parents and to his brother William, George now wrote to Mary, 'tho' last, believe me, not the least in my affection since that never to be forgot parting under the Kilns,' in Cartlett Road that survived well into the twentieth century. Two letters written by Mary, soon after her marriage, that awaited him on his return to barracks, 'had been in the West Indies and back so that the postage amounted to something considerable.' He writes to her next, 'after an unusual long silence' on June 9th noting that *The Cambrian* had informed him that Lord Milford had been elected again as member of Parliament for the county of Pembroke but would 'neither express regret or joy, not knowing the sentiments of our friends.'

On July 14th, he writes, from the Royal Marine Barracks at Plymouth, to his brother, William, at 'Kensington Place', stating that, when next he has leave, he will 'go to Bideford and take the chance of a vessel crossing for limestone' from the south Pembrokeshire quarries. He expresses his admiration of Miss Jane, of Penlan, but has to content himself with the situation in which he finds himself. His 'upper country friends,' from north Pembrokeshire, may be 'down at the races' but the society in which they mixed would prevent William speaking to them. Perhaps it was because Mary had got married, or that he was anxious to establish good relations with his brother, that he now kept writing to William. On August 26th 1807, he writes to him to say that he has embarked on HMS *Garland*, 'a fine new ship rated 22 guns but mounting 34.' On October 13th, he writes to Mary expressing some surprise that John Mathias, possibly a relative, is to be the next mayor, which reminded him of 'a little story of Whittington and his cat'. Mathias was mayor in 1808 and again in 1810 during which year he held the distinction of being the only mayor of Haverfordwest to be 'removed by mandamus,' that is, removed by an order of the Court of King's Bench.

George writes to his sister, on November 10th, from Cork, when they were 'under weigh with a fine wind for Jamaica,' confessing that he regretted having left HMS *Fisgard*. On April 26th 1808, writing from Port Royal, he complains that he has not heard from her since September and ends by saying 'as I am not much inclined to write from your "supposed" silence, I will conclude with duty, love and affection.' This was his last letter to her and, sadly, it did not contain the warmth of previous letters.

On July 16th, on *Garland* 'off Santo Domingo', he writes to William, who was still at home, saying that they have left Port Royal four days earlier, escorting the Packet carrying that letter 'clear of the islands'. He had met 'three or four neighbours, one a boy belonging to this ship of the name of Jones,' a quiet boy whom he had got the Captain to take on as an assistant to his steward. He wants to know how James fared and advises him, if in England, 'to pass at the Trinity Board for a master,' which was a rank below that of lieutenant. His desire to know 'what ships the Evanses of Mabws belong to, as I should like to see them on the family's account,' must remain one of the unsolved mysteries, and so must the message to 'the Captain', that is, William Davies, informing him that 'his mahogany coloured friends in this part of the globe say that he ought not to neglect the little ones' and that Miss Sophy is grown a very fine girl and very likely soon to have a 'man for true'. He wishes to be remembered to his 'dear sister and her little family,' and requests that his brother should, 'to my adored and affectionate Parents say everything for me: a short time yet I hope to meet their warm embraces.'

This was not to be as, on October 3rd 1808, while boarding a prize of HMS *Garland* off Jamaica, Lieutenant John George was 'killed in action'.

Dillwyn Miles

Haverfordwest 2001

The Letters

1. Rev^d Mr Cleaveland, Haverfordwest.[1]

London
Jany 23rd 1799

Revd Sir,

After a long silence I take the liberty of addressing these few lines to you hoping it will meet your forgiveness for the neglect which I have taken in not writing sooner. I should have wrote long since but desiring my Father to shew you the contents of my letters to him which I thought would be equally the same.

I went to the Admiralty[2] the day after my arrival in Town when, enquiring for Admiral Young was shewn up to his apartments, the Admiral asked me a few questions relative to my age and what business I was brought up to, and if I was a pretty good scholar, &c., when appointed me to attend at a further time in the course of the same day which accordingly I did and upon giving up my name was ordered to one of the offices and getting the recommendation took it up before the Lords, there being only three in the room, and after asking me a few questions similar to Admiral Young's, they approved of me, and have the satisfaction to say that I was immediately passed.

I should have left Town long before this if I had my Commission which being with several more before the King for this fortnight and not yet signed: however, I intends leaving Town at any rate by this evening's Mail for Plymouth without the Commission nor the Official Letter which I ought to bring to the Adjutant General – the Letter can't be wrote till the Commission is signed and Mr Coombe promising he will forward it immediately – together with the Letter and until then I can't do any duty.

I yesterday executed a Power of Attorney to Mr Coombe to act for me as an Agent, he being an Agent for most of the Marine Officers. My pay is 4s.8d. per day and his charge for Agency is 6d. in the Pound: after I had appointed the Agent I delivered Mr Sykes's letter to him who upon looking at it said it is a long story on the same subject and without reading it put the letter in his pocket, he being seemingly very busy with some Gentlemen and I took no further notice of the contents but walked off very deliberately after wishing him the Good Morning. I also yesterday purchased my accoutrements, being accompanied by one of the Clerks in the Admiralty, which cost me £12.19.6, the particulars is: for the Sword £4.4.0, Plate £1.7.0, Gorget £1.3.0, Belt 12s.6d, Sash £2.12.6, Sword Knot 10s.6d, and the Epaulets £2.10.0, which in the whole is £12.19s.6d. I shall purchase nothing else till I join the Regiment which Mr Coombe tells me he expects to forward the Commission and Official Letter in the course of a week at farthest under cover to Captain Wier[3] who bears an excellent character at the Admiralty. I received your letter to Captain Wier which I am greatly obliged to you for.

Please give my love to Patty and also any friend that should enquire of you after me and accept these few lines with my best wishes for your health and also thanks innumerable for the very great kindness you have done in getting the Commission for, Rev[d] Sir,

Your most obliged H[ble] Serv[t], John George.

P.S. My next will be from Plymouth. Since I wrote the above I was informed that the expense attending the Commission and Power of Attorney is £7. JG.

*

2. Mr Stephen George,[4] Blue Boar Inn,[5] Haverfordwest.

Stone House Barracks
Jany. 28th 1799

Dear Father and Mother,

After a long and fatiguing Journey I arrived safe here and got every thing settled as much as I can do at present as you see by Mr Cleaveland's letter. Had I known as much as I does now I think I should not have joined the Marines being so expensive. I thought by Mr Powell's discourse that a mere trifle would fit one out but I see it much now to the contrary, however, I will endeavour to make it do without any further assistance. My clothes will be ready by Wednesday evening there being no lace to it only the two Epaulets. I mean by my clothes,[6] Coat, kerseymere Waistcoat & Breeches and several other little things such as Stock and roses for the Gorget and Hat. The Bed, Bedding, &c. I shall see about in the course of a few days being obliged to get them but shall consult first with Capt. Wier.

I finds it quite lonesome in a strange place and all strangers but hopes in a few days to pick acquaintance with some of the Officers.

I paid from Exeter to Plymouth per Heavy coach 17s.0d. and the carriage of my trunk I paid in London for all the way. The Mess is not at all extravagant. Dinner is only 1s.8d. with the beer along with it and you may drink wine or anything as you please or might rise immediately after dinner and drink nothing. Cold meat for supper is only 4d. besides drinking. Breakfast is charged as in other Inns; the Lodging I know not what as yet.

A few days before I left London I spent the evening with Doctor Morgans late at Mr Ayleway's and the day I came off spent the day till about 6 in the evening with Miss Fields at Mr Davies's house,[7] being invited by Mr Davies. I'll assure you that Miss Fields is improved much for the better and as to her being apprenticed to a Milliner is all a falsity for there can't be more respect shewn to any person than what is shewn to her. Mr Davies also seemed very agreeable and as to what Mr E. B. Phillips said before I left H'west is I think a falsity. Mrs Davies was confined to her bed being very ill but sent down her compliments and was sorry to leave Town so soon hoping to have had my company at a future period.

Miss Fields is much the same in temper as when she left H'west open and of good nature; she did not know how to treat me good enough. She is by some means deprived of writing home but would be extremely glad to hear from Mary or any other of her old acquaintances.

Dear Parents, I beg you'll write by the first post for the only thing that will give me pleasure is in hearing from you. Direct for me:

Lieut. John George of Marines, Stone House Barracks, near Plymouth.

Please to give my love to Mary, Bill, James, &c. – Grandmother, also Miss Gould, Miss Davies, John Potter and in short all my old acquaintance and accept this from, Dear Father & Mother,

Your ever Aff[te] & Dutiful Son, John George.

P.S. I shan't go into Barracks till I'm provided with every necessary article.

*

3. Miss Mary George, Blue Boar, Haverfordwest.

Stone House Barracks
Jany 29th 1799

Dear Sister,

I wrote to my Father by yesterday's Post which I suppose is received, and since falling in discourse with some of the Officers about their Linen I understand that they call it but a very small stock to have 2 dozen shirts and other clothes in proportion: 2 pair of Kerseymere Breeches and Waistcoats and a pair of Leather Breeches. I should be very glad if you would consult with my Mother about it and also with Mr Cleaveland and let me know by the first or second post at furthest their opinion. I find it very expensive and am almost sorry I ever thought of it. I gave my measure for one suit of clothes and shall be obliged to get a second dress when my first is made. I also shall be obliged to get bed & bedding, towels, clothes brush, blacking brushes and in short a great number of different things; tea things & tea kettle, plates, knives and forks, &c., &c., &c., and a boot jack. It will not be so expensive when I am once rigged out.

I beg you will not mention what I am going to say to any one, not even Father or Mother, that I was necessitated to write to Uncle George in Bristol for the loan of £10 being in immediate want of cash & shall remit it back in the course of a few days, being told by him when at Bristol to send to him if I should want. Once more I beg you will not mention it as I am sure I shall have my Father & Mother's displeasure.

You'll excuse me in stopping so short, the Post being just going out. Adieu with love to all.

Your Aff^{te} Brother, John George.

*

4. Mr Stephen George, Blue Boar Inn, Haverfordwest.

Stone House Barracks
Feby 9th 1799

Dear and Hon^d Parents,

Yours I received last night under frank[8] and was greatly shocked at the sudden death of poor Mr Cleaveland, my best of friends, but I have not the least doubt but what his morals in this life entitled him to the world of everlasting happiness, also I was greatly shocked at the death of Mr Kitchin & Mrs Webb; however I will say with you, let us be thankful for the blessings that is left and try to pass through this life as we may have a blessed reward in the next.

I received an inclosure of £10 in yours which makes your goodness too much; I did not expect it and indeed I am not pleased for your sending it being willing to do the utmost in my power without distressing you, but to say the truth I was quite reduced in cash and you must pardon me in saying that sooner than troubling you I was necessitated to draw a Bill on my Agent for about ten guineas before hand having a long bill in Plymouth for my uniform, cot bed & bedding, towels and Breakfast Clothes and also for my hat and numerous articles too tedious to mention, but will send you every particular in a short time. However, you might rely upon my word that I shall not be in the least extravagant in my way of living.

I wrote by the next post after I wrote to you, to Mary to consult between my Mother and poor Mr Cleaveland about shirts, being told that 2 dozen shirts was but an indifferent stock to take to sea, there being on board some ships no women allowed. I should be glad to know as early as possible your opinion whether you could get them for me or for me to get them here, as for the carriage of a small box would be but trifling from H'west to this first getting it sent to George in Bristol and for him to forward it here. There is no necessity for anything else but shirts as the General does not allow any colour clothes to be wore at any time but the uniform. I shall be obliged to get a large trunk, or a sea chest, very soon having no room for my clothes, and also in the course of a fortnight, 2 silver table spoons and 2 tea spoons not being in immediate want of them on account of my Servant buying some metal spoons, without being ordered.

I have got a room in the Barracks & hopes to make myself pretty comfortable in a short time, but have not got my cot bed or bedding yet, I don't know how I shall find it in sleeping on a mattress rather odd, I should think, being never used to lay on such a thing before but shall soon come to it.

Dear Father, don't wait to receive letters from me as I shall write every opportunity but write very often as you can get franks. I was very impatient this 2 or 3 days to receive yours, there being a great delay from Bristol to Plymouth, but received it with a great deal of pleasure altho' the contents shocked me much. When you write to me always direct as before:

Lieut. John George of Marines, Stone House Barracks, near Plymouth –

because the greatest pleasure I receive is from home and I should wish you would put Billy[9] to write to me in order that he might improve himself: you can get 2 or 3 franks or more if they are wanted and it is no more than trouble, if so I call it, but I hope you won't call it trouble.

Please to give my kind love to my Sister & Brothers, Grandmother, Price and all my old acquaintance, also remember me to my relations at Hook and elsewhere, and also to John Potter, Mr M Phillips, Mr Duberlin, Mr Thos. Rees, writer, and in short remember me to all that enquire after me. I shall write to Mary by tomorrow's post, it being rather late and expecting an answer to mine relative to the shirts.

Accept those few lines with my prayers for your health from, Dear Parents,

Your ever Aff[te] & Dutiful Son, John George.

P.S. I have purchased a Pocket Bible.

*

5. Miss Mary George, Blue Boar Inn, Haverfordwest.

Stone House Barracks
Feby 9th 1799

Dear Sister,

I received yours of the 1st inst. late yesterday evening and should have wrote by this evening's post, only being preparing for Drill where about 8 of us attends every day, but have wrote to my Father & Mother which is all the same: however I am now seated in my own room by a good fire embracing every opportunity in writing to you, hoping to find you all in good health as I am at present.

I have been here almost a fortnight already and spends my time pretty agreeable being got acquainted with some of the officers. I very seldom sits down to drink wine without it is of a chance day, there being what is called two Grand Days in the week when wine is put on the table with the dinner and then it is impossible for any officer to avoid it. I expect to lay in my cot about Monday next for the first time and intends subscribing to a circulating library when I shall pass part of the evenings more comfortable. I have already had one lot of books in 3 vols. called *The Castle of Burktholme*: it is rather a foolish book. In looking over Steel's List I find there is a great many below me and most of them have joined the Division. There is one Mr Perkins, a very agreeable young man just joined, plays on the flute exceeding well: he is one from Leicestershire and the distance from this to his home is upwards of 300 miles.

I wrote in my last to you saying that I had wrote to Uncle George to send me £10 and accordingly in a few days afterwards I received a letter with an inclosure of £5 from him being fearful to send more till I acknowledged the receipt of it doubting the letter might be mislaid and immediately I wrote back informing him I had received it and also desiring him to forward me no more, not being in want of any more cash, and intends returning the £5 by tomorrow's post with this. I am very much obliged to you for offering me to forward £5 but indeed I am not in want and am sorry it is not in my power to repay you for the very great attention you pay towards me. I shall have a very long bill to pay at Plymouth but have enough of money and some spare and if I should want I will immediately let you know. I shall call on Mr Wier next Monday and give him the melancholy account of the death of poor Mr Cleaveland. I dare say he will be very much shocked at hearing of his old friend's death. I beg you'll not wait for my letters before you write as you now perfectly well where to find me, and it will be my greatest pleasure in writing home. Put Billy in the method of writing letters, and let him write often to me as he have no occasioned to be ashamed and it might be a great improvement for him I shall write to him in the course of a few days, and also let James write.

Sunday morning, 9 o'clock

I was obliged to lay down my pen last night, being interrupted by some of the Officers calling on me. I suppose you would scarcely know me in my uniform with a great 3-cocked hat. I very seldom dress before 4 in the afternoon on account of my going to drill with several others in the morning from 11 to near one o'clock, and we don't dine till 5: there is no lace on our dress, only the two epaulets. I have had one pair of kerseymere breeches & waistcoats and have spoke for another, and I shall be obliged to get a pair of doe skin breeches, being very lasting and serviceable. When I come down to H'west I will bring my whole dress with me when I shall have the pleasure of your opinion on them. It is a black feather we wear in our hair. I expect an answer to the letter I wrote you daily whether it is your opinion for to send the linen here or for me to get them myself. There is waggons goes constantly from this [place] to Bristol.

You must think I find it very odd in dining at 5 o'clock where formerly I used to dine at 1, but I very seldom eat any supper afterwards, without it is of a chance I should fall in company with some of the Officers, then it is impossible for me to avoid it. I have breakfast for nearly a week in my own room on tea have bought ¼ of C^a Tea[10] and ½ lb. White and ½ Brown Sugar and gets fresh rolls every morning and some cream so that in a short time [shall] make myself pretty comfortable.

My room is facing Mount Edgcumbe where you might have heard so much talk of and indeed I calls it a very pleasant room having a full view of the sea and the country. I was seeing the Dock the other day where some very large ships are building and repairing, amongst them was the *Robust*, a ship that fought very gallant off Ireland lately. I have bought all my tea things consisting of 2 cups & saucers, tea pot, slop basin, sugar basin, cream jug, spoons and tea board together with a tea kettle so that I breakfast quite in style. My paper is going short.

Please to give my love to Miss Gould, Miss Davies and all your acquaintance, make use of my name with my love altho' not inserted here – also give my duty to my Father and Mother, love to my Brothers, Grandmother and Price and accept this, Dear, Dear Sister, from,

Your ever loving & Aff^{ate} Brother, John George.

*

6. Mr Stephen George, Blue Boar Inn, Haverfordwest.

Stone House Barracks,
Feby 13th 1799

Dear Father and Mother,

I received yours of the 6th inst. late this evening and am just now seated, altho' 10 o'clock at night to answer it, hoping it will meet you in good health as I am at present. I have wrote 3 letters home within this week which I suppose is received.

Your goodness is too much, my dear Mother, in getting me rigged out as you does. I shall want nothing but a few shirts which you are so good to mention you are getting ready to send me, having got a mattress, 3 blankets, 2 pair sheets, pillow and 2 pillow cases and 6 towels from a shopkeeper in Plymouth by the recommendation of Capt. Wier. I am heartily obliged to you for your kind offer in sending me a bed but I really don't want any thing at present. I have also got 2 Breakfast Clothes from the same man in Plymouth. I have given him an order on Coombe, my agent, for £20 (being about 6 weeks pay before hand, there being now due to me about 11 guineas) not being willing to distress you but have not settled the bill on account of there being no answer from my agent & not having called at Plymouth for this 3 days. I dare say his bill is near £20, he paying for my hat and the making of 1 suit of uniform and 2 waistcoats & breeches by the desire of Capt. Wier's brother. As soon as I settle with him I'll send you the bill to look at under cover to Lord K.[11] which I expect will be tomorrow. There is a great number of Officers in Barracks at present and mostly very agreeable. Most possibly I shall come down early in the summer for 2 or 3 months on leave of absence, if I don't embark before, which I don't think I shall as there are so many Officers here and no great call for them. However, I am pretty certain I shan't leave Barracks not these 2 months to come at any rate. I am provided with every thing till I embark except 2 tablespoons & 2 tea spoons which would be very thankful if you would send them with the shirts in a small box per Mail to George in Bristol and to be by him forwarded here, and also I will be very thankful if you will send me a small folding bag for holding my dirty linen and desire Mary if she will make me half a dozen rosettes for the hair as they cost 1s.0d. here and have had 2 already: I was obliged to get a false tail, my hair having been too short to tie.

I shall be obliged when I embark on board ship to get 2 large table cloths, 4½ yards long, but there is no necessity for them at present as they might be easily got at a minute's warning. I have not bought a trunk not having time being obliged to attend the Drill-Serjeant daily with several other young officers who after drilling us is to receive half a guinea from each. I have got in my trunk £16 which will last me a long time and should esteem it a very happy thing if I could repay you for your very great kindness to me. I find my complaint as I had getting a great deal better, quite well, and makes myself comfortable in my room, breakfasting on tea and seldom eats supper after dinner on account of our dining so late, and indeed very seldom goes out of the Barracks after night without a great deal of persuasion from some of my fellow Officers and then only to Plymouth or to Dock and some times to the Play.

I mentioned in one of my letters that I had remitted Uncle George the £5 which he sent me back to him, and hope you'll pardon me for borrowing it as I did not know at that time the expense which I might be put to.

In looking over my Papers I fortunately met Mr Allen, the shoemaker's memorandum to enquire after his son and I intend tomorrow to make every enquiry that lies in my power and shall know in my next what intelligence I can procure.

I am quite astonished in your mentioning the depth of snow with you as this part of the kingdom is quite fine: we have had but little snow and that is all thawed.

Since I wrote my last we are obliged to wear our uniform clothes always and the Officers in the Division are allowed to wear nothing but boots and when I came here was obliged to get a new pair as the old ones [I brought] from home is quite gone out of shape. I gave for the boots £1.5s. and indeed they are quite short for me but as Captain Wier was as good as to approve of them I could not refuse them.

I have not called on Capt. Wier yet to give him an account of the death of his old friend but shall today or tomorrow.

I'll also be thankful if Mary will make a black velvet stock as the one I have got is charged 3s.6d., for you will see 2 on the bill but one is for Perkins, one of the Officers, which he has paid me for.

Please give my love to my Sister, Brothers, Grandmother & all enquiring friends and accept this, with my prayer for your health, from,

Your Dutiful & Affec^te^ Son, John George.

If I can get every thing settled to my satisfaction I shall write by this post as it does not go out for some hours yet. JG.

*

7. Miss Mary George, Blue Boar Inn, Haverfordwest.

Stone House Barracks
Feby 19th 1799

Dear Sister,

    I have got a large bundle of letters tied up in my trunk from home and all my dear Sister's hand writing. How happy should I be if I could repay you for the many great obligations I am laid under: indeed against I settle every thing my pay of £1.11s.6d. per week will look very small at the week's end; however, I can live very well upon it here everything being very reasonable in the Barracks and if Fortune should have it for my going into a reasonable Mess when I embark, then I hope I shall be able to shew the affection of a brother. I have wrote home two letters a few days ago and in one inclosed my bill being to a very great amount but as I have drawn on my agent for £20 I shall have some spare cash (I suppose near £14) after discharging the bill. It is far more expensive than what I first thought it and indeed had I known of its being so I should have preferred any inferior provision sooner than distressing my dear parents as I have already done.

    I have not done any duty yet but was appointed this morning to the command of Company and intends tomorrow to fall in for the first time and shall in a few days go on guard. I have often thought of mentioning a few words in my letters home, but always forgot, that is for my Father to ask Captain Dobbins some time before the summer that if he should come in his Cutter (and I not being embarked) some time about June or July to Plymouth if he would be so kind as to write me a note with an invitation of a passage to Milford as very possibly I might have a leave of absence of a couple of months as there is Officers which have not been here but a very short time and has had leave already, however it is time enough yet to think of it for I only mentioned it that in case an opportunity should offer.

    I go to church every Sunday constantly with most of the officers, there being a separate apartment for the Marines with a seat in front for the officers, and beautiful singing, indeed there is no organ in the church, but our Band which is much more beautiful. I have been told that this barracks is far more preferable than either Portsmouth or Chatham it being nice and open. The General has got his house in the barracks where the Band plays opposite both morning and evening. There is some very agreeable officers here and amongst them is my inseparable companion Lieut. Tucker, he who copied the Bill that I sent home. We are always together: he spends one evening with me in my room and I also spend the other in his, reading – the book I got now is called *The Life and Adventures of Joe Thompson* in 2 vols., a very good book & I have just returned the *Scotch Tale of Duncan & Peggy*, a book I recollect you praised much: they charge very high for reading here, 2d. for a small volume and subscribers are obliged to leave the value of the books when they are brought out of the Library but I suppose it is only strangers does so.

When I came here first of all I found myself very unpleasant not knowing any person but have got acquainted since with a great many officers and find myself quite comfortable. I breakfast & mostly drink tea in the evening in my own room and sleeps in my cot, as if I was in a cradle. It is impossible for me to accuse you in neglect of writing, let me know as early as you conveniently can how affairs goes on at home, that is, what run has the chaise and how does Colonel Edwardes[12] and other Bills stand and what custom is there in the house and in short let me know all and let me know John Potter's[13] determination whether he is for the Marines or what, and what Billy is thinking of as he is advancing in his youthful years, and how does Price agree and let me know if John Gibbs is come home. Tell Adams, Colonel Edwardes's servant, that I have got his cane and if possible will keep it till I deliver it into his own hands. I left a very good stick behind me in London to take Adams's along with me.

When I come home I will take with me my uniform and dress to see how you like me: we wear no lace, only two epaulets and don't be surprised when you expects my coming home to see me full dressed. I suppose you won't know me & there will be such a stare after me as they does mostly after strangers in H'west and seldom sees Marine Officers. I should have been much ashamed when I left home to wear Regimentals but now if I was in H'west I could wear them just the same as if I was wearing my coloured clothes. The Marines being the most Honourable Corps under the Crown; I have no very strange news to tell you. It shall always be my greatest pleasure in writing home and trust you will keep a constant correspondence with me.

Please to give my love to all my old acquaintance and make use of my name as if they were mentioned in this letter to all your friends & acquaintance not forgetting my relations in Hook, Miss Gould, Miss Davies, Mr Moses Phillips, Mr Duberlin, J. Potter, Mrs Bloss & in short remember me to all enquiring friends; tell Mr James of Hook that I should be very sorry if I had the command of such a Division of Men on the Poop as what he is, as I think he is of a cowardly disposition.

Please give my duty to my Father & Mother, love to my Brothers, Grandmother & Price and be pleased to accept of my love to yourself who am, Dear Sister,

Your Affectionate Brother, John George.

P.S. Since I left home I can't write at all. I have taken the greatest pain with

this & am ashamed almost to see it. I should have put a cover on this to Lord
K. – only being quite out of paper, which begs you'll excuse.

*

8. Miss Mary George, Blue Boar Inn, Haverfordwest.

Stone House
Feby 26th 1799

Dear Sister,

Yours I received under frank together with Miss Gould's letter with a great
deal of joy and am happy of hearing of your being all well particularly you
with your eyes, being quite uneasy about your illness. I wrote to William 2
days ago, which I suppose is received. I send you the enclosed strip of paper
as a kind of measure for the stocks. I have wrote the description of the length
and breadth on it: the stock I now wears is black velvet sowed on some linen,
and am obliged to wear always a white handkerchief under it. I think if you was
to make them with a place to put a pad in would be much more comfortable and
also save expense of washing.

I assure you I approve of your taking Miss Blethin as an acquaintance being
to my opinion a very decent good natured girl. Please to return my love to her.

Yesterday morning I marched with my Company to see two poor men
flogged: one had 200 lashes & the other had 50: they bore it very well: my
feelings was so much that I could not look on but turned my head aside.
Afterwards I met with Captain Wier and communicated Mr Cleaveland's death
to him, who was very much shocked at it. He asked first after Mr Cleaveland
and told me he was going to write to him, but I soon stopt him.

I should be exceeding happy to see you but it would not be proper for any
modest girl to come to Barracks as there is so many officers here and some
are apt to take too much liberties, but in the evening when the Band plays the
Court is sometimes full of ladies walking.

I fancied yesterday I saw Capt. Kean of the *Chapman* at Dock. I should think
if Mr Wakelin is on board he would call to see me. I was on board the *Ramillies*
of 74 guns, a very fine ship indeed but there is much larger ships in Dock.

I have been studying yours & Miss Gould's letters for some time and can
make neither head nor tail of the Shopkeeper's name you mentioned that live
at Plymouth, but know who you mean very well. Plymouth is quite close to the
Barracks but have not the pleasure of being personally known to him and for
that reason shan't call except you should have any Commands, or perhaps
Miss Gould might. I shall not be able to write to Miss Gould by this evening's
post as it is rather late being just returned from Drill. Altho' we are reported

35

fit for duty, the Colonel that inspected us advised for to still practice as it might be a very great improvement to an Officer.

I this morning bought a small sea chest and gave for it 11s.6d.; it is a very strong one and is new, I am better off in getting a small one than one that is over large, being so encumbersome in lugging about when I embark. How happy I should be if the ship that I embark on was to put in to Milford and should have the pleasure of shewing a ship which I am clearly convinced you never seen before. I have not the least doubt of my getting (much to my sorrow) on board of a line of battle ship as all young subalterns do, there being 3 or 4 officers on board them ships.

I saw Mr Saunders of the *Phoenix* yesterday in the Dock he is left Prize-master of my Prize.

Please to give my duty to my Father & Mother, love to Brothers, Grand-mother, Price and all enquiring friends & accept this with my warmest affection from, Dear Sister,

Your ever Affec^te Brother, John George.

*

9. Mr Stephen George, Blue Boar Inn, Haverfordwest.

Stone House Barracks
March 1st 1799

Dear and Hon^ed Parents,

I have taken up my pen with a great deal of pleasure embracing every opportunity in writing hoping it will meet you all well as I am at present. I am sure it is out of your power to accuse me of neglect in writing for I always make it my utmost endeavour in writing home & should be glad if you would inform me how many letters I wrote since I left home for I am certain there must be a great many, as I mostly writes every other day and am glad the postage costs you but very trifling.

I wrote to my Sister 2 letters a few posts ago which I suppose is received. She desired me in one of her last letters to let her know what tails we wear: it is but a single tie and no Club. I have sent her a description of the stocks in my last.

I was greatly surprised in receiving such a letter as Billy sent me, he is much improved since I left home & thinks him capable of transacting any business whatever. I desired in a letter I wrote to him to write often but have received not a one since.

You might recollect of Mr Moses Phillips's application to Mr Cleaveland for his interest in getting a Lieutenancy in the Marines: it was for Mr William Phillips I suppose as he told me the other day he was very desirous of getting a Commission but was dubious if they would pass him at the Board on account of his age. He said he could get the Earl of Warwick's interest. You have no occasion to take notice to Mr Phillips of what I have been writing as Mr William Phillips told me as a secret.

I am indebted to my Agent yet, a little better than a month's pay when we shall be even: my stock of cash is £10 having purchased several things lately. I gave £1 for a writing case yesterday, most of the Officers having one: it is very handy thing, with a drawer to it.

I shall be obliged to pay towards the Income Bill[14] £1.7s.8d., being the 60th part of my pay after deducting the Agency.

I have settled my bill with Harries: the mistake was in the copy I sent you relative to the scarlet cloth for instead of the 1 yard it was 1⅜ yard at 27s which makes £1.17.1.

In your next should be glad to know how you comes on with Colonel Edwardes. I should suppose if he has not yet settled his bill it must be to a very great amount. I got a furlough for my Servant of six weeks, he first asking me if I would permit him to go as he had a servant for me till his return.

I should have went to Mount Edgecumbe on Cawsand Bay yesterday but was prevented on account of the weather being very bad. We have had rain almost every day since I first came here, if it should chance be a fine day it is sure rain in the evening.

I have nothing very particular to say but shall write again in the course of 2 or 3 days: begs you will write often for it gives me the greatest pleasure in hearing from home.

Please to give my love to Brothers & Sister & Grandmother & remember me with my best respects to Mr Duberlin, Mr M. Phillips, Mr E. B. Phillips & Mrs Fields and in short to all enquiring friends & accept these lines from, dear Parents,

Your Dutiful & Affte Son, John George.

*

10. Miss Mary George, Blue Boar Inn, Haverfordwest.

Stone House Barracks
March 4th 1799

Dear Sister,

I am sorry to say I have experienced within this two or three days a very great loss by my watch being stolen out of my room from over the chimney piece, suspecting it to be my servant, but after every endeavour it is all to no purpose for he still declares he knows nothing of it, however, I have just turned him off. I of late kept the key of my room over the door; it was between 4 & 10 of the clock last Thursday evening. Upon all my enquiries it proves quite fruitless & indeed I am much afraid I shall never see it again.

I am writing home constantly but of late seldom receive any letter. This loss has quite disheartened me and begs for the present you'll excuse me writing any more.

Please to give my duty to my Father & Mother. Love to Brothers & Grandmother & accept this with my warmest affections from,

Your Aff^te & loving Brother, John George.

*

11. Miss Mary George, Blue Boar Inn, Haverfordwest.

Stone House Barracks
Mar 8th 1799

Dear Sister,

I received yours of 28th Feby last Tuesday & I should have answered it sooner only being on guard for the first time and having no time to write. It was very late before I went to bed last Tuesday being obliged to go the Patrols at 10 & 12 o'clock all around Stone House, as you see the Militia go in Haverfordwest but am obliged to be more sharper than what they are. I was obliged to give the Guard on my first mounting, 1 guinea being customary.

I wrote several letters home since the date of your last which suppose is all received. I mentioned in my last of my watch being stolen. I have given up all hopes of ever getting it again; after every endeavour it proves quite useless: the General knows of it being stolen.

You desired me to give a description of Captain Wier & his 2 daughters, which I can easily do. The Captain is old & infirm being afflicted much with gout, and as to his daughters, there is neither of them handsome in my opinion but might be called passable. It won't do for a young subaltern to look out for a wife without he has a good fortune besides his pay, for the pay will scarcely support himself without a wife to look after, and as to rich ladies, they are seldom to be found.

Please to give the enclosed to James it being the favourite tune with the Band. I think it is a beautiful one if it is well played.

In my walk yesterday evening I met Mr Wakelin, he looks exceeding well and tells me he belongs to the *Childers* brig, but in what situation I had no time to ask him. I appointed to meet him in Dock this morning but did not see him.

I this morning received my Commission from the General.

I beg you'll excuse the shortness of my letter having an appointment with an Officer to have a little chat. I remain, with my duty to my Father & Mother, love to Brothers & Yourself, from,

Your Aff^te Brother, John George.

I have just this inst. received the Frank dated Mar. 5th and having no time to open it: if there is any answers requested I will write them the first opportunity; begs you'll not wait for such answers but write constantly.

*

12. Mr Stephen George, Blue Boar Inn, Haverfordwest.

Stone House Barracks
Mar 17th 1799

Dear Parents,

I have just this instant received yours of the 13th inst. and in answer would be glad to know as early as possible what you mean by desiring me to give the enclosed to Mr Wakelin, there being no enclosure at all in your letter which surprises me much whether it was intended to enclose some cash to him, or what. I am quite confident there was no enclosure for I am always very cautious in opening letters having opened it on my table.

I never saw Mr Wakelin only once and then he told me he was quite impatient in expecting letters from home. The *Childers*, as I was informed, sailed a week ago and also the *Chapman* which I have mentioned in some letters home. I wrote to you a few days ago and also to my Sister by yesterday's post.

It being late, being just come out of church which prevents me making any inquiry after Mr Wakelin' letter in time for this post but will let you have every information possible by tomorrow's post.

I also received by today's post an account from George of his having received the box from Richards and of getting it booked by the Coach for me, which I expects tomorrow morning.

I have wrote an acknowledgement to your present. I have no particular news to insert, am sorry I offended James in not writing, will write very soon. I remain, with love to Brothers & Sister,

Your Dutiful Son, John George.

Please to give my compliments to Mr Phillips and make use of my name to any friends that should enquire after me as if they were inserted. I should have been very glad to have known how Mr W.'s letter was addressed and what time it was sent.

*

13. Miss Mary George, Blue Boar Inn, Haverfordwest.

Stone House Barracks
Mar 24th 1799

Dear Sister,

I wrote by yesterday's post which suppose is received and mentioned in the bottom of desiring you to make enquiry about getting me a small sum on good int[erest] in order for to get the necessary articles which I am occasioned for. Upon consideration I wrife these few lines to remind you, finding the situation that I am now in very uncertain for I don't know the moment of my embarkation as there are a great many shipping in here, altho' I write such I hope not to embark before I get leave but at present and doubtless shall meet with a refusal upon asking but no opportunity shall escape. I have no particular news to acquaint you with: begs to be excused as the post is just going out.

I remain with duty to Father & Mother, love to Brothers & accept this with my kind love from, Dear Sister,

Your ever Affte Brother, John George.

Pray send a speedy answer.

*

14. Miss Mary George, Blue Boar Inn, Haverfordwest.

Stone House Barracks
March 31st 1799

Dear Sister,

I am almost ashamed to answer yours of the 26th inst. which I have received just this evening but in hopes of gaining your affection have taken up my pen to address these few lines to my dear Sister hoping it will meet you all well as I am at present.

I am really sorry to have troubled you about the same thing so often; it was on account of a mind so flurried as the General sent to me to know if I was ready for embarkation, upon my answering him in the negative, desired me to get ready as soon as possible as the situation I was in was very uncertain, – he wanted me to go on board the *Dragon* but fortunately did not; the officer that went in my room was obliged to launch out 20 guineas towards 3 months' mess on his embarking. I think myself very fortunate in not going, the Mess being so extravagantly high, but it is not so in all ships.

You might be well assured that I am not in the least extravagant and I can very well say that there is not an officer in all Barracks that lives more upright than what I does. I never enter into any vice whatever and always makes it my maxim to refrain any officer's company who sees they are going astray. I speak without flattery.

It was the General's desire for me to get 2 coats upon my first arrival here, he spoke to me but was willing to do without one as long as possible; have just been given an address for one at £3.10.0; indeed the coat I now wear is rather gone bad for a best coat. The Adjutant has just spoke to me to get everything in readiness and being obliged to get 2 Cloths I have bespoke them at 11 yards at 3s.10d. being 2 yards wide. I am sure I am not too hasty in making preparations, for it is a thing which I must do & not being willing to be pestered on the moment; to my opinion have acted right.

As to my application for a frigate is quite useless for it a thing which I don't expect. Would you suppose that I should be appointed to one to have the whole command upon myself knowing nothing of duty? No I am sure my dear Sister would hold no such thoughts. There is now in Barracks several old 1st Lieuts. who have applied long since for frigates still waiting. If Mr Meyrick was so good to arbour such thoughts to my Father, why didn't he offer to make application? I dare say his interest is as powerful as any gentleman in Pembrokeshire but it is mostly the case in general not to trouble themselves in any affair without there is something to their own interest.

Dear Sister, I am very well satisfied in your enclosure and hopes for the future to no more trouble you, and soon hopes to return it with interest.

I am quite angry to those friends of mine who are troubling themselves regarding my conduct. I am sure it is out of the power of any man to say I am extravagant; if you would wish I can send you my whole expenses since I joined Barracks: then I hope you'll be convinced to the contrary.

My pay for April is due tomorrow and my Agent is good to write to me if I want cash upon my embarkation that he would accept of a Bill for £20. We stand even in accounts and tomorrow my month's pay will go to my credit.

I wrote to you and to my Mother to remind you on the purport of the business to which your answer agrees please to burn them for I can't endure the thought of such letters being kept; I also wrote to my Brother in answer to his (and at the same time received one from you) which suppose is received. I have been told that the clothes which I have spoke for is very cheap, it being huckaback and very strong: there was another Officer at the same time bought the same quantity. they are selling off at prime cost. My month's pay is always payable to first day of the month.

If any thing particular should happen you shall immediately know. I remain with duty to Father & Mother, love to Brothers, Grandmother & Miss Gould, Dear Sister,

Your ever Aff^{te} Brother, John George.

I would write to Miss Gould but am quite at a loss what to say: will write very soon: should be glad to receive a few lines very soon after the receipt of that from you.

*

15. Mr Stephen George, Blue Boar Inn, Haverfordwest.

Stone House Barracks
Apr 1st 1799

Dear and Hon^d Parents,

Unexpectedly yours of the 28th inst. just arrived together with the enclosure and will assure you it was far beyond my expectations for instead of such a letter I expected no other than a sharp letter respecting my conduct but hopes you have a different opinion to what some friends have, as mentioned in my Sister's letter. I would have given a great deal could I have recalled the letters I wrote home within this week but trusts you'll forgive as at that time my mind being so much flurried preparatory to embarking. I never thought any thing of the kind till was roused by the General (as mentioned in a letter to my Sister by yesterday's post). I never should have thought of troubling you had I received my Agent's kind letter before but at present shan't draw till I am necessitated so to do. The Officer that embarked on board the *Dragon* was obliged to pay 20 guineas on his first going on board and indeed that was the cause of my writing such letters which I am now ashamed to acknowledge: trusts that when the time of my embarking arrives shall find a more fortunate ship and a more reasonable Mess: a short time after I embark shall see how matters stand and you might rely upon my word that all the remainder of my purse will immediately remit to you and hopes shall prove as dutiful a son as ever Mr Perkins have.

Was I remaining in Barracks should be able very well to save some pay after paying for every thing my expenses don't exceed a guinea. I mostly pay at the canteen from 10 to 12s. per week and the remainder will clear all other expenses. My purse is now worth 16½ guineas; will have 5½ to pay out of it for coat & clothes and hopes the remainder will do without any more drawing. My Agent has got my month's pay in hand today (being payable the first day of the month): his address is George Coombe, Esq., No. 20 Great Marlborough Street, London: he has an excellent character among the Officers and dare say if he was asked would advance any sum. When I saw Mr Phillips here he told me that Mr F. Williams drew upon his agent 6 months' pay before hand: you see I was not the only person. Will endeavour in the future to keep even in accounts, if not make him debtor.

Dear Parents you might be well assured in regard to my conduct that it is not injured in the least since I was under your eye. I never go to any idle places nor enter into any vice whatever, it is greatly to my credit in behaving in a proper light for the General is that sort of a man that he privately inspects into our conduct; you can't do a thing without his knowing through some channel and since I first joined I always made it my utmost endeavour to gain his good will: those that behaves well he takes a great liking to and those who behave the reverse he detests: it was only the other day he spoke to me not to keep company with one of the officers he mentioned and desired me to transmit this to all the rest of my brother Officers to do the same. This officer has injured his character much in whoring and other vices; without flattery I have every reason to believe that I am amongst the number that are in his good opinion.

I must drop my pen for the present being on guard today. The duty is far more tedious than it is in the Militia, am obliged to be in readiness all night and scarce can get a nap of sleep. We are always 2 days confined to barracks and dare not stir out without being brought to a General Court Martial for quitting the Guard. The first day we call it In Waiting & the second day, Officer of the Barrack Guard. I go the Patrols with a Party at 10, 12 & 2 o'clock tonight, as always careful to put my greatcoat on, drinks tea between 11 & 3.

I hope this will gain a speedy answer for nothing gives me greater pleasure than hearing from home. Please to give my love to Sister & Brothers, Grandmother and all enquiring friends and accept those few lines with my hearty prayers for your health and happiness from, Dear Parents,

Your ever Dutiful & Aff^{te} Son, John George.

*

16. Miss Mary George, Blue Boar Inn, Haverfordwest.

Stone House Barracks
Apr 19th 1799

Dear Sister,

Yours of the 14th inst. I just received and am happy to find you are all well as I am at present. I wrote to you the 13th. inst. requesting to know as early as possible how the shipping goes on at Milford, particularly the *Lavinia*[15] it being the report here that she is ready for sea. If you have not wrote, please to let me know if it is a fact and how many men are working in the yard as I promised an officer in Barracks that I would make every possible enquiry.

This is going to be the rendezvous for the Channel Fleet this summer and a few evenings ago part of the Fleet came in; it is supposed there will be a great call for Marine Officers this summer in the fleet, however there is plenty of Officers in the Barracks wishing to embark. I thought of dining with Mr Birch[16] today but on receipt of yours declined it finding far more pleasure in writing to my dear Sister than discoursing over a glass of wine.

I am very thankful to my dear Mother in offering to send me boots, but at present I want nothing: had I thought of it before the box was sent I should have liked to have had a few pair of yarn stockings as such an article here is not to be got, but must drop it till such time as I shall be able to fetch them myself. I makes use of my 2 pair of boots in Barracks; when I embark shall be allowed to wear any thing except the coat which must be uniform.

Please to give my kind love to my old friend John Potter and congratulate him on his return home. Tell him I shall be extremely happy to hear from him very soon. As for Miss Fisher, otherwise Mrs Evans, I have nothing more to say of but blot her out of my mind entirely.

Dear Sister, you must excuse me going any lengths to this as it is very late for the post; my next I hope will be longer. I shall wait for your answer to your last letter which expects tomorrow or Sunday. Please to give my respectful love to Miss Davies, Miss Gould and in short to all yours and my acquaintance not forgetting Mr E. B. Phillips and sister. I remain with duty to Father & Mother, love to Brothers & accept those few lines with the warmest affections of,

Your ever loving Brother, John George.

Please to let me know if you have wrote to Miss Fields: her address is Miss Fields at Mrs Davies, No. 64 Pall Mall, London: when you next write give her my love: in remembering me to my old acquaintance, don't forget Mr M. Phillips & Mr Duberlin, tell them I wish them a speedy riddance of their old acquaintance (Gout). Adieu. JG.

*

17. Miss Mary George, Blue Boar Inn, Haverfordwest.

HMS *Bellona*,[17] Hamoaze
Apr. 25th 1799

Dear Sister,

I wrote to my Father 23rd inst. which supposed is received. Yesterday morning Mr Watson & myself embarked on the *Bellona* and have every reason to believe shall make it very agreeable. We shall go out of harbour in the course of ten days: her destination is not known. If you should write you must not delay but write very early upon the receipt of this & let me know all the news you can think of. We are to take in 8 months stock of provisions, &c., for the Mess. Mr Birch is the Cater.

Mr Wm. Phillips called on me yesterday evening, but several others were left behind at Portsmouth, the *Phoenix* sailing very unexpectedly for Plymouth. – they were obliged to travel Post from Portsmouth, – the *Phoenix* is going on her old station again (the Irish).

I also called on Mr Curgenven yesterday, he looks exceeding well & was very glad to see me. He informs me he is in a very extensive line of business: he pressed me much to call upon him very often. He desires his love to you. I beg you'll excuse my hurry having my things on board just now.

I remain with duty to Father & Mother, love to Brothers & all friends,

Your Affte & loving Brother, John George.

Pray don't fail to write. I am prepared with every thing for embarkation. Direct for me as I have desired my Father his letters till such time as you hear further from me. JG.

*

18. Mr Stephen George, Blue Boar Inn, Haverfordwest.

Bellona, Hamoaze
Apr. 30th 1799

Dear Parents,

We unexpectedly received orders last night to join the Channel Fleet immediately: shall go out of Harbour in the course of a 2 hours. When you write please to direct for me as desired by a letter which I wrote home. The ship is all in uproar and begs you'll excuse me saying more than I am very well and hopes this'll meet you the same.

Please to take notice of Mrs Birch. Mr Birch expects her round. I expect we shall come in again in the course of a fortnight. All letters will be forwarded to the ship.

I remain with love to Sister & Brothers & all friends,

Your ever Aff[te] & Dutiful Son, John George

*

19. Mr Stephen George, Blue Boar Inn, Haverfordwest.

Bellona, Cawsand Bay
May 1st 1799

Dear & Hon'[d] Parents,

I wrote to you by yesterday's post, which suppose is received. We sailed out of harbour this morning to this place and are likely to remain here some days. When I wrote to you we expected to proceed to sea instantly to join the Channel Fleet having received intelligence that the French fleet were at sea and that Lord Bridport's[18] fleet were only 5 leagues distant from them, since we have been ordered not to proceed to sea till such time as we receive further orders, it is reported that the French fleet have gone into Brest again; there is 7 sail-of-the-line[19] lying here waiting for further orders besides the *Bellona* which makes the whole 8 sail a pretty good fleet.

Yours of the 28th ult. I have just received & am happy to find you are all well as I am at present. You might rely upon my word that no opportunity shall slip in writing. The ship is paid today and suppose we shall soon join the Channel Fleet.

Mr Birch desires his compliments to you and will be obliged to you if you could send to Mrs Birch that we are going to sea and that he would wish her to go to Haverfordwest and take lodgings till such time as we comes in again and would thank you to assist her in getting comfortable lodgings for her.

I have no particular news to inform you at present. I have not been sick yet we are quite in the open sea and the ship rolling as if we were in a cradle.

I can't ask you to write an answer for we shall certainly sail before such time as it could arrive. I'll let you know again how to direct to me. I don't want any thing and am very thankful for your enquiry.

Please to give my love to Sister & Brothers & Grandmother, Price and all friends, particularly my Sister's female acquaintance & also J. Potter, Mr M. Phillips & Mr Duberlin and accept those few lines with my prayers for your health and happiness from, Dear Parents,

Your ever Aff[te] & dutiful Son, John George.

I have received letters from Mr Phillips & Mr Robbin, the *Phoenix*, to meet them in Dock but never could have the opportunity as there were no Marine Officers on board besides myself and being obliged to remain on board. They are very well. Excuse my writing. Adieu. JG.

*

20. Miss Mary George, Blue Boar Inn, Haverfordwest.

HM Ship *Bellona*
May 4th 1799

Dear Sister,

I have just this moment received 2 letters under frank of the 28th & 30th ult. and embrace this favourable [opportunity] of returning those few lines by the same boat to say I am very well and hopes this will meet you the same. I have not time before the boat sails to open the letters otherwise should lose this opportunity of writing. You may be assured that I'll write again by the very next opportunity.

It is Sir T. Thompson's[20] express orders that no officer shall go out of the ship and that we are to get ready to sail at a moment's warning.

Mr Birch has wrote to his wife by yesterday's post and I also wrote to my Father at the same time. We are to join the Channel fleet for a short time and afterwards to have a better station . . .

I remain with duty to Father & Mother, love to Brothers and all friends, and accept this with the warmest affection of,

Your ever loving Brother, John George.

*

21. Mr Stephen George, Blue Boar Inn, Haverfordwest.

HM Ship *Bellona*, Gibraltar
May 20th 1799

Dear and Hon^d Parents,

We are just now arrived after a very pleasant cruise: embrace the favourable opportunity of sending this by the *Childers* who is going home with dispatches. We got information of the French fleet passing the Gut four days ago and of Lord St Vincent's[21] fleet pursuing them, and since the Spanish fleet is come out and steered the same course so that shortly you may expect, I hope, the capture of both fleets. Our squadron consists of 5 sail-of-the-line & 2 frigates. Suppose we shall not come to an anchor on account of this intelligence.

The climate agrees with me very well, hope this will meet with you all well as I am at present. The *Childers* is already weighed: you must excuse the shortness of this. You might rely upon my word that the first information I get shall be immediately transmitted to you.

Mr Birch is very well, desires his respects to you and love to Mrs Birch. He is very busy doing the duty of the ship otherwise would write.

Please to write directly upon receipt of this & address for Lieut. John George, Marines, HM Ship *Bellona*, Lord St Vincent's Fleet, Mediterranean. I remain with love to Brothers, Sister & all friends,

Your Aff^te & Dutiful Son, John George.

Enclosed is a letter for Mrs Birch being desired to enclose it since I wrote the above. When you write to me under the above address whether we join Lord St V's Fleet or not, will always be received. Adieu. John George.

*

22. Mr Stephen George, Blue Boar Inn, Haverfordwest.

HMS *Bellona* at sea
May 26th 1799

Dear and Hon'^d Parents,

I am now going to take up my pen to write a few lines to you in hopes of getting a speedy opportunity of sending them from Minorca, as we are not far distant from it. The distance we are from each other makes me very anxious to hear of your welfare. I hope the time will yet come when I shall meet your embraces which in my opinion will not be long as we have both the French and Spanish Fleets before us. I wrote to you the 19th inst. from Gibraltar by the *Childers* brig informing you of the above fleets passing by & also of Lord St Vincent's Fleet, the time I mentioned of their sailing through the Gut was false for upon further information I find the French Fleet sailed the 5th inst., Lord St Vincent's the 11th, the Spaniards the 15th & our Squadron the 19th so we get them all before.

We received information a few days ago from the *Caroline* frigate that she had seen 10 sail-of-the-line of Spaniards not far ahead of her and that three out of the ten were dismasted. We were counting out our Prize Money; unfortunately the wind shifting unfavourable for our getting up with them, have neither seen or heard of them since; suppose they have reached Cartagena or some other Spanish port; we got everything cleared for action. The *Phoenix* has parted with us prior to our arrival at Gibraltar; suppose she is sent & with dispatches. We stopped but a very short time off Gibraltar waiting for orders from the Governor . . .

I have the Command in Action of all the cannonades on the quarter deck, which makes me perfectly satisfied with my station. Mr Hall has also command of all the cannon on the quarter deck and Capt. Betty and Mr Watson have the command of the Marines on the Poop. I have dined with Sir T. Thompson twice and think him to be a very agreeable good-natured man.

The climate is not so warm as I had expected but fine, mild & healthy weather, & thinks it will agree with me very well. This is a fine country for fruit but have had no opportunity yet to get any except a few oranges which the Captain got off from Gibraltar. When I wrote to you from Hamoaze, Plymouth, I little thought of going abroad so soon: had I known I might have provided myself with boots & shoes and several other things I shall be in need of, particularly if we stay out here any length of time, without a very extravagant price & of a very bad quality.

I am quite angry with you for sending me the £10 bill in your last letter, having just before taken up all the cash from my agent which he had in my favour,

27th May at sea

We have just spoke with a Swedish brig from Minorca. She informed us that it is reported there that the French fleet is gone to Toulon and that the Spanish fleet is all dispersed in a heavy gale of wind. She also informed us that Lord St Vincent sailed from Minorca about 9 days ago to cruise off Toulon with 26 sail-of-the-line.

I beg of you to write immediately upon receipt of this and let me have all the news. I believe there is no postage charge after it goes on board the Packet, but not before direct thus

Lieut. John George, Marines, On board HM Ship *Bellona*,
Lord St Vincent's Fleet, Mediterranean.

Believe me there will be nothing give me more pleasure than receiving letters from you at the distance we are from each other – ever so short will be joyfully accepted – you may depend that no opportunity shall slip in my writing to you, and I beg of my dear Parents to write very often and not wait for my letter s as I shall not have so many opportunities as what you'll have.

We keep very regular hours on board: we dine at half past one, sup at 8 and breakfast at half past seven in the morning – and as to our drinking is very modest, mostly wine. I always goes to my bed between 9 & 10 o'clock and rise about 6.

I wrote to my Sister under the same cover with this. Please to remember me to Mr Phillips, Mr Duberlin, Mr E. B. Philips, all relations at Hook and elsewhere and in short all friends.

May 30th We have just now arrived off Minorca but not yet come to an anchor: it seems to be a very fine island. I suppose we shall remain here a very short time but proceed to Toulon.

I must conclude with my prayers for your health and happiness,

Your ever Affte & Dutiful Son, John George.

Please to give my love to Sister & Brothers. Mr Birch desires his respects to you.

*

23. Miss Mary George, Blue Boar Inn, Haverfordwest.

HM Ship *Bellona*
May 30th 1799

Dear Sister,

After a long silence I take up my pen to write these few lines in hopes of meeting you all well as I am at present. We are just arrived off this place but not yet come to anchor nor don't think we shall but proceed to Toulon. I have given my Father all the news I know of. Please to write very soon and let me know if John Potter's eyes is any thing better. You must excuse the shortness of this, my next shall be longer.

Please to remember me to Miss Davies, Miss Gould & all your acquaintance & John Potter. I remain with duty to parents, love to Brothers, Grandmother & friends,

Your ever Affte & Loving Brother, John George.

I am in hopes of boats coming along side so that I may send this on shore to be forwarded by the first opportunity.

June 1st 5 o'clock a.m. We joined Lord St Vincent's Fleet off Toulon yesterday evening. We are about 24 sail-of-the-line and several frigates among which are 7 three-deckers. I can't exactly say the number. The French Fleet, I believe is nearly the same number. What a beautiful sight it is to see the Grand Fleet.

I am now in my bed finishing this to send it by an opportunity which now offers. I had no opportunity from Minorca.

*

24. Miss Mary George, Blue Boar Inn, Haverfordwest.

HMS *Bellona*, Minorca
July 10th 1799

Dear Sister,

After a long silence I have taken up my pen to write a few lines in hopes of meeting you all well as I am at present. Our Fleet arrived here last Sunday where we yet remain watering, most of the ships being very short; prior to our arrival we were joined by a reinforcement of 12 sail-of-the-line under the command of Sir C. Cotton[22] which makes our fleet nearly 40 sail-of-the-line amongst which are 12 three-deckers. I have not been on shore nor am thinking; shan't as we are at anchor of the harbour, most of the Fleet are gone in. I am not at all anxious about it, it being so excessively hot on board and must be much more so on shore. We enjoy all the varieties of the Island which is mostly fruit and vegetables. The bullocks are very poor and small, however we have had a few on board as fresh provision.

We hear that the French fleet is at Cartagena; if so we shall soon sail; also we hear that the Russians & Austrians are cutting all before them on the continent, and all Italy is completely restored. When we were off Genoa we sent a flag of truce for an acceptance of prisoners which were taken out of the frigates and brigs taken by us, accordingly cartels[23] came out, took them all.

The republic of Genoa were in a dreadful situation at that time, there being 40,000 Austrians within 40 miles of the frontier, so that I expect before long Genoa is retaken with great slaughter: the Russians and Austrians give no quarter. Leghorn is also retook after putting every Frenchman to death. There is nothing wanting to put a conclusion to this war but the capture of the French fleet which I hope we shall soon compass. The Spaniards are easily brought to.

I dare say Mr Phillips is anxious to hear of the *Phoenix*: you might tell him she got into harbour yesterday after cruising. Mr Birch [who] is just returned from shore spoke with Mr Bèule, a brother Officer, who informed him that Mr P. was very [well] and the other gentlemen on board. I must lay down my pen for the present being called to supper.

The Fleet are all coming out of harbour, suppose we will soon sail. I hope you have answered some of my [letters] before this: believe me I am very uneasy in not hearing from you since we left England: please to write on receipt of this and direct as before, only say Lord Keith's[24] Fleet, Lord St Vincent having resigned his command to Lord Keith and gone down to Gibraltar. Please to give my love to all your acquaintance, Miss Davies, Miss Gould, John Potter and all relations & friends. Tell Miss Davies she might have had my sash & gorget had I known when I embarked, having had no occasion to wear it on board. Let me have all the news you possibly can think of in your next. Mr Birch is very well, desires his compliments to the family.

Everything here is extravagantly dear; you can't get a skein of thread under 2d.; they gain by clothes which is brought from England cent per cent. I thought once to get scarlet cloth for a coat but have since declined it on account of the price. I am going about a job which was never done at home, that is to turn my coat: that is the way with soldiers, particularly Sub-Lieutenants.

I remain with duty to father & Mother, love to Grandmother, Price & family and accept this with the warmest affection of, Dear Sister,

Yours ever loving Brother, John George.

P.S. I am well seasoned against sea sickness.

*

25. Miss Mary George, Blue Boar Inn, Haverfordwest.

HMS *Bellona*, off Gibraltar
July 29th 1799

Dear Sister,

Here we are with a very strong westerly wind trying to work out of the Gut but of no purpose, the wind being so much against us and until such time as the wind shifts, here we are likely to remain, It is really very disheartening to the Fleet to hear of the combined Fleet being at sea and we confined here as if were in a gaol, but I hope to God the wind will soon change and then I think it will be likely of our soon seeing Old England. The enemy are actually sailed from Cadiz and that we have frigates dogging them. The Admiral have received intelligence but what can't say. We have been for this 8 days waiting for a fair wind, it blowing fresh which obliged us to go over on the Barbary Coast and there came on an anchor to water. We were obliged to send a party of Marines with an Officer on shore to cover the watering place. I was on shore 3 times, the country seems very wild and mountainous and the inhabitants are truly frightful: they at best seemed to resent our watering without their Governor's permission, or a present from each of our ships. Gunpowder soon brought them to and never attempted to molest us afterwards. We hear that the Russians & Austrians are very [active] on the Continent, that they are clearing all [before] them and after restoring all Italy, &c., are advancing into France.

I wrote to you the 11th inst. from Minorca & hopes you have received. Believe me, my anxiety is great to hear from you, not having had any letter since we left England. If you write, all letters will be forwarded after us, wherever we go.

Herewith is a letter for Miss Gould. I have left open for your perusal. Please put a [frank] to it and give it to her. I know she will be very glad to receive it as she likes to correspond [often] with the young men. I am not like Mr Curgenven who was obliged to break off his correspondence on account of business for I have not the least thing to do on board only to eat & [sleep].

Mr Birch is very well & desires his compliments to the family. I send this by our Purser who is going to England. Please to give my duty to Parents, love to Brothers, Grandmother, friends & acquaintances & accept this with the warmest affections of,

Your affte & loving Brother, John George.

P.S. I am greatly surprised I have not received an answer to my letter of the 19th May as gentlemen on board have received answers to theirs sent the same time. I think there must be a great delay in some office or another. Adieu. JG.

*

26. Mr Stephen George, Blue Boar Inn, Haverfordwest.

HMS *Bellona*, Torbay
Aug 16th 1799

Dear Parents,

We are just this instance come to an anchor and embrace the opportunity of acquainting you of our arrival. We met here at anchor the Channel Fleet under the command of Lord Bridport. Our whole force here is upward of 50 sail-of-the-line: such a fleet was never collected together before. I really can't say anything about the Combined Fleets, no more than suppose them to be in Brest.

Please to write by the very first post and let me know how you all are. Address for me on board HMS *Bellona*, Torbay, Devon. How long we shall stay here God knows: we are in expectation of either going to Plymouth or Portsmouth to victual, however letters will be forwarded after us, wherever we go.

Mr Birch desires his compliments to you, begs you'll by the first opportunity inform Mrs Birch of his arrival, and is sorry he can't embrace this opportunity of writing, the signal being just made for him to prepare on board one of the ships on survey. He will write as soon as he can get an uninterrupted half-hour.

I enjoy a very good state of health on board. Please to give my kind love to Sister and Brothers, Grandmother and all friends. Tell Mary I have wrote several letters to her but have received none in return. It is all owing to delay in the [Letters] Office I suppose.

I remain with all my prayers for your health & happiness,

Your ever aff^te & dutiful Son, John George.

*

27. Miss Mary George, Blue Boar Inn, Haverfordwest.

HMS *Bellona*, Cawsand Bay
Aug 27th 1799

Dear Sister,

We have been here nearly 7 days without receiving letters from you. I am greatly surprised what can be the reason; be assured I am anxious to hear from you. Please to write as early as possible as we expect to sail very soon and perhaps on a foreign station again.

I am very well and hope you are all the same. I remain with duty to Parents, love to Brothers and acquaintances,

Yours affectionate Brother, John George.

Consider what my uneasiness must be in not receiving any letters for this four months.

*

28. Miss M. George, Blue Boar Inn, Haverfordwest.

HMS *Bellona*, Cawsand Bay
Sept 4th 1799

Dear Sister,

Yours of the 29th ult. is just received and am glad to find you all well. Since the date of yours I wrote twice to you, which hopes you have received. Don't suppose that I am ill for I never enjoyed a better state of health in my life. The reason for my silence upon our first arrival was that I was determined to have an answer to mine sent from Torbay before I wrote the second time: 'twas not from neglect but merely anxiety.

I mentioned in my last of inspecting the ship to go abroad again but since, our minds are entirely changed for we expect now to join Lord Bridport's fleet in the Channel. The ship is ready for sea and expect we shall sail very soon. The *Princess Royal* arrived yesterday evening and is going into harbour if possible. I will see Wakelin and will let you know for the satisfaction of his father.

I have been on shore several times since our arrival and went to the play one evening to see Pizarro, a very excellent play and well performed.

I enclose a letter for John Potter which you will please to give to him. He seems determined of coming into the Marines. I really thought there would not be the least delay in getting his appointment by his talk before I left home, but take them all together there is none equal to poor Mr Cleaveland.

I took a walk to the Marine Barracks a few days ago and amongst all my old acquaintance could see but one, the others being all embarked.

John Potter mentioned in his letter that Capt. Allen had promised him his advice, which I advised him to pay the greatest attention but was a friend to ask me what Division I could recommend: I would prefer Plymouth to either Portsmouth or Chatham.

Lord Bridport is gone down Channel from Torbay 2 days ago with upward of forty sail-of-the-line. We expected a signal for us to weigh: we certainly shall ail very soon. If it should be convenient for you to write upon receipt of this, believe me it will be most welcoming accepted. Please to give my duty to Parents, love to Brothers, Grandmother and friends, and remember me to Mr Lloyd and his sisters and all your acquaintance, also to Mr M. Phillips, Mr Duberlin, &c. I remain, dear Sister,

Your ever affectionate & loving Brother, John George.

P.S. Pray what does Miss Gould mean by her Postcript of Miss George and a Mr N.: don't blush.

*

29. Miss Mary George, Blue Boar Inn, Haverfordwest.

Plymouth Dock
Sept. 5th 1799

Dear Parents,

I am just come on shore and immediately sent a note to Mr Wakelin: have the satisfaction of saying that we are now in company together: he is really a fine young man and is improved much since I last saw him.

We have no news. Stop. Beg your pardon: we have just received the confirmation of the Dutch Fleet being given up to Lord Duncan[25] for the Stadholder – glorious news.

I must conclude with love to Sister, Brother, &c.,

Your affectionate & dutiful Son, John George.

Mr Wakelin desires his compliments to you, Sister & Brothers.

*

30. Mrs George, Blue Boar Inn, Haverfordwest.

HMS *Bellona*, Cawsand Bay
Sept. 8th 1799

Dear Mother,

It was not until this instant that I received your ever welcomed letter altho' arrived yesterday owing to an Officer taking it up and not coming off. Believe me it made me quite happy to see the handwriting: hope this correspondence might be kept up.

You are too good in offering me things but really I am not in want of anything at present: accept my hearty thanks for your great attention to me, indeed I wish I could see you and have the pleasure of taking my dear Mother's arm for a walk, but patience is required as I am afraid we shall not meet very soon except we should have a General Peace, then I would go and live with you.

I have wrote twice by the last two posts which hopes you have received. I have got none of the letters which my Sister mentions of; suppose they are sent out to the Mediterranean, perhaps they might be received in a twelve months' time. We expect to sail in the course of a few days to join the Channel Fleet: shall be in again in the course of a few weeks. Any letters which you may write, direct them as your last, they will be forwarded to me.

I find by John Potter's letter that he intends coming into the Marines: he has not informed me who applies for him but suppose from my sister's letter it is Lord K. I wish him success on account of his situation.

We have no particular news here, except Lord Duncan's victory. It is thought we shall have an illumination here this evening.

Mr Birch desires his compliments to you. I must conclude with prayers for your health. Love to Sister, Brothers, friends & relations.

Your ever affte & dutiful Son, John George.

*

31. Miss George, Blue Boar Inn, Haverfordwest.

HMS *Bellona*, Torbay
Sept 29th 1799

Dear Sister,

I received yours of the 24th inst. and am exceeding happy to find you all well as I am at present. I was much shocked at Mr Fortune's rash exit,[26] and of poor Mr Phillips's death. I understood Mr Wm. James was in the West Indies having a commission in a regiment there; pray when did he come home? I have also received since my last, two letters which has been abroad; altho' they were of an old date it gave me great pleasure to find you all well at that time. We still remain here waiting for a fair wind, at present there is no appearance. When we sail it will only be for a short time. I suppose we shan't be much at sea all the winter; it is not likely we shall go abroad again but remain in the Channel.

We made a small party to go ashore and walked to Dartmouth, about 4 miles from here, where we spent most part of a day. Dartmouth is a small town, neat and clean: it is situated at the bottom of a hill, with hills all around We returned to Brixham, Torbay, where we slept and came on board the following evening. Mr Birch has just informed me of the death of a countryman, Lieut. Roch, of HMS *Formidable*, a brother of Mr Roch of Butterhilll, perhaps you might have remembered him. He went ashore to sick quarters and died at Dartmouth about thirteen days ago.

Mr Birch received a letter from his wife since our arrival informing him that she was coming round: he has been expecting her daily ever since: she was to take her leave of you before her departure.

I am sorry you are deprived of James's company. I hope it's all for his own advantage; was I at this moment but that short distance from you, how soon would I meet your embraces: it is my whole desire to see you. God knows when. This war has been the means of separating many a son from his parents and brother from his sister. Peace, I hope, will bring us all together again. Until then we must endeavour to make ourselves comfortable in our separation. I am heartily thankful to my dear Parents for wishing to send me a present, but really could not wish any thing of the kind: in the winter season a little game would be very acceptable, but the uncertainty we are on board will not permit me to beg of you to send some, unless we go into dock, when you shall have timely notice.

I am sorry for Mr E. B. Phillips and Mrs Jenkins's indisposition: I wish them a speedy recovery with all my heart. I hope this fever, which you mentioned of, is not infectious: do take care of yourselves: it is my constant prayer for your health and happiness. Have not heard any thing of Miss Jenkins for this long time. Do you associate with her as usual: please to remember me to her and to that family.

My apology for the shortness of my last is merely that we arrived just before the post went out and willing to inform you of our arrival. There could be no lady in the case as I had not put my foot on shore at that time. I'll endeavour for the future to write longer letters.

I find that John Potter has not got his appointment into the Marines yet, neither Mr Jones. I wish J. Potter success with all my heart; as to Mr Jones, was he fortunate enough would soon get tired of it. What is Jones about? Does he do any thing or is he quite a Gentleman?

Please to give my love to Miss Gould and all your acquaintance; let me know how Miss Gould relishes my not answering her letter yet. I shall drop the correspondence a little. I have not heard a word of Miss Davies for this long time; pray where is she; remember me to her.

My paper being almost filled, I must therefore conclude with duty to parents, love to Brothers, Grandmother, relations & friends and accept this yourself with the warmest affections of,

Your ever loving Brother, John George.

Please to write as soon as convenient.

*

32. Miss George, Blue Boar Inn, Haverfordwest.

HMS *Bellona*, Torbay
Oct. 6th 1799

Dear Sister,

At last I take up my pen to address these few lines to my dear Sister. I have been waiting this week for a letter from William, having wrote to him the 23rd of last month and at the same time to Bristol to Uncle George, otherwise would have written sooner. The signal was made a few days ago for the fleet to unmoor, the wind being fair; soon after, the wind shifted; moored again. I had wrote a letter to send to you if an opportunity offered to inform you of our sailing; have the satisfaction to say the wind still continues against our sailing, for really I don't like myself to be rolling about the seas this dis-agreeable weather; in fine weather, it is very pleasant. I don't know of a better place which I should like for cruising than the Mediterranean, was it not for its distance from you, it being as smooth as a mill pond, except when a gale of wind comes on which is very severe but continues for a short time, when all is smooth again. I have no news to give you except the arrival of Sir J. B. Warren's[27] Squadron. We shall certainly sail the first fair wind & you may expect our arrival again the first strong westerly winds.

The day's post boat is returned but no letter for me. I must expect one tomorrow. Perhaps I might not have the opportunity of sending this to the post till after the return of tomorrow's boat, therefore will leave it open.

7th I again resume my fun. The post is just arrived but no letter; I suppose it's owing to you being busy. Mr Birch is very well, desires his compliments to the family.

I conclude with duty to parents, love to Brothers, Grandmother and friends,

Your ever aff^{te} & loving Brother, John George.

Please to write when convenient. You may leave out the word Devon on the directions as Torbay is sufficient. One of your letters was sent to the Downs in a mistake. Adieu. JG.

*

33. Miss George, Blue Boar Inn, Haverfordwest.

HMS *Bellona*, Torbay
Oct. 10th 1799

My dear Sister,

Yours of the 4th inst. I have just received and am exceeding happy to find you all well. I have had no account of my letter to William neither Uncle George yet which I wrote the 23rd ult. I suppose they are lost through the neglect of the boatman which took them on shore, fortunately there was nothing particular in them. You mentioned that Lord Keith is going out to the Mediterranean which I have been informed before as a fact, also a squadron with him. I really can't say whether our ship is intended for one, or what ships are going.

I dined with Sir Thomas [Thompson] 2 days ago when he informed me that he expected a letter daily with orders to go to Spithead to fit out, but it is the opinion of my messmates that we shan't go out of the Channel: how it will terminate, God knows.

I am just come down to my cabin after seeing a party of ladies out of the ship who came on board to see one of the gentlemen. They dined with us and nothing afterwards would do but clear a way for dancing and a very agreeable dance indeed we had, till within this half hour when the party broke up. I could heartily hope my dear sister was one of the party: hope I shall yet have that pleasure of being in her parties. After seeing the ladies over the side I could not rest content till I sat down to pen these few lines to you.

I was anxious to hear from you this some days; had sent you a letter under cover the 7th to enquire if you received any of my letters: have the satisfaction to find you got mine of the 29th for I conceive that my letters would give you as much pleasure as what yours would me, which is the greatest satisfaction I receive in hearing of your welfare.

I have been wishing often I had brought with me my Blue Cyphering book as I am getting quite ignorant of part which I have gone through and which might be useful to me yet. I will thank you to desire William to take care of it for me.

There is nothing particular going on here since my last. The wind still continues against us. We received by this day's post the confirmation of the capitulation of Alkmaar[28] by our able troops. I really wish them every success.

I am really sorry that John Potter's application for commission in the Marines proved fruitless. I find Mr Masterman is appointed to the Portsmouth Division. I forgot to enquire before: you informed me Bloss was married, please to let me know in your next to whom, and where Colonel Edwardes's regiment lies.

Please to send an acknowledgement of this with all news going on with you in H'west and its vicinity. Mr Birch desires his compliments to the family.

I must conclude, with duty to Parents, to Brothers, Grandmother and friends, dear Sister,

Your ever affectionate brother, John George.

P.S. Please to remember me to my old acquaintance John Potter, also.

*

34. Miss George, Blue Boar Inn, Haverfordwest.

HMS *Bellona*, Torbay
Oct. 20th 1799

Dear Sister,

Yours of the 13th inst. I have just received and am exceeding happy to find you all well. I have wrote since the date of yours which suppose you have received. I am glad William got his letter which I was so doubtful of. I must therefore expect Uncle George got his which I sent the same time. I have not heard from neither yet. I thought yesterday morning we should have sailed before this, the wind being fair, but since, the wind is come round to its old place again.

I should have been very happy to have seen Mr Green[29] when at Plymouth and more so in asking him on board. I am really sorry for Wakelin's indisposition. I would write to him if I knew his address.

We made up a party a few days ago to Dartmouth and returned on board the same evening after spending the day very agreeable.

I am made exceeding happy since writing the above in having received yours and my Brother's letter of the 15th I have heard nothing particular since my last about going abroad. It is the opinion here yet we shall not go but remain at home agreeable to you wish.

In respect to the yarn stockings, an article which might be comfortable in the winter, if you promise me you will not send any thing else, I'll direct you how to address them. I have not the least doubt but what my dear Sister will give and keep her word, well then you might send them to Bristol by some opportunity and Uncle George to forward them for me HMS *Bellona* to be left at Mr Hair, Shopkeeper, Torbay.

I wish John Potter success as landlord in his inn. I should like to know Mr Wakelin's appointment. You say Mr David Evans is going to send his son round here as a midshipman: don't give him my address as perhaps he might be too troublesome. Please to write soon.

I must conclude with duty to Parents, love to Brothers, Grandmother and friends. Dear Sister,

Your ever affectionate Brother, John George.

P.S. I should be glad to have Mr Frank Williams's address. I'll write very soon to my brother. JG.

*

35. Miss M. George, Blue Boar Inn, Haverfordwest.

HMS *Bellona*, Torbay
Oct. 24th 1799

Dear Sister,

I embrace the opportunity of letting you know that the signal is made for the Fleet to get under weigh, the wind being fair. Any thing particular which you should wish to write whilst we are out, you may address my letters Torbay as before; if they are not forwarded out, we shall receive them upon our arrival, which I expect will be very soon. Look out for a strong westerly wind and you'll soon hear of Lord Bridport's fleet being in Torbay. The men are now employed getting up the anchor.

Mr Birch is very well, desires his compliments to the family. Dear Sister,

Your ever affectionate Brother, John George.

*

36. Miss George, Blue Boar Inn, Haverfordwest.

HMS *Bellona*, Torbay
Nov. 14th 1799

Dear Sister,

I again take up my pen to address these few lines to you in hopes of meeting you and the family all well. I wrote to you upon our arrival and have been expecting a letter this two days but have not received one yet. I must lay the fault to the bomb-boat man who had the letter to put in the office.

We have had very bad weather ever since our arrival and very little communication with the shore. I don't expect to go ashore at all without the weather clears up very fine. The last time I was ashore was the day before we sailed. I had engaged with one of our Lieuts. to go to Dartmouth together: upon landing at the beach who should I see standing a little way off but Mr Woodcock, the hawker. I went up to him: he did not at first recollect me: upon letting him know who I was, he seemed very glad to see me and we chatted together for a short time. He told me his wife was here and wanted me to call and see her. I could not with decency leave my messmate at that time, who was waiting for me, but promised I would call on my return. Whilst we were at Dartmouth the wind came fair, which obliged us to return on board with all possible dispatch, and without fulfilling my promise to Mr Woodcock. It was 10 o'clock in the evening before we got on board, and sailed early next morning.

I think I have well tired you with this trivial meeting, but you must lay all the fault to the weather not having heard any news worth relating, and if I am not mistaken it is my Sister's wish for my writing long letters.

Since my last I received your letter of 15th July last which have been abroad: you mentioned of Miss Bevan's marriage with a Militiaman: I suppose much against Miss Gould's consent. Pray give Miss Gould my compliments and congratulate her on her niece's marriage, but don't take notice that I knew to whom Miss B. was married as I would not wish to displeasure Miss Gould.

I have heard nothing respecting the Mediterranean since my last: believe it to be all knocked in the head. If we remain in the Channel we shall be seldom out this winter except in very fine weather and then for a short time.

MR BIRCH, MY PARTICULAR FRIEND

Please to write as early as convenient on receipt of this. If you have answered my last which is not yet received, I will write directly after I get it.

Mr Birch is very well, desires his compliments to the family. When you next write to Miss Fields, remember me to her.

I must conclude with duty to Parents, love to Brothers, Grandmother and friends Dear Sister,

Your affectionate & loving Brother, John George.

*

37. Miss Mary George, Blue Boar Inn, Haverfordwest.

HMS *Bellona*
Nov. 15th 1799

Dear Sister,

Your ever welcomed letter of the 10th I have just received with a great deal of pleasure and am exceeding happy to find you all well. I wrote with yesterday's post which hope you'll receive before you get this.

The wind is come to the eastward and the signal is just made for the fleet to unmoor, therefore expects we shall go to sea this evening, without the wind shifts; at present there is no appearance. I can say with pleasure that all thoughts are given up of going abroad. Please to write and address as usual when I shall receive them upon our arrival.

Mr Birch received his letter with great satisfaction and bid me say everything that is affectionate for his wife. He would write but is obliged to attend the duty of the ship. I respect Mr Birch as my particular friend: begs my dear sister will do everything to contribute to Mrs Birch's happiness.

I'll write again the first opportunity. You must excuse me saying more than I am, with duty to Parents, love to Brothers, Grandmother and friends, Dear Sister,

Your ever affectionate Brother, John George.

Pray excuse faults if any.

*

38. Miss George, Blue Boar Inn, Haverfordwest.

Bellona, Torbay
Feb. 1st 1800

Dear Sister,

Yours of the 21st inst. I received yesterday evening with a great deal of pleasure, am happy to find you all well. I wrote upon our arrival which hope you have received & can't conceal the happiness I felt upon perusing part of your letter wherein you mention that our dear Parents were perfectly composed respecting the parcel. I should be extremely sorry at any time to offend them particularly at the distance we are from each other.

I took a walk to Dartmouth yesterday with one of my messmates and had the pleasing satisfaction of meeting with Capt. Richards who commanded one of the packets from Milford to Waterford. I believe he is building a packet at Dartmouth when he'll go on his old run. I have asked him on board: hope I have the pleasure of his company before we [leave]: we might converse about dear Pembrokeshire: he saw my Father in good health the day before he left the county which is now 2 months ago.

As it is likely we shall have a long cruise when we once sail I would wish, if it is convenient, for you to write once a week or a fortnight addressed Torbay or Plymouth, when I shall get them by the Cutters who are coming out to the Fleet every week. In return, be assured, I'll embrace every opportunity to write.

If William is determined to go to sea and agreeable to the family, I should wish him to go nowhere but the East Indies; after a length of time he may perhaps get on in the world. As for the West Indies and other parts, it is nothing but slavery for a young man; even mates are obliged to slave themselves. Supposing Lady Kensington could procure him a cadetship to India he is then sure of promotion. One of our Lieutenants has a brother in India, a Captain, in the Artillery, who went out a few years ago as a Cadet: in short I think it is time for my brother to think of something.

In a few days I shall expect an answer to mine of the 25th ult. At present there is no appearance of a fair wind to go down Channel, therefore I will trouble you to write when convenient after you receive this as the latest news is the most acceptable. Mr Birch is very well, desires his compliments to the family.

Please to give my love to relations of Hook, John Potter and all old acquaintances. I must conclude with duty to Parents, love to Brothers, Grandmother and friends,

Your Affte & loving Brother, John George.

*

39. Miss George, Blue Boar Inn, Haverfordwest.

HMS *Bellona*, Torbay.
4 a.m., Feb. 6th 1800

Dear Sister,

At this early hour I have the mortification of taking up my pen to inform you that we are now getting under weigh for sea, the wind being fair. I received your very agreeable letter of the 20th, ult. and was made exceeding happy to find it left you all well. I showed part of your letter which concerned Mrs Birch to her husband. I don't know well what steps he has taken. You mentioned of a Miss Jones having seen me at Plymouth. I don't recollect of meeting with such a person nor don't know of a woman of that name near St Martin's. Pray, who is she? I expected by yesterday's post an answer to mine of the 25th ult., it must arrive today, too late I am afraid; however, I shall get it by one of the Cutters in a few days. Please to write and let me know what is it you mean of suspecting my Mother having told something to me of you. If it is not an impertinent question and as you have promised some time to tell me, may I presume to ask what this secret is. I shall expect your next will contain my dear Mother's promised letter.

Mr Birch desires his compliments to the family.

I must look out for an opportunity to send this to the Office, therefore, my dear Sister, please to excuse me saying more than I am, with duty to Parents, love to Brothers, Grandmother and friends, Dear Sister,

Your Aff^{te} and loving Brother, John George.

*

40. Miss George, Blue Boar Inn, Haverfordwest.

HMS *Bellona*, Cawsand Bay
Mar. 29th 1800

My dear Sister,

I have just received your 4 letters of the 7th Feb., 17th Mar., 2nd & 16th, all which gave me infinite pleasure.

In respect to a berth for William, I beg to be excused giving my opinion. I would with the greatest pleasure but really am not able to think of a situation suitable for him. A 2nd. Lieut. of Marines is certainly a very poor provision for a young man, and half pay is only 1s.9d. a day. I only ask you when a peace comes, what he is to lay his hands on to support himself: surely his pay couldn't do it: the only prospect he has, and that a very distant one, is promotion: indeed, he must see a number of years pass over his head before he'll rise to any rank. Have you considered a Marine Officer's prospects? God knows what I am to do when I can [marry]. I am not at all surprised at Lady K.'s reply to Father when he asked her for her interest. It would have been just the same if he had asked for me before poor Mr Cleaveland [died. He knew] those kind of Gentry. I trust William will do very well to whatever he takes to, having spirit enough to fight his way through Mr Press. I hope with all my heart he will arise to his expectations, let them be what they will. I'll say no more on the subject but proceed on something else.

I feel extremely sorry for poor John Potter, I wish him reformation with all my heart. I have been ashore but once since we arrived and in my walks have met with a character which I suppose you have not heard of for a long time, no other than Davies the Jew[30] I have met him frequently with a box under his arm, but a very small one, indeed. The poor fellow looked poor and shabby and seemed distressed at the sight of me, therefore I think he must have known my [predicament] being in uniform and in company with Gentlemen, I did not like to take him by the hand in the public street but will embrace a future opportunity of falling in with him in coloured clothes to know what he is about.

Since writing the above we have received orders to go to sea immediately on report of the French fleet being at sea, also the other ships are fitting out as fast as possible. We expected to be paid before we sailed; as we are not, we shall come in again shortly. I would not advise you to believe such reports: if it is a fact, you'll soon hear.

Mr Birch desires his love to his wife and compliments to the family. He is busily employed stowing the provisions, &c., at present otherwise he would write, has desired me to say that should he have an opportunity to write he'll endeavour to save evening post. I wrote last Sunday to you. It is proved our mast is not sprung therefore we have only to get provisions, &c., before we are ready. I expect we'll sail this evening. I had not seen Mr Mullins since we arrived.

Dear Sister, remember me to all acquaintance, Mr Duberlin & Miss Gould. If we should fall in with the *Chapman* I should like to see George Jenkins[31] very well as he would be able to give me [the latest?] news of H'west. Remember me to [my dear] sister. Since Miss Gould has wrote me that letter I don't intend writing to her till she has a better opinion of me. Please to write: you haven't told me this secret yet which you mentioned in a former letter, as you promised you would, I shall expect it yet. My paper is going short, must conclude with duty to Parents, love to Brothers, Grandmother and friends. Dear Sister,

Your ever Aff^te & loving Brother, John George.

Pray, what is become of Price?[30] I don't know well what I have written; you must excuse all errors.

*

41. Miss George, Blue Boar Inn, Haverfordwest.

HMS *Bellona*, Cawsand Bay
Apr. 19th 1800

Dear Sister,

I have just received your very welcome letter and am exceedingly happy to find it left you all well as this leaves me. I also received a few days ago your letter of the 20th March. Dear Sister, what will my Mother think of me for not fulfilling my promise in writing to her: do make some excuse: I have attempted several times to put pen to paper, but can't collect my senses to write such a letter as I should wish them to receive. We are to be paid today and tomorrow we shall go to Torbay. By that time I'll write to Mother and send it by this first post.

I am extremely obliged to you for the entertaining correspondence in yours of the 20th ult. relative to the Delf, &c. I think the Delf might as well have made a private Ball instead of going to the principal inn and exposing themselves to the ridicule of the China. I hope my dear sister was not one of the party. I should be very sorry if she was. I have spent most of my time ashore since we been in. I called on Mrs Mullins one day and found Mary in the shop: you can't conceive how happy she was to see me: she looks remarkably well and both she and Mrs Mullins particularly desired me to give their love to you: they expected Dyson down daily: suppose him to be arrived by this time. I did not hear of George Jenkins being on board the *Chapman* till the receipt of yours of the 20th ult. I wrote to him three days ago but have received no answer, whether he has received it or not can't say. I have not seen Mr Curgenven yet. I always thought Miss Gould would prove inconstant: her poor Beau is rivalled. I don't know what would be the consequence if I was on the spot. It is an old proverb and a very true one – Out of sight out of mind – therefore must leave it rest on that. I yet wish her every happiness heaven can bestow and if ever I should see H'west I will certainly do myself the pleasure of paying her a visit. Make my love to her. Please to give my respectful compliments to Mr Duberlin and Mr Thos. Rees. I am obliged to draw to a conclusion on account of the bustle upon deck. Mr Birch desires his compliments. Please to write.

I am, dear Sister, with duty to Parents, love to Brothers, Grandmother & friends,

Your ever Affte Brother, John George.

*

42. Mr Stephen George, Blue Boar Inn, Haverfordwest.

HMS *Bellona*, Cawsand Bay
Apr. 20th 1800

Dear & Hon'[d] Parents,

At last I take up my pen with the greatest pleasure in hopes of finding you all well. I wrote by the last post to my Sister where I mentioned the ship being paid yesterday.

This morning I was surprised at seeing Davies the Jew with three more in a boat along side with slops, &c.[32] I acquainted the 1st Lieut. at the time who did not approve of such gentlemen coming on board, upon which I went below; soon after a message was brought me that a man along side had a letter for me from my father. I knew 'twas Davies and was positive he had no such letter. I sent back to say I was not on board; at the time he delivered such a message he was some distance from the ship. He spoke in the hearing of the whole ship's company to Sir T. Thompson who was standing on the gangway & who sent down to me which has hurt'd me much and have been very uneasy ever since to think that a man of that description should come along side & deliver such a message. After the answer was given to him he behaved in a most outrageous manner and made use of expressions which I was ashamed of; he even said so much as we were relations and at last took off one of his shoes, got upon his legs & slap'ed it on his hands towards the ship and immediately pulled off. What he meant by that I don't know. Had he come on board by himself instead of having 3 Jews along with him, I should have no objections to come to a meeting, but as he has behaved in the manner he did, I am provoked almost to blow his brains out. The principal thing on board of a man-o'-war is for an Officer to keep his dignity with the Ship's Company: this day that scoundrel has hurt mine much to think that he should come on board to annoy me in the manner he did. I dare say Wolfe has told him I am on board this ship. Dear Parents, I'll drop the subject as I am sure I have well tired you and leave you to consider whether I have acted right or not.

We expect to sail tomorrow for Torbay; as the wind is now we shall make a short passage of it. Lord Bridport has resigned his command which is given to Sir A. Gardner[33] for the next cruise when it is expected Lord St Vincent will take the command if his health will permit him.

I have received by today's post a letter from my Agent informing me that he is obliged to give up the agency on account of his holding an official situation at the Admiralty Office and has recommended Capt. Kempster of the Marines to act as an Agent, from whom I have also received a letter.

From what I have heard of Capt. K. I intend appointing him, being a very good and honest character. The balance of my account with Mr Coombe is in his favour a little, but that is immaterial as it can be transferred to the new Agent and the balance paid by him to Mr Coombe. You see I have opened my concerns to you. I should suppose you have a bad opinion of me if I did not. I can partly tell what my Mess account cost me the last year: it is £40 more than I expected when I embarked into the ship. It is likely to be higher next year as every thing is so very high. Mutton is 9d. per lb. in the Dock market; beef 8d. & every other thing in proportion. I mentioned in my sister's letter yesterday that I spend most of my time ashore: you may think that I am spending my money all the time at taverns, &c., but be assured it is not; what I means by that is going ashore after breakfast & returning to dinner. I have just paid 3s.0d. since we came in to a tavern, surely that is not extravagant. I have an excellent stock of clothes; in short, I want nothing – but a rich Prize so that I night be enabled to pay the debt of obligation which I am laid under to you and my Dear Sister. Please to write when you receive this to Torbay & let me have all the news, how William comes on and if the farming business is pretty favourable this season. I dare say you'll be able to fill a sheet of paper. I don't know what to think of losing my old sweetheart Miss Gould having heard that she is to be married to Mr Charles. I believe the ladies about the Blue Boar are all inconstant, this being the second I have lost. The first is Miss Fisher. Pray let me know what has become of the latter, not having heard of her for a long time.

Mr Birch who was in company a few days ago with the Surgeon of the Marlborough, told me that the Surgeon had been in Wales very lately and was at your house and had the pleasure of seeing you

[Last page missing.]

*

43. Miss George, Blue Boar Inn, Haverfordwest.

HMS *Bellona*, Torbay
May 17th 1800, 10 at night.

Dear Sister,
    I have the satisfaction to say that we have just come to an anchor on account of a severe gale of wind: best part of the fleet are out, some of them have lost their top masts &c., but none have received material damage.

May 18th

The remainder of the fleet is now coming in, the weather is yet very boisterous. I have just received by the Boatman the two letters of the 27th April & 12th instant, which has given me a good deal of pleasure to find it left you all well. This, be assured, leaves me the same.

The affair of Davies the Jew I have forgot am sorry to say that he behaved at that time with very little delicacy in coming along side with two others of his tribe to pay me a visit. You may judge my feelings were not altogether pleasant, – enough!

I wrote from off Ushant the 10th inst., to you, at the same time to Bristol. I little thought to see Torbay so soon; suppose we shall sail the first wind: have heard no news yet from shore. The letter of the 27th which my dear Parents dictated I am very thankful to them for it. In respect to their kind offer, upon reflection I am ashamed to say I have disburthened them of a great sum since I took up my Commission. How can I look into their faces & say 'I want more'? My feelings won't allow me to do it. I have wrote to Capt. Kempster, as you'll see in my last to you.

I am glad William improves in his Navigation. I dare say he will do well. Between you & me I yet think had he chosen a Trade 'twould been more comfortable both for himself & the family. I can't say it is altogether a pleasant life rolling about the seas: in a short time I'll write to him.

In my last I desired you to forward your letters to me thro' Mr George Jenkins: as we are come in, address to me here & when we sail do it agreeable to my last.

Please to write as early as convenient. You must excuse the shortness of this. With duty to Parents, love to Brothers, Grandmother and Friends,

Your ever Aff^{te} & loving Brother, John George.

Miss Gould & Mr Duberlin & Mr Thos. Rees is among the Friends which you'll remember me to. Mr Birch desires his compliments; he has received a letter from his wife.

*

44. Miss George, Blue Boar Inn, Haverfordwest.

HMS *Bellona* at sea off Dartmouth
May 27th 1800

Dear Sister,

You'll be surprised to see me date this at sea: this morning we left Torbay with orders to proceed to Plymouth: I can't conceive what it is for. The Fleet are also sailed on a cruise. There are a large East India convoy in Torbay, which made things extravagantly dear, waiting for a fair wind down Channel. The both fleets made a fine appearance.

The country looks beautiful, every thing in the most flourishing way. I have been on shore several times in Torbay: upon inquiry I find there is every appearance of a good crop of hay, the wheat is very fine: in short every thing. I dare say the country is as forward with you. It gives me great satisfaction to see it so, as the present scarcity must distress the poor very much.

The Postmaster of Plymouth Dock have promised to send our letters out when we are at sea, therefore I think you had better not trouble Mr Jenkins. I shall probably have an opportunity of seeing him if he is still at the Admiral's Office. We left most of our Lieuts. behind us. Mr Jauncey he is gone to Sick Quarters at Dartmouth in a fever. Mr Birch thinks we'll get in this evening, I hope in time for the Post. Dinner is ready. We had no sooner sat down than the wind came directly against us: the well-wished Post is in view but am afraid shan't reach it before tomorrow noon. William must think me very ungrateful in not fulfilling my promise in writing. I shall write if possible a post or two after this. Indeed I should have wrote from Torbay but the weather was so fine that the short time I was on board I was obliged to be on the look out, being Officer of the Guard & the rest of my time, I am ashamed to say instead of writing walked ashore – you must pardon me.

The convoy are coming out. I hear mates of West Indiamen have no protection from the Impress service: perhaps I am misinformed. If it is the case, I cannot consent for William to go to sea: indeed, I think, could he settle himself ashore 'twould be much better. However, if it is his choice & have our dear Parents' approbation, make the strictest inquiry into the Captain's conduct he goes with. I should wish to see him but have it not in my power. I am sick of the [sea?] myself at times, with the idle life I had: don't mention what I have said to our Parents as I am not capable of being consulted upon the subject. nor neither would wish it. I could not conceal my sentiments from you, the height of affection that subsists between us is so strong that I should call myself unnatural if I did.

May 20th, 2 o'clock p.m.

We have just come to our lines in Cawsand Bay. There are several ships here, have heard no news; please to write & add The Dock. I must conclude with duty to Parents, love &c., dear Sister,

Your most Affte Brother, John George.

Mr Birch's compliments.   *

71

45. Mr William George, Blue Boar Inn, Haverfordwest.

HMS *Bellona*, Cawsand Bay
May 31st 1800

Dear William,

At last I take up my pen with infinite pleasure to address a few lines to my dear Brother. I need apologise for my long silence but I think the long correspondence that has been carried on between Mary & me will convince you that it was not neglect for when I wrote to Sister I expect she'll conceal nothing from the family without being desired: however, you say I am a letter in debt to you. I hope that this will be acknowledged as an answer.

By my Sister's letter I find you have an inclination to be a sailor. Now before you must go too far upon what plan to proceed: if you should go on board a West Indiaman, of course, after a certain time you'll expect to be a Captain; if in an East Indiaman the same recollect you may be a long time before you arrive to the command of a ship & may experience many difficulties in that time. Certainly some have the good luck of making a speedy fortune, but for one that is so lucky there are a hundred that comes to nothing at the end. On board of a man-o'-war you must serve 6 years, must be a really good sailor before you can attempt to pass & require a great deal of interest before you arrive to promotion. I have laid these things before you just to consider a little. You are a fine boy & I have not the least doubt of your doing well. I am happy to find you improve in your Navigation & would not wish to check your inclinations, let them be what they will.

It is reported by a Cutter that is come in that a squadron is sailed from Brest. We are making every preparation for sea, suppose we will sail this evening. There has been so many reports that you can't trust to it. Lord St Vincent is off Ushant with a formidable fleet, much superior to theirs.

I expected little Charles Phillips (Doctor P.'s son) on board to dine with me yesterday from the Warrior[34] with another Midshipman but did not come. The way I knew he was there was through a Midshipman from the *Warrior* who dined on board the day before & told me Charles was on board. I desired him to come on board as yesterday & bring C. Phillips with him. Some of our youngsters went to bathe yesterday evening & met Charles: he sent his compliments. I am surprised those letters which I wrote from off Ushant are not arrived: there was one [written] at Bristol: please to [hear] Mr Birch wrote [to me]. Please to write [to me] I shall always be made happy in hearing from you and should you leave Haverfordwest be assured I'll carry on as regular correspondence with you as I do now with my Sister. Remember me to all my old acquaintance: John Potter, Mr Duberlin, &c. the enclosed is for Mother, please to deliver it.

I must conclude with love to Sister, Brother, Grandmother & friends & be assured you have the warmest affections of, Dear William,

Your loving Brother, John George.

Mr Birch's compliments – excuse this scrawl.

*

46. Miss George, Blue Boar Inn, Haverfordwest.

HMS *Bellona*, off Ushant
July 1st 1800

My dear Sister,

I have been impatiently waiting to hear from you this length of time, am astonished that I have received no answer to my former letters, certainly there must be a great delay somewhere but can't accuse my Sister to be the cause of it. I embrace this opportunity of writing in hopes 'twill find you all well. Your last letter which I answered immediately upon the receipt was dated the 23rd May which acknowledged having received mine of the 11th May. Since that time I have written from different places no less than 4 letters which I am doubtful if they are received: pray don't keep me in suspense as I am particularly desirous to hear from you.

We have been out upwards of four weeks & can't form the most distant idea when we'll go in. The weather has been most beautiful. I really envy you in having all the produce of the garden in your power every day while we poor fellows are cruising off here with the only vegetable a potato to eat with our provisions & them very short: but stop, before I go further, 'twas but two days ago that we had a fine dish of green peas at dinner & yesterday a gooseberry pudding which we purchased of a vessel from Plymouth at a most enormous price you may be sure, therefore don't laugh at our situation as we are not entirely destitute with the good living of Old England: when we'll have another feast God knows. We have very little news. I saw the French fleet in Brest a few days ago: they don't appear to be doing any thing. We have an inshore squadron at an anchor off the harbour in sight of the enemy's fleet, therefore it is impossible for them to come out without being observed. Our latest newspaper on board is the 24th ult. I am sorry to say that the Austrians are in a bad way on the continent. Bonaparte seems to clear every thing before him: it is the opinion on board that this defeat by the French will occasion a peace with our Ally, if not a general one. Part of the Fleet are at Quiberon, with a number of troop ships. It is useless for my writing the particulars, as I hear no more than what I have seen in an old newspaper & that, I dare say, you have perused. Mr Birch has desired me to give his compliments to the family & his love to his wife: he wrote the same time as I did (June 12th) to Mrs Birch but has not received an answer. Please to give my kind love to Miss Gould & to all my acquaintance, relations at Hook & elsewhere.

Sir Thomas Thompson has said that he expects the ship will go to Portsmouth to be dock'd next winter. Who knows but that I may spend the next Christmas with you: do most sincerely wish it. I find part of the Pembroke Militia[35] are gone home to be disembodied. I dare say poor John Argent is one of them, give my best wishes to him. I was not ashore when in Cawsand Bay last otherwise would have called on Mr George Jenkins who perhaps might have told me some news from home. If it is convenient I will thank you to write as I am now anxiously waiting for a letter. I have nothing more particular to say.

With my prayers for your happiness, duty to Parents, love to Brothers, Grandmother & friends, I am, Dear Sister,

Your most Affte & loving Brother, John George.

*

47. Miss M. George, Blue Boar Inn, Haverfordwest.

HMS *Bellona*, off Ushant
July 16th 1800

Dear Sister,

Your very welcome letter of the 8th inst. I received enclosed in a letter from Mr George Jenkins a few days ago which has given me a great deal of pleasure to find it left you all well. I wrote the 3rd inst. which hope you have received. A few days ago we were looking out with a prospect of going in; today unfortunately we received orders to complete the ship with 4 months' provisions from the *Windsor Castle* who is going in, therefore we have little hope of seeing Old England soon.

Mr Jenkins has been good enough to say that he'll send all your letters out which I have not received I wrote to him the 14th I shall esteem him as a particular friend for his kind attention. He has offered to send any thing out that I should want if we are out a long time perhaps, I may trouble him.

I have no news. The weather is beautiful. Mr Birch is well, desires his compliments. You must excuse this short letter as an opportunity now offers to send it in: my next shall be longer. With duty to Parents, love to Brothers, Grandmother & friends, I am, Dear Sister,

Your most Aff^te Brother, John George.

Please to write.

*

48. Miss George, Blue Boar Inn, Haverfordwest.

NB. To be read by my Sister only

Bellona, off Ushant
Aug. 8th 1800

Dear Sister,

With extreme pleasure I received your kind letters of 3rd, 21st & 27th July: am happy to find they left you all well. I wrote the 2nd inst. to you through Mr Jenkins & having no news since: I must endeavour to make such answers as your letters will require.

In yours of the 3rd ult. you mention an offer being made by Mr Simon to you & £45 after his death if you did not marry, a tempting offer – you must pardon me when I say that I really don't understand you. It struck me at first that it was an offer of marriage between you and him, now upon recollection how foolish I must call myself when I know he has a wife already & supposed he was single. I must have a better opinion of my sister than to accept the hand of any old fellow, him particularly. If it should be agreeable please to write in your next your meaning respecting this offer: don't be angry for the liberty I have taken. I trust you would do the same in a similar situation.

I never heard before of Mr Colby being broke of his commission: please to write me the particulars.

I am obliged to you for your kind offer to send me Ale or Porter [by packet] to Plymouth. I rather it should remain in the cellar: a drink of Welsh ale is certainly a very great treat to me, but only consider what a quantity we must have so as to give 13 of us a taste & after all to have no thanks for it: I have often been asked to send for some but am determined not to do it & it is my particular wish that you'll not think any thing of the kind.

I am glad our Parents agree in opinion with Mr Birch respecting William. You seem certain that he will go with Capt. Lunn to America. I can say no more than it is my earnest prayer that he will do well. I am sorry for Capt. Coldstream's misfortune.

So you was surprised at the unexpected arrival of Uncle George in H'west. I am sorry I was not present to receive the great man: please to give my kind love to him. If he can crack a joke as formerly, Grandmother must be very happy with his company. I believe the seal of my last letter was torn a little: you must excuse it & the hasty way I concluded: the reason of its being so was on account of the signal being made for all letters & I wishing not to lose the opportunity. Please let me know what is become of Essex Smith, Market House, as I see he is of the list of Marine Officers, whether is he dead or what.

In my last I mentioned something of our [departure] but I am sorry to say that we are still in the same situation: today ships are expected out every hour. We shall go in, in the course of this month, to be paid.

Mr Birch is well, desires his compliments to you & the family.

Please to give my respects to Mr Duberlin & to Mr Thos. Rees, – the last time you mentioned him he was very ill: I hope he is better, – to Miss Gould & John Potter. remember me to all acquaintance & in short to all friends.

I suppose Mr Thomas Davies of Broomhill is one of your good Volunteer Men now: he was just making his appearance, I recollect, as I left home. Pray what commission has he?

I must beg you to destroy this after you have perused the contents as there are things I should not wish to be known to any person but yourself. I am sorry I said so much in the first part on a certain subject.

Please to write. My paper reminds me it's time to conclude, therefore accept this with duty to Parents, love to Brothers & Grandmother, from, my dear Sister,

Your most Aff^{te} & loving Brother, John George.

*

49. Miss George, Blue Boar Inn, Haverfordwest.

HMS *Bellona* at sea
Aug. 20th 1800

My dear Sister,

With infinite pleasure I take my pen to inform you that we are now on our passage for Plymouth, having parted company with the Fleet yesterday. There is very little wind at present, am afraid we'll not get in today. I received your kind letters of the 2nd & 16th inst. a few days ago which has made me quite happy in being assured of your welfare.

I suppose William has left H'west before this: I really feel as if I was present at the parting business, our dear Mother, I am sure, was much affected on the occasion. It is hoped he will do well. I do most anxiously wait for your letter.

I am sorry for my father's illness: I hope before this he has got rid of his troublesome companion – the Gout, as you mention that to be his complaint.

I can't give you any news of the Belle Isle expedition[36] as they have succeeded in taking it: it will prove a very advantageous thing to our Fleet, there being an excellent watering place, good anchorage & shelter from a westerly gale. An important affair happened on board about a fortnight ago: a poor inoffensive good man in a state of insanity jumped overboard & never was seen: he was servant to the Gunner & it appears he waited on his master who was in a very low state in his cot: about 7 a.m., on going out of his cabin, the Gunner fancied he heard a splash in the water as if somebody had jumped overboard: he called for his servant, but no answer, neither was he heard by any person; at last somebody going in he mentioned what he had heard: the poor fellow was immediately missed & on searching all over the ship could not be found. It is very evident that he was the person the Gunner heard. It blew almost a gale of wind at the time & by the time it was discovered, the poor man was some miles astern, this being the only accident that has occurred this cruise.

You say Miss Fields is arrived in H'west: pray remember me to her. I shall leave this open till we come to an anchor to acquaint you of our safe arrival: we don't expect to be in above five days. I shall certainly see George Jenkins if he is still at the Admiral's office. Mr Birch is very well: desires his compliments to you & the family.

31st 10 a.m. I have the satisfaction to say we have just arrived in Cawsand Bay once more after a 15 weeks cruise. There are a great many ships here. No news. Please to give my kind love to all relations & enquiring friends & conclude with duty to Parents, love to Brothers & Grandmother, dear Sister,

Your most Affte & loving brother, John George.

Let me know if Mrs Birch is well & if convenient send down to her to know if she intends writing to her husband. He is at present employed about the duty of the ship.

*

50. Miss George, Blue Boar Inn, Haverfordwest.

Bellona, Cawsand Bay
Sept. 5th 1800. p.m.

Dear Sister,
I am under the disagreeable necessity of informing you that we are going

to sea immediately on account of orders received from Earl St Vincent, also the other ships that are here ready for sea. We were to be paid tomorrow: I suppose we'll be in again in the course of a few days. It is very singular that as sure as we come into this Bay we are sure to be hurried to sea on some false alarm. I really can't pretend to say what this is for. I wrote to you on our arrival. Mr Jenkins is very well, I spent an evening with him.

I received your letter of the 28th ult. I do most seriously wish I was with you when William took his leave, to console my dear Mother who, I am sure, was much grieved on the occasion: his letter I do most anxiously look for. I think it very unfortunate that you should be disappointed in your passage to Bristol, however, between you & me, I think it much better in William's going alone, for had you gone it would have caused a second parting. I have been ashore a good deal considering the short time we have been in: the weather is fine but very dry. Please to write as usual. Excuse this short letter as the men are now employed in getting up the anchor & suppose in a few minutes we shall be under weigh. With duty to Parents, love to Brother, Grandmother & friends. I remain dear Sister,

Your most Aff^te & loving Brother, John George.

Mr Birch desires his compliments. he is surprised Mrs Birch has not written to him, so am I.

*

51. Miss George, Blue Boar Inn, Haverfordwest.

Bellano, Torbay
Sept. 26th 1800

My dear Sister,

With extreme pleasure I take up my pen to acquaint you that we are this instant anchored here after some very boisterous weather without any material injury done to the Fleet. We arrived at this place yesterday evening, it being very late which occasioned us to anchor outside. This morning we got under weigh in order to proceed off Ushant, the weather being fair, fortunately for us the wind [changed].

My last letter to you was the 16th inst. from Cawsand Bay. At the same time I wrote to William the answer to which I do most anxiously look for. I should have wrote from sea had not the weather been so bad. I have no news to communicate: when your letter arrives I'll write again.

Mr Birch is very well, desires his compliments to you & the family. I believe he writes to Mrs Birch.

Please to write. We shall sail with the first fair wind. With duty to Parents, love to Brother, Grandmother & friends, I am, my dear Sister,

Your most Aff^{te} & loving brother, John George.

Love & compliments to all acquaintance.

*

52. Mr George, Blue Boar Inn, Haverfordwest.

HMS *Bellona*, Torbay
Sept 29th 1800

Dear & Honble Parents,

A long time has elapsed since I last wrote to you; with heartfelt pleasure do I take up my pen in hopes of finding you all well as this, be assured, leaves me.

I have the satisfaction to say that I have received a letter from William this morning; he is very well & I think very lucky in finding out the Captain's conduct that he was to have gone to America with before he sailed; instead of grieving I rejoice at his first disappointment that it has so happened. I have not the least doubt but what he'll do very well. He expects Mary in Bristol by Whittam's vessel with Mr Havard who he says he has promised to apply to some friends to get him a pleasant ship. It is needless for me to write what you must be well acquainted with therefore I'll say no more at present than I hope he'll succeed in getting a most comfortable ship.

My sister's letter of the 14th I also got this morning, altho' it is rather an old date it gives me equal satisfaction in being assured of your welfare at that time. There is nothing particular going forward here. The weather is very squally and disagreeable. The prospect of seeing you is not so mean as I first expected. Our ship it is supposed will go to Portsmouth in the winter to be docked. If it is the case you may rely that I'll do the utmost in my power to get leave as I am longing to see you, particularly at this moment :should I succeed, with what pleasure would I fly to meet your embraces.

I have one request to make to my dear Mother, that is, that she will not make herself unhappy on the parting with another son. It is all very natural for the moment, but why make the remaining family unpleasant. I have spies out who tells me every thing, therefore, I hope you'll put on a cheerful smile & say 'I have done every thing for William which I hope is for his good.' If you don't comply with this request, I must be angry, as I feel myself very awkward on your account. Do write me a letter and convince me you are once more happy.

I write this day to William & shall make it my constant study [*sic*] to continue the correspondence. I wrote to Mary the 26th inst., being on our arrival. I hope to have an answer in a few days.

Tomorrow morning 3 Marine Officers goes ashore for 24 hours to guard at the watering place. I [expect] 'twill be quite a novelty to do the duty as [we have been] so long embarked.

My paper reminds me to conclude as I have no particular news. I will, with love to Sister, Brother, Grandmother & friends. I am, dear Parents,

Yoor most Dutiful & Aff^{te} Son, John George.

I must beg of you to answer. Mr Birch desires his compliments to you; he writes to Mrs Birch by this post.

Should be glad to know if it is agreeable to Lord K for me to address your letters under cover[37] to him yet: I send this under cover.

Pray is Mr Thos. Moore of Ramascastle[38] appointed Lieutenant of Marines yet. I see there is a Thos. Moore in Steel's list. JG.

*

53. Miss M. George,
    To the care of Mr G. Mathias at Mr Peter Williams
    Maudlin Lane, Bristol.

HMS *Bellona*, Torbay
Oct. 6th 1800

My dear Sister,

I have just received your kind letter of the 2nd inst. from Bristol & am made extremely happy to find it left you, Brother & relations all well. I was not at all surprised in seeing your letter from Bristol as William had told me before of your intention of visiting the great city. I certainly must congratulate you on your safe arrival & upon my word agree with you in preferring the comfortable town of H'west to the great mercantile city of Bristol.

I wrote to our Parents on the 29th ult. But have received no letters in return since we arrived; shall expect one by the next post.

Don't be surprised if I should have the pleasure of conducting you home, it being firmly believed here that a Naval Armistice will take place between England and France & it is probable 'twill conclude with a general truce. Should it be the case, with what great pleasure should I accompany my dear Sister to the embraces of our dear Parents.

We are no sooner in port than we are off again. Since I have begun this letter, the wind has come round to the eastward & the Admiral has just made the signal to unmoor: the men are now employed getting up the anchor. Please to write & address your letters Plymouth Dock.

When I wrote to William I did not intend it should be handed to a third person: as it has so happened, you must pardon for what I have wrote to offend you. I must beg of you to write to our Parents to let them know we are going to sea & desire them to write to me as above. I would write myself but time does not permit as a shore boat now awaits for the letter. You must excuse me saying more than I am, my dear Sister,

Your most Aff^{te} & loving Brother, John George

I hope this cruise will be no longer than the last.

*

54. Mr George, Blue Boar, Haverfordwest.

Bellona, Torbay
Oct. 7th 1800

Hon^d Parents,

I received your kind letter of the 2nd inst. & am made extremely happy to find it left you all well. I also received a letter from Sister the day before yesterday from Bristol. She says Brother & all relations are well. I wrote an answer to her letter yesterday: at that time we were unmooring & expected to have gone to sea: in a short time after I sent it, the wind being for down Channel, it blew so hard into the bay that none of the ships were drove from their anchors: we were one of them but the consequence were trifling as we had other anchors to let down: the Admiral waited for the weather to moderate: fortunately towards evening the wind shifted again to the Wester^{ds} which caused us to moor afresh: my time would not permit me to write to you at that time, I desired Mary to tell you we were going to sea. Now I must beg of you in your letter to her to inform her we are not sailed. I shall wait today & tomorrow before I write to Bristol for William's letter as he has promised me to write.

The Lieutenant you speak of belonging to the *Chapman* I have seen on board this ship; should be very happy to see him. I may some time perhaps take a passage round with him.

I have not heard from George Jenkins since we left Plymouth: will perhaps write today to inquire about W$^{m.}$ Davies.

You seem to approve of William's being a Midshipman. I'll only ask you one simple question: do you think the war will continue six years longer? – as he must serve that time before there is the least likelihood of a promotion. I wish he was comfortably settled ashore. As for gales of wind to be frightened at, is foolish, for there is not the least danger in an open sea: all the danger is vessels inshore.

Mary's letter was very short & scarce of news. She seems tired of Bristol already. I am very glad Mr Wakelin is made Purser & should be more so if I heard the same of poor Phillips: pray enquire what ship Wakelin is made into: there are not any news going forward here: the weather is bad & disagreeable: the first fair wind we are off.

Please to write & address Torbay & after we are sailed on a cruise I'll thank you to send them to Plymouth Dock as the Postman forward our letters out to us. Mr Birch is very well; desires his compliments.

Please to give my love to Miss Fields, Miss Gould & all inquiring friends: was I to insert the whole it would take up a whole sheet of paper. My dear Parents, I must draw to a conclusion but once more must beg you to write. With love to James & Grandmother, I am

Your ever dutiful & Affec^te Son, John George.

*

55. Miss George,
    To the care of Mr G. Mathias at Mr P. Williams
    Maudlin Lane, Bristol.

Bellona, Torbay
Oct. 12th 1800

My dear Sister,

I received your kind letter of the 11th yesterday evening: am extremely happy to find it left you all well. I am again under the disagreeable necessity of informing you that the wind is fair down Channel & the Admiral has the signal up to unmoor I am afraid the wind is not likely to shift as before, the weather being fine & seems settled.

After sending that trifling note, why should you wish me to take it back: no, my dear Sister, 'twas not of the least inconvenient to me: I only wish it had been a more valuable one.

I write home by this post. Our relation W^m. Davies is on board the *Doris* frigate, I understand. Our Parents will inform you how he was known to belong to that ship as I have wrote them the particulars. You must excuse me saying more than I am, with love to Brother & relations, dear Sister,

Your Aff^te & loving Brother, John George.

Address Plymouth Dock.

*

56. Miss George, Blue Boar Inn, Hav^dwest.

Bellona, Torbay
Oct. 28th 1800

My dear Sister,

With extreme pleasure do I at last take up my pen to address these few lines to you in hopes 'twill find you all well. I received your kind letter of the 20th inst. from Bristol yesterday evening, also one of the 17th inst. from my Mother: by yours I must think you'll be in H'west by the time this arrives: have assured this accordingly.

My anxiety, which I felt for a long time is eased by being assured of all your welfare & of William being satisfactory settled. I would write but must think he is sailed before this: his letter I shall be very happy to receive & should there be a prospect of falling in with him at any time, I'll do every thing to make him comfortable. Should this meet you at any time I must congratulate you on your arrival.

I suppose for a short time you'll not reconcile yourself to the small town of H'west after paying a visit to Bristol & Bath & spending your time so very agreeable. You'll be able to amuse our Parents round the fire of a cold evening with telling them your travels I wish I could do so; the prospect of seeing you I am sorry to say is very distant at present; however, I'll not despair as there is a long time to elapse yet till Christmas

I expected to have heard of Miss Green's marriage[39] long before this: how has it happened that such a fine girl should remain single so long. You say Mr Powell[40] is going a-recruiting: he may like it but I'll assure you was I offered a Party tomorrow I should certainly refuse it as it requires a great deal of attention & trouble & finally it runs a very great risk of losing money: it is not a difficult thing, I believe, to go round recruiting, but I would much rather stay on board a comfortable ship. Don't mention this to Mr Powell, I only give you my own opinion & what I have heard from a brother officer.

My mother's letter says Miss Gould & Miss Fields are more confined than ever. I pity the poor girls: please give my love to them. Miss Davies, I understand, is going to Ireland to be married. I am glad of it as she has been looking out for one long before I left home 'No longer Mrs Edwardes'.

Now I am come to the pleasantest part of the story. This morning our Captain's signal was made & on his return we were given to understand that Lord St Vincent intends hoisting his flag on board the *Bellona* as soon as the wind should become fair for the Fleet to sail. He is ill & does not intend going to sea, therefore he'll keep us here as, it is supposed, best part of the winter. What say you? In my opinion 'tis much better than cruising off

Ushant, – as we have been promised, the ship should be dock'd this winter, I rather think he'll not keep us here long but take us to Portsmouth. I'll assure you we'll be quite gay in having the Commander-in-Chief on board. Mr Birch is now on shore sounding for a close berth for the ship by the Earl's order.

I wrote the 26th to Father, being on our arrival. I do heartily wish he has got rid of his troublesome companion (the Gout) before this.

I have not been ashore yet, altho' the weather is at present very fine. There is nothing to attract a person's notice here: was the ship at Milford I should have been ashore long ere this.

I have neither heard of the Dr. or Mr Wm Davies yet, altho' he seemed to inquire so anxious after me to George Jenkins I am come to a resolution not to go on board his ship to see him should an opportunity offer & not even write to him unless he does first. I must think this long letter will tire you in the perusal. Please to write and if you took a passage by water let me know if it agreed with you & in short all the news your time will permit.

Hyde Parker[41] is expected from Portsmouth to take the command during Lord St Vincent's absence.

I have not heard of John Potter for a considerable time: please remember me to him. Mr Birch is very well.

If I should get leave of absence from quarters, I intend going across Devonshire & take an opportunity of the first vessel going over to Wales. As I am not acquainted with the country, I will thank you to ask Mr George of Hook where the most likely place is to get a vessel going for culm, &c., to Milford or Carmarthen . . .

Your most Affte & loving brother, John George.

Remember me to Mrs Rees, Market House: she just came into my mind: pray has she any children yet?

*

57. Mr George, Blue Boar Inn, Haverfordwest.

Bellona, Torbay
Nov. 5th 1800

Dear Parents,

With extreme pleasure have I received your kind letter of the 31st ult. this morning; am very happy to find it left you all well. I wrote to my Sister the 20th addressed H'west which I hope she was present to receive.

84

My last informed you that Lord St Vincent intended hoisting his flag on board the ship as soon as the Fleet sailed. We have his flag on board now, the Fleet having sailed, returned on account of contrary winds & are gone again. I have not had the pleasure of seeing his Lordship yet: he has taken a house ashore, where he lives. There are only two ships, *Terrible* & *Robust*, in the Bay, besides *Bellona*, and they only wait for fair wind to join the Fleet.

I have been ashore several times: the weather has been pretty fine considering the country.

We understand all the frigates under Lord St Vincent's command are ordered in here, very likely I shall see Davies as the *Doris* is one of them. We Troop the Guard every morning, having a most excellent band on board belonging to the *Ville de Paris*, & all day long hearing nothing but musick.

I shall wait for my Sister's answer before I write again. Please to write. Mr Birch desires his compliments I must conclude with love to Brother, Grandmother & friends, dear Parents,

Your most Aff^{te} & dutiful son, John George.

*

58. Miss George, Blue Boar, H'west.

Bellona, Torbay
Nov. 14th 1800

Dear Sister,

I have been so long waiting for your letter that I concluded you had not left Bristol till yesterday a letter which I received from Uncle George informed me you had left this fortnight. The wind has certainly been against you but I hope you'll be safe arrived before this can possibly reach H'west. Your last letter from Bristol, I do certainly agree with you in the affair you mentioned respecting William. I dare say he has forgot it before this.

I received my brother James's last letter informing me of William's arrival at Portsmouth: tell him I complied with his request made to W^m but have not heard from him yet; I am surprised he does not write.

I told you in my last Lord St Vincent's flag was on board. I am under the disagreeable necessity to say that on the Fleet's last arrival he shifted his flag into the *Ville de Paris*, therefore our hopes are all done away and we are going to sea with the Fleet the first wind.

I had the pleasure of having an unexpected friend to dine with me yesterday, Mr George Phillips, the physician's son. I was surprised to find he was appointed Chaplain to the *Formidable* & when he sent his name on board I

85

could not conceive who it was. He looks very well & seems to like his situation very much.

All the news I have is that the *Triumph* is just arrived from off Brest with intelligence that there are 45 sail in the harbour with sails bent & every thing ready for sea. This has been said so often that I little think they'll ever come out with an intention to fight.

The weather has been very bad till within this 3 days it being pretty fine. We still expect to be docked this winter. I have only to request that you'll write when convenient as it gives me at all times infinite pleasure in perusing your letters. Please to give my love to Miss Fields & with wishing you a safe arrival, I am, dear Sister,

Your Aff^te & loving Brother, John George.

*

59. Miss George, Blue Boar Inn, Haverfordwest.

Bellona, Torbay
Dec. 4th 1800

My dear Sister,

I have just received your very kind letters of the 20th & 28th ult. & am extremely happy to find it left you all well. We arrived here the evening before last: should have wrote but expected your letter

As to Peace, there is very little prospect of, as the Russians[40] have laid an embargo on our shipping in their ports, consequently we have done the same by theirs. There seems to be something going forward in the Fleet but am perfectly unacquainted with it. I only wish we may be removed from under the command of the noble Earl, time will explain the whole, if we are to have a Russian war (which God forbid for the country's sake) it is very likely this Fleet will separate: the *Bellona* is likely to be sent to the North Sea. Should my being docked at Plymouth, be assured, with the Captain's permission, I shall immediately write to the Admiralty for leave & should I obtain it, with what pleasure would I fly to the embrace of my dear sister & our parents. God grant that it may be soon. You have no occasion to forward your intended present, which you are so good to mention. I am in hopes of receiving it from your own hands.

I dined on board the *Formidable* today: Mr Phillips is very well.

I trust in me you'll find a real confidant, respecting Miss G. & in one letter you seem to say that you are not on good terms, in another you seem to contradict it. May I beg you will in your next explain to me more fully as I am not at present capable of judging or at least give you my opinion, excuse my freedom, as a Brother & as you have been pleased to appoint me a confidant I have taken the liberty so far to write. I have, agreeable to yours of the 28th, burnt your former one.

I shall certainly embrace every opportunity to write to William: will thank you to let me know when he is likely to arrive at Tobago & also his address in full.

Mr Birch is very well: desires his compliments to you & the family; he wrote to his wife by yesterday's post. I have no particular news. Please to give my kind love to Miss Gould & Miss Fields & in short to those whom you should think proper. With duty to Parents, love to Brother & Grandmother, accept this from, my dear Sister, from,

Your Aff^{te} & loving Brother, John George.

Please to write. It is late. Good Night.

Dec. 5th 6 a.m. I again resume my pen: a great change since yesterday evening: the wind is now fair for the Fleet to sail & the signal is up to unmoor. I hope this will be as short as the last. Admiral Whitehead & a squadron is to remain here, am sorry the *Bellona* is not in the same. I must beg you'll write every opportunity as the greatest satisfaction I receive is from the perusal of your letters be assured. I shall make it my constant endeavour to write by every opportunity. I am sorry I said so much in my letter yesterday morning, you must pardon me. I would write it over again but time will not permit as opportunity now offers of sending this ashore. My dear Sister, once more, adieu. J. George.

Pray who lives in the late Mr Savage's house? It blows hard at present, altho' we are unmoored 'tis not likely we'll sail till it moderates, perhaps not till tomorrow morning. Mr Birch says there is every appearance of a westerly wind; if we don't sail tomorrow I'll write again, address Torbay [please reply] by return of post. Adieu. J George.

The 68th Regiment are here, going to the West Indies.

*

60. Mr George, Blue Boar, Haverfordwest.

HMS *Bellona*, Spithead
Jan. 1st 1801

Dear & Hon^d Parents,

With extreme pleasure I received my Sister's letter of the 24th ult. This morning & am happy to find it left her & you all well. I wrote the 25th to Mary acquainting her of our arrival & should have wrote a second time before this only wanted to hear of our destination.

The surveying shipwrights came off to survey the ship a few days ago, their report being sent up to the Admiralty. Have the satisfaction to say that orders arrived this morning for the ship to be docked here. The wind at present is unfavourable for our going into harbour. I fancy we shall go in the first wind.

This being the first time of my being here I like the country, considering being ashore but once, pretty well: when I get a little acquainted, perhaps I shall like it better. I should be extremely happy could I obtain leave to spend some time with you. I have my reasons for not asking at present, some future time will explain it, perhaps not long; be assured I shall write to Wm by the first packet to the West Indies after I receive your promised letter.

We have already expended a little powder since our arrival: last Sunday, Prince Augustus Frederick[42] embarked on board the *Endymion* for Lisbon: we gave him a Royal Salute & today we are going to have another on the Union[43] taking place between Great Britain & Ireland.

I must think Wm is nearly arrived at Tobago by this time. I called at Quarters to inquire for Mr Powell but thro' the stupidity of the Clerk in the Office, could hear nothing of him, 'till this morning your letter informed me of his being at Chatham.

Tell Mary I have not received her letter of the 18th ult. yet, which she addressed Torbay. The Plymouth & Torbay letters are not arrived yet but the ship is expected hourly; very likely I shall receive them with the rest.

This being New Year's Day I do most sincerely wish you all a happy & many returns of the season, altho' we are separated we must endeavour to enjoy a pleasure in corresponding one to the other: believe me it is the greatest satisfaction I receive is in hearing from you. I always made it my study to write at all opportunities & I shall continue to do so.

Please to make my kind love to Mr George, Hook, & family, in short to all friends and relations. Mr Birch desires his compliments, he wrote a few days ago to his wife.

I must beg you'll write. My paper reminds me to conclude, therefore with warmest prayers for your welfare, I remain dear Parents,

Your most Affte & dutiful son, John George.

*

61. Miss George, The Blue Boar Inn, Haverfordwest.

Bellona, Portsmouth
Jan 12th 1801

My dear Sister,

At last I take up my pen with the greatest pleasure to address a few lines to you in hopes it will find you & the family all well. Since I wrote my last (Jany 4th) to Parents I received no less than 4 letters; you can't conceive the pleasure they gave me in the perusal & just now yours of the 8th. I received with the rosette & purse enclosure for which accept my warmest thanks. I shall expect in a day or two an answer to my letter of the 4th upon consideration, I think as an opportunity now offers for my seeing you, I ought not to let it slip; the Captn is (God knows where) upon leave & has promised as soon as he is settled to write to the 1st Lieut.; he has been gone this week; I have been consulting with our present commanding officer who has promised that as soon as the Captn's letter arrives, which is expected daily, he'll write by return of post & state my affair to him; the Captn's answer, when it arrives, will determine the business. He certainly can have no objections to my applying to the Admiralty. I shall ask for a month but should I obtain no more than 14 days it is doubtful if you'll see me. Mr Birch has written for leave to go to Town; he expects Mrs Birch will meet him there.

If the Captn's letter was to arrive tomorrow it would be impossible to know the result of it for at least 6 days; perhaps I may surprise you. We shifted on board the *Hulk* yesterday, can't say when the ship goes into dock. Having crammed you pretty well on one subject it is time to inform you of my seeing an old friend, Lieut. Wm. Davies. I accidentally met him in the street a few days ago, he seemed exceptionally happy to see me & took me to his lodgings where he introduced me to his wife, a nice little woman, & a very fine child. I call there every time I go ashore & spent a very pleasant evening with him at his lodgings; he left the *Doris* this some weeks past & was on half pay till this moment when he received his appointment to the *Tigress* bomb at Harwich; he goes off this evening to join her, his wife still remains; what I have seen of her I think you must like her, if you had an opportunity of being acquainted with her. Cousin W^{m.} has particularly desired me to give his love to you and the family.

I received your letter of the 4th, with W^{m's} address too late for my writing to him by this month's packet, shall wait a few days to know if I have leave, if not shall certainly write by the next.

It is a thing impossible to say where the ship is going when docked; at least we shan't be ready for sea this two months; when that is expired perhaps I shall be able to inform you. Suppose we shall join the Fleet again: it is rumoured here that all the ships that can properly put to sea are to be put on commission immediately: every appearance of a Russian war. I am going to take my leave of Davies before he goes off. I like the place better than when I wrote my last, having the society of Mrs Davies & a few of her female acquaintance.

I thank you for your recommendation for a wife in Miss Fields; give my love to her; tell her I hope to see her shortly.

Please to write. My paper is almost full, therefore with duty to Parents, love to James, &c, I conclude, my dear Sister,

Your most Aff^{te} & loving Brother, John George.

I am thinking of making such answers as you requested in your yesterday's letter; am astonished that you should think any thing of the kind. One thing I agree that in the course of the next summer perhaps I may trouble you to get me made a dozen shirts but shall insist on purchasing the linen: our dear Parents has done so much for me already.

*

62. Miss George, Blue Boar Inn, Haverfordwest.

Portsmouth
Jan. 15th 1801

My dear Sister,

I received our Parents' kind letter of the 8th two days ago & am excessively happy to find it left you all well. I wrote the 12th inst. respecting leave: I have given up all hope: the Captain has written to the 1st Lieut. but not at all satisfactory. Mr Birch went to London on Tuesday last: he applied for 14 days but could obtain only 7: he will be greatly disappointed if he does not meet Mrs Birch there. Our relation Davies is gone to join his brig: I have not seen his wife since, shall call on her today.

Excuse this short letter; when I last wrote to you I really expected to have seen you. Whether it is from the Russian business or what, Admiralty will not grant leave for any time. We must put up with disappointment.

Please to make my kind love to all friends, with duty to Parents, love to Brother, Grandmother, &c., I remain, dear Sister,

Ever your Aff^{te} Brother, John George.

The ship is to go into dock tomorrow.

*

63. Miss George, Blue Boar Inn, Haverfordwest.

Portsmouth
Jan. 23rd 1801

My dear Sister,

With extreme pleasure do I at last take up my pen to address these few lines to my dear Sister in hopes it will find you & the family all well.

I should have wrote sooner only waited for the Captain's arrival: he says 'tis quite useless to apply for leave as he has been informed the Admiralty will not grant leave at this moment: he could not get his own renewed: so particular they are that an order is given to the ships in the harbour, as well Spithead, that all officers are to sleep on board their respective ships every night. We think it hard as we are now in a Hulk & not likely to go in to the ship this fortnight: she comes out of dock in the course of ten days.

I have not heard from Mr Birch since he left us; a gentleman who has been in Town saw him; he had his leave renewed for 6 days longer which time is nearly expired. I suppose he'll be down in a few days & Mrs B., if she acted agreeable to his letter which he wrote her before he applied for leave; you have not mentioned her in your last letters, therefore must suppose she is with her husband.

Every preparation is making here for a vigorous war. There are 6 or 7 sail in this port to be put in commission & I have been informed, how far it is true can't say, there are too a fleet of 25 sail-of-the-line ready for the North Sea by the middle of March: indeed, it is my wish our ship may be one as we stand a great chance of making prize money & at the same time have as great an opportunity of corresponding with you as if we were off Ushant.

The last augmentation in the Marines has given me 15 steps. I suppose if the war should continue another 12 months, 'twould bring [closer] the Peace establishment.

I had engaged to drink tea a few days ago with Mrs Davies but was obliged to be excused as I was wanted [on board]. Wm. Davies has written to his wife that he likes life aboard the Brig very much. I have begun writing to W^m shall finish it by tomorrow.

[I shall convey] all the news you have given me & shall finish it in such a manner that I trust he'll be pleased with the perusal.

Please to inform Mr Adams that, agreeable to his wish, I called at the Custom House & am extremely sorry to say that the box which was detained is condemned long ago.

Please to make my kind love to all friends & with duty to Parents, love to James & Grandmother, I conclude, my dear Sister,

Your most Aff^{te} & loving Brother, John George.

Yours of the 15th I have just received.

*

64. Mr Wm George,
   on Board the *Nautilus*, Scarboro in Tobago West Indies.

Bellona, Portsmouth
Jan. 26th 1801

Dear William

With infinite pleasure do I at last take up my pen to address this to you, have the satisfaction to say that the family in H'west is well, myself am well; this I hope will find you the same.

We arrived here 3 weeks ago to be docked; she is at present in dock & expect her to come out in the course of 10 days. I expected at one time to have got leave to go home; as I can't get sufficient leave to spend some time with our parents, I have given up all thoughts of it. My last letter from Mary is the 8th inst.; she has been part of the Christmas at Llanunwas with Mrs Harries. In every letter from home I receive, they speak highly of you. I trust you'll prove that dutiful son which they are now in opinion of. The only news which I can collect from their letters is the death of poor Miss James of Sodson, Mr Tasker of Upton Castle & Mr Davies of the Isle de Barry.[44] Among the marriages is Miss Anthony, our labourer's daughter, to a man belonging to the *Chapman*. There is nothing else from that part of the country except the exorbitant price of provisions. The poor suffer very much. I did not at all like this place at its first appearance, but meeting with a few old acquaintances I now like it better. The second day after we arrived in the harbour, I met with our relation, Wm. Davies. He seemed very happy to see me, took me to his lodgings & introduced me to his wife, a nice little woman, & a very fine child. He has left the *Doris* these some weeks past & a few days ago received his appointment to the *Tigress* bomb at Harwich where he is gone to join her. It was not altogether his fault in not seeing me as he had made several inquiries in different places without gaining any information. His wife and child are still here. I call very often to see them, and had you & I the great good luck of being here together, I trust we should have spent some very agreeable time.

Every preparation is making here for a war with the Northern Powers no less than 5 or 6 sail-of-the-line from this port are ordered to be fitted and for sea, & I have been informed that by the middle of March there will be a fleet of 25 sail-of-the-line ready for the North Sea. There is an order now in force to detain all Russians, Swedes and Danes. In short, there is everything but a Declaration. A squadron of the enemy sailed from Brest a fortnight ago but were obliged from the hard pressure of the inshore squadron to take shelter in a bay adjoining, the remainder in Brest amounting to 55 sail are perfectly ready for sea. I give you this intelligence from the *Star*. There is no doubt but that we shall have plenty to do the next Spring. Since writing the above I received a letter of the 19th inst. from Sister: the family were all well. Little Pegg, our old servant girl, is to be married to a militiaman. You must smile at the idea of that 'dwarf' getting a husband. Prior to Mary's writing, she received a letter from Bristol who informed them Mr Fisher had not heard of the ship since she sailed. I must entreat you'll write every opportunity to me or our Parents & upon consideration I think you had better address my letters to Haverfordwest as by the time an answer to this can possibly arrive it will be uncertain where we shall be, perhaps abroad. They will receive equal satisfaction in opening my letter as if it was addressed to them & should I be at [sea] will be an easy matter to forward it to me in a Frank. Let me know how you like your situation: in short, every little matter that you think you may interest me with. Since giving you an account of a squadron in Brest having sailed & drove into a bay adjoining, I read in a paper since that they returned to Brest.

I must think of drawing to a conclusion, my paper being almost filled. I certainly shall communicate anything particular that should occur at home: beg you'll not neglect writing to our Parents, as it is their greatest desire to hear often from us. Let me know how you like the Captn.

Dear Brother accept this with the warmest prayers for your health and happiness from,

Your Aff^{te} & loving Brother, John George.

*

65. Miss George, Blue Boar Inn, Haverfordwest.

Bellona, Spithead
Feb. 28th 1801

My dear Sister,

[Once] I again take up my pen to address this to you in hopes it will find you all well. We came out of harbour on Thursday (26th): our stay I am afraid will be very short here. We are at present under the command of Lord Nelson[45] who hoisted his flag on the *St George*. Sir Hyde Parker's ship is getting ready for him and in the course of a few days it is supposed a Squadron, of whom we are one, will sail for the North Sea under his command. Our ship will be in course of pay tomorrow: suppose we shall be paid on Monday: after that we may say farewell to Portsmouth. I intend, if I possibly can, to take my leave of Mrs Davies today or tomorrow, her husband being at Yarmouth: 'tis very probable I may see him.

93

It is doubtful what port we shall make our rendezvous in the North Sea: some say Yarmouth, others again Leith: let it be any port whatever, be assured I'll embrace the first opportunity of writing on our arrival. My last to you was the 22nd which hope you have received before this. I have been waiting for this few days past to receive your answer to my letter which I wrote about the 11th inst.; our short stay only has induced me to write this, not having received your answer yet. Please to continue to address Portsmouth till you hear again from me which shall be before we sail.

Mr Birch was on board yesterday morning: desired his compliments to you and the family: he has had his appointment as Surveying Master this 6 weeks & not seen his wife yet: I am surprised at the woman. There are many things which he can do here for our Parents: if any thing should be wanted, don't forget to write to him, as he'll do every thing to the utmost of his power as well as yours: as my Acct we have agreed to correspond.

Please to make my love to Miss Fields, Miss Gould, in short to all friends: tell Miss Gould I was dreaming of her last night, that we were taking some pleasant walks together: I hope it may be realised in course of time. Is L. Jenkins married yet?

My paper reminds me to conclude, therefore, with duty to Parents, love to James & G'mother, I am, my dear Sister,

Your Affte & loving Brother, John George.

*

66. Miss George, Blue Boar Inn, Haverfordwest.

Bellona, Spithead
March 2nd 1801

My dear Sister

Again I take up my pen & do acknowledge the receipt of your kind letter of the 23rd ult. & am extremely happy to find it left you all well. I wrote as late as the 28th ult. to you respecting the troops I mentioned: 'tis the 49 Regt that is embarked in Lord Nelson's squadron. We have 80 on board here with 2 officers, very fine, pleasant young men. The whole Regiment are about 800, a small force to go upon any expedition let it be what it will; we are perfectly unacquainted with it except that we are to proceed from this place to The Downs; there perhaps we shall leave them. Part of the squadron are sailed, the *Warrior* for one. I'll not ask you to write till you hear again from me, which shall be the first opportunity. I am now going ashore to take my leave of Mrs Davies & if possible get Mrs Birch to dine with us for the last time.

Please to make my love to all friends & with prayers for all your welfare. I am, my dear Sister,

Your most Aff^te & loving Brother, John George

Since writing the above, I think you may as well write to me to this place again as the letters for the ship will be forwarded after us. I mean if you should have any time.

We sail tomorrow.

*

67. Miss George, Blue Boar Inn, Haverfordwest.

Bellona, Yarmouth
March 10th 1801

Dear Sister,

With extreme pleasure do I take up my pen to acknowledge the receipt your kind letter of the 2nd inst. which I received yesterday evening & am happy to find it left you all well. I wrote to you the 6th, being the time of our arrival, under cover to Lord K., which hope you have received. Respecting the expedition that is going forward, we are perfectly in the dark: it is generally supposed by the preparations that are making that it is for the Baltic; time will explain; 'tis not exactly known when we shall sail: our fleet will consist of about 22 sail-of-the-line & about thirty frigates, bombs & gun brigs, a very formidable fleet to salute the Danes & Swedes.

I have made repeated inquiries after the *Tigress* without gaining any information, as I promised Mrs Davies I would see her husband the first opportunity. I certainly shall make every inquiry as there are a great many gun brigs lying here. I was ashore but once: Yarmouth is a clean but a very curious built town, only one principal street with a great number of alleys turning out off it: 'twas originally built by the Danes or Swedes: the appearance of the country I like very well. The gentry of H'west in my opinion, deserve a great deal for their very great attention to the poor. We expected when we left Spithead to have found things cheap here: upon inquiry every thing is full as high: veal & mutton is 9d. or 10d. a lb. and every thing else in proportion.

I do most sincerely wish you'll very soon hear from William, you could hardly expect a letter before this; I dare say a short time will produce this very welcome letter; pray let me have the earliest information; hope he has received my letter.

Since writing the within, the signal has just been made to prepare for sailing which in my opinion smells strong of going to sea & it is rumoured we shall sail tomorrow; how far it is true can't say. In any case I shan't conclude my letter till the morning, when I shall be able to know if it is really so. I write to Birch by this post. Please continue to write to this place as all letters will be forwarded after us: in return be assured I'll embrace every opportunity of writing to you.

11 a.m The signal is now up for all Officers to repair on board their respective ships: we sail today. Please to make my love to all old acquaintances, with duty to Parents, love to Brother, Grandmother & friends. I must conclude, my dear Sister,

Your ever Aff^{te} & loving Brother, John George.

*

68. Miss George, Blue Boar Inn, Haverfordwest.

HMS Bellona, Danzig
June 4th 1801

My dear Sister,

With extreme pleasure, I take up my pen to answer your letters of the 20th & 28th ult. which I received a week ago off Bornholm and am very happy to find they left you all well. My last was the [letter] from Revel which hope you have received; we unexpectedly left it two days after as we were forming parties for the shore on what account can't say , . . We joined Admiral Totty, who was cruising with a squadron off the island of Bornholm & put ourselves under his command. Lord Nelson, with the greatest part of the fleet, went to Rostok. After cruising a week we received orders to proceed to this place with the Raisonable & Ramillies & arrived yesterday morning. We lay 3 miles from the shore: a large party are gone ashore today & tomorrow I take my turn, till then I shall leave this open as I mean to send it over land by post. I like the appearance of the country. The ships that have been here before say they met with every reception by the inhabitants. I forwarded Mr E. Phillips's letter to the Commander-in-Chief to the Warrior, she being then at this place but had joined the Fleet before we left it. I have not a doubt but what he has got it.

Every thing appears very pacific here: we are informed the Emperor of Russia has taken off the embargo on our ships without any preliminary, liberated our men & lastly has sent an invitation to Lord Nelson to Petersburg, being anxious to see the Hero of the Nile: if it is actually the case our stay I think will be short in the Baltic. You seem rejoiced at our success in the *Squirrel* taking a valuable Prize but I tell you in a few words that we have not taken a single thing since we left England that the Fleet will share except in Copenhagen on the 2nd April & that will be very trifling, – so much for your congratulations. I have seen a drawing of the action: they were very kind to us, giving the *Bellona* a peaceful Berth: it is a very incorrect thing allowed by most in the Fleet.

I received a letter from Mr Birch with yours, he said he had received your letter & was extremely thankful for it. I mean to answer it today. I shan't say a word of Mrs Birch: am astonished at her conduct.

This being the King's Birthday, the Yards[46] were manned at 8 this morning & saluted at 1.

We negotiate our Bills here at a very great disadvantage, from 12½ per cent. Every thing is pretty reasonable: the beef is much superior both in size & quality to any we have yet had in the Baltic, but not equal to the English. When we return to the Fleet, which will be, I dare say, in the course of a week, I shall expect a later letter from you.

You mentioned in a former letter that you had entrusted one to Mr George Jenkins for me. I believe that is the only letter which I have not received of yours.

June 5th, The party have not yet returned from the shore: expect them every minute as a boat has gone some time for them. The Hamburg mail goes out this afternoon, therefore won't miss the opportunity of sending this: I said I would leave it on till my return from the shore: must keep you in suspense for an account of our excursion till my next, or perhaps till we all sit round a fire at H'west, which I hope will be before next. There have been great many gentlemen aboard already to see the ship, no ladies, but expect some tomorrow or next day.

Please to make my kind love to Misses Fields & Gould; in short to all my acquaintances. I am anxious to receive your answer to my last letter as it requested one. I hope you have heard from Wm. before this. Dear Mary, I must think of drawing to a conclusion, first requesting you'll write & continue to address Yarmouth. Accept this with duty to Parents, love to James & Grandmother from, dear Sister,

Your ever Aff^te Brother, John George.

*

97

69. Miss George, Blue Boar Inn, Haverfordwest.

Bellona, off Cadiz
Nov. 1st, 1801

My dear Sister,

I can't lose a moment in answering your very welcome letter of 11th September which I received a week ago & am being made extremely happy in being assured of your welfare. My last was as long ago as the 18th September which hope is received, it being the last opportunity for writing: of course, you have a right to expect a great deal of news since that period but nothing has transpired here worth mentioning, except the glorious news of Peace[47] which you must be better acquainted with it than I am. The first I heard of it was about the middle of October in a Flag of Truce being sent out from Cadiz by the French Admiral rather unexpectedly, but at the same time most warmly received. The vessel that came out saluted the Commander-in-Chief, which was returned by him: the Ship's Company after cheering threw their hats overboard, which I am told is customary on these occasions. I believe there is nothing officially arrived yet but is expected. We have received late papers & also heard of the ratification of the preliminaries. Hostilities have not yet ceased nor do we know when we shall raise the blockade: suppose about the 12th inst.: it is doubtful whether we go to Lisbon, or to England, at once: I hope the latter. You must look out for a comfortable lodging for me in some cottage, as I expect to be anchored by April next at farthest: recollect my half pay will be very small. I am told the newspapers gave an account of a very valuable Prize which the *Bellona* captured & took into Gibraltar, which is a very great false-hood. We certainly took a Spanish sloop in a prize to the Fleet but of no consequence as for Prize Money. My Agent has received, I believe, 6 & 8£s for the frigate & one captured in the Mediterranean and if I get 4 or 5 dollars more I shall be perfectly satisfied, except for the Copenhagen business, which I have dropt all thoughts of for the present.

The weather has been very fine since we came on the station; latterly squally at times, which obliged us to get under weigh, but at the same time far from disagreeable.

I feel the pleasure you must have had on William's arrival, particularly his returning in good health. I only hope I had been present, do most sincerely wish he'll retain his health as well as the last voyage.

Doctor Phillips's death I do really lament: the *Warrior*, I believe, is off Lisbon: was she here I should certainly see Charles Phillips the earliest opportunity.

I am rather surprised I have not heard from Mr Birch since our arrival here. Mrs B. is still at Milford by your last letter.

When I received your letter the perusal gave me that pleasure that I feasted on it for a considerable time before I could lay it down, not having received one since June before & the news of my Father's leg being better than for many years, increased it infinitely. I hope to God it will continue so.

The ship is expected to be paid off at Chatham. I must join my Division, of course, must look out for a march.

Please make my kind love to all your acquaintances, particularly Miss Fields and Miss Gould: tell the latter I shall see her soon: also to Mr Duberlin, Mr Rees & those you wish among my male acquaintances; Mr George of Hook & all relations & with duty to Parents, love to James & Grandmother, accept this with the warmest affections of, dear Sister,

Your ever loving brother, John George.

P.S. If William is still in England, make my kind love to him: if it is possible for him to receive my letter before he sailed I would have wrote to him. I have heard the Natty Schooner has taken two galleons coming out here, fortunate fellows: a foremast man will make his fortune. We wait for a confirmation. Once more, adieu. JG.

*

70. Miss George, Blue Boar, Haverfordwest.

Gibraltar
Dec. 3rd 1801

[First page missing.]

. . . don't see any harm in getting a letter ready: as you well know, the wind is very uncertain and there are ships here ready to start the first favourable puff. The Rock appears much more pleasant now than when we were here 4 months ago getting our mast repaired: fine cool weather & everything flourishing, when at that time the weather was disagreeably hot & the Rock completely scorched up.

We hear Lord Cornwallis is gone to France to settle the Definitive Treaty. I hope everything will be settled soon as we look from that for our return. The uncertainty of our stay won't permit me to beg you'll answer this here as you well know we must return & most likely very shortly.

Peace is welcomely received by every body here, particularly the Spaniards who are crowding in already, quite a new thing for every body.

Please to make my kind love to Mr Duberlin & all your & my acquaintances. Having almost filled my paper it reminds me to conclude, therefore, with duty to Parents, love to Brother & G'mo^r, accept this as a mark of the warmest affection of, dear Sister,

Your ever loving Bro, John George.

I was ashore for an hour yesterday and ran by Robbin who is very well.

*

71. Miss George, Blue Boar Inn, Haverfordwest.

Bellona, Gibraltar
Dec. 20th 1801

My dear Sister,

I can't lose a moment in addressing a few lines to my dear Sister in hopes of finding her and the family all well. I wrote the 1st inst. which hope is received. We have been ever since daily in expectation of seeing England but are greatly disappointed. The Squadron remain here nearly the same as in my last account excepting a few ships which have since sailed. The *Ajax* and two troop ships are arrived from Lord Keith's fleet and are now waiting for a wind to go home. I was rather disappointed yesterday on the arrival of a schooner from Lisbon with letters in not receiving any from you: am confident it is not your fault: you must suppose I am rather anxious to hear from you now, your last being so long back as the beginning of October.

Since my last I have had the pleasure of dining with Colonel Edwardes who received me very friendly, He desired Captain Propert of the *Cambrian* to let me know he should be happy to see me. We had a fine round Welsh party: Chas Phillips & Mr Robbin were present. Mrs Edwardes seemed to be very pleasant indeed. I have also dined at the *Cambrian*'s mess with Captain Propert who has paid every attention to me that I could possibly expect: in return I have asked him on board but he is rather loath to trust himself on the water after being cast away. I still hope to have his company on board. I saw him yesterday, as well Mr C. Phillips & Mr Robbin who are all very well. I have met with several I knew in the *Cambrian*'s: Howells the Pedlar's son & your neighbour Dicky Harries: they look very well & all seem glad they are likely to go home soon. We have received late papers but very little news respecting the Definitive Treaty.

Sir James Saumarez[48] has received dispatches by a frigate which arrived two days ago: there are five sail-of-the-line ordered to complete immediately with five months' stores, provisions, &c. and ready to sail the first fine wind with sealed orders, it is supposed for the West Indies. We are lucky enough to escape: the ship being very bad is the reason, I suppose, their destination is quite a conjecture. We heard Bonaparte means to send a force out; of course, we must send an equal force to cope with them. I have not exactly heard the name of the ship yet. Captain Danby of the *Spencer* is to be the commander of the squadron, I believe: one satisfaction we are short of is the number. The communication with Spain is not yet completely opened, passports are not granted to any body. I walked one day to their lines but had not the opportunity of forming an opinion of their works.

The weather is delightful for this time of the year, every thing appears as if it were late in spring: vegetables in great plenty, flowers in full blossom, a chance orange tree loaded with fruit & hedges of geraniums in bloom. I don't much like The Rock but if it is possible for any thing to attract my notice, 'tis what I have already mentioned.

We have heard of dreadful gales happening in different parts but have not experienced any severe weather here. I believe in my last I requested you would not write till you heard from me: upon consideration must beg you'll write, recollect all the news as I have a great deal to expect, paying the Inland postage as it will then come out by the Lisbon Packet, our stay being very uncertain, some say till March.

My paper is almost filled. This being Christmas time, accept the compliments of the season & please make them to Parents, Grandmother, Brothers, Miss Gould & Miss Fisher, in short all friends, & may you all enjoy many happy, happy returns, is the earnest prayer of, dear Sister,

Yours very affect^{ly}, John George.

Wakelin's ship is with Lord Keith aloft. The *Warrior*, I believe, is not one of the ships going away.

*

72. Miss George, Blue Boar Inn, Haverfordwest.

Bellona, Gibraltar
Jan. 19th 1802

My dear Sister,

With extreme pleasure, I embrace the opportunity of writing by a troop ship going home. It is so long since I heard from you that I almost despair of hearing from you at this place as our stay, of course, can't be long. I don't at all accuse you with inattention, very far from it I assure you. My last was dated about the latter [end] of last month, which I hope arrived safe.

There is very little going forward here: we hear the Definitive is going on very favourably, supposed to be signed before this. Lord Keith's fleet are still aloft excepting 2 or 3 frigates and troop ships which are gone by. We expected Lord Hutchins here in the *Egyptian*, which called here on the passage home: he was so very ill that he was obliged to stay at Malta.

The ships which I mentioned in a former letter supposed to be going to the West Indies went to Tetuan Bay on account of contrary winds but, I believe, are since sailed: the ships are the *Spencer, St George, Vanguard & Parsifal*. Charles Phillips dined on board here yesterday: he is very well and is happy the *Warrior* was not included in the above squadron. He is in the same predicament with myself not having heard from his friends for a considerable time.

The weather has been very boisterous here indeed for this last week till today, but of no serious consequences. I have not been ashore this 9 days: the last time I went I saw G. Robbin & all my *Cambrian* friends. Since I came here I got acquainted with two neighbours, officers of the *Cambrian*, people I had not the least recollection of in Wales: Smith of Jeffreston is one & the other's name is Lewis: I really forget the place he comes from, somewhere in Pembroke side: two very agreeable young men.

Birch has made for all the lost time in writing: I received a few days ago from him 3 very friendly letters, with a large packet of newspapers. He mentioned having heard from you Mrs B. is still at Milford, he says – what can the woman be about?

The communication with Spain is not yet opened so much as to grant passage to officers; a few commanding officers have been as far as St Roch. I was going to Algeciras with a party in a fortnight by water, but the Captain altered his mind.

We have a Portuguese squadron here, under a Commodore. I don't know what they are going about: they saluted the Admiral & Garrison, which was returned. A French man-o'-war, lugger & cutter arrived here yesterday evening but are since sailed: very pacific, to be sure: 'twas not the case four months ago.

I heard some thing from Birch: Captain Frank Williams's marriage to Miss Picton of Poyston[49] a very good match I think: he is now in the *Robust* & relieved his namesake, our Captain of Marine's brother.

You must judge entirely by the Definitive Treaty. If I have time to receive your letter before the signalling as it is not likely we shall leave this place before it is really settled: should a favourable opportunity offer & plenty of time, will thank you for a letter.

This being my first for this year, must wish you all as happy a one as heaven can bestow, and may you all enjoy many happy, happy returns is the earnest prayer of, dear Mary,

Your most aff^te & loving brother, John George.

*

73. Miss George, Blue Boar Inn, Haverfordwest.

Port Royal, Jamaica
Feb. 16th 1802

My dear Sister,

I fancy you'll be surprised in finding me writing to you from this place. We arrived here yesterday evening with the *Warrior*, *Defence* and *Zealous* after a short and pleasant voyage of 26 days and have the satisfaction to say in very good health. Our departure from Gibraltar was very sudden indeed. I wrote the day before we sailed to you and meant to have done it after we received orders to proceed to sea but as our destination was so very uncertain, I thought it more prudent in desiring Mr Robbins to write & mention our sailing, which I dare say he did. The Island as we passed along was very beautiful, almost as fine as any part I ever saw in my life: I can assure you I am much altered in my opinion of the country since our arrival: instead of burning hot weather as I expected, found it very pleasant, rather hot to be sure but not unpleasant. Admiral Duckworth[50] commands: he has 16 sail-of-the-line under his command, 12 of them are here, the remainder are cruising. Our coming here is occasioned by four sail-of-the-line sailing from Cadiz for St Domingo to join the French squadron from Brest in order to quell the Negroes. We have just heard with great pleasure that they have landed in three divisions and every thing appears so favourable that there is no doubt but what our stay will be here very short. Respecting the yellow fever, I have not a thought of it: the Island is particularly healthy: at present no such a thing as the fever: as long as I enjoy my health, should [not] have any dislike to the country but at the same time should have no objection to seeing old England once more.

I was on shore this morning and meant to have gone to the capital, Kingston, about 7 miles off, but was surprised in hearing of our being ordered on a cruise tomorrow morning with a squadron, between this island and St Domingo, it is supposed not longer than a fortnight, therefore I have the pleasure to come yet. Everything appears so very different here that 5 or 6 months will soon elapse: surely we shan't be much longer here. Fruit is very reasonable: the first thing that saluted my eyes this morning was a dish of pineapples and several other fruit which are not met with at home. Stock is very dear: mutton ½ a dollar a lb., fowls 3 dollars a pair & turkeys 4 & 4½ dollars a piece. A serious thing: no Prize Money.

Poor James, I find, is to take his departure yet before William. I thought he was not inclined for the sea, but it seems we are all to be seafaring men. The Merchant Service I don't much approve of, for reasons I should be glad to explain if we were together, but our Parents' approbation is sufficient to satisfy me in every respect. I am extremely sorry for poor Green's[51] death.

You say our relation Davies is at Bristol: when I see him I'll take care to give him a good rousing for not writing to you, indeed I haven't heard from him or his wife yet no answer to mine: suppose returned like all yours for postage. I have not seen C. Phillips since we arrived

The *Elephant* is on a cruise: Capt. Foley[52] is left her & is gone home.

Pray make my compliments to all female acquaintances, in short to all friends. My paper reminds me to conclude, therefore with duty to Parents, love to Brothers & Grm[mr], I remain, dear Mary,

Your very aff[te] brother, John George.

I must beg you to write immediately and address to me Port Royal, Jamaica as we expect to leave the country by the 1st June, therefore it will be as much as I can expect to receive your letter by that time. 'twas my intention to have written to Birch but time won't admit of it. Adieu. JG.

*

74. Miss George, Blue Boar Inn, Haverfordwest.

Port Royal, Jamaica
March 12th 1802

My dear Sister.

I can't for a moment lose an opportunity of assuring you of my health, particularly in this country as I can't possibly expect to hear from you soon. I write by almost every opportunity trusting they will not be thrown aside unopened. My last was about the 15th ult. on our arrival here. We sailed the following morning & joined Admiral Montagu[53] off Navassa, a small island between Jamaica & S[t] Domingo, and remained with him till the 5th inst. when we were ordered in to refit. We have no authentic account of the proceedings for the French at S[t] Domingo. My last informed you of their being successful: the report now is very different and I believe pretty much credited: they made good their landing in three different places but met with great opposition. Toussaint[54] has destroyed S[t] Francois, the capital, and other places to prevent them falling into the hands of the French: it is uncertain how long this business will be before it terminates our stay here; depends a great deal on Peace unless relieved. A French frigate arrived here a fortnight ago & sailed soon after; nothing transpired: they have 20 sail-of-the-line in this country, we have only 17. Admiral Campbell is expected daily with 7 more, therefore the superiority will be on our side. There is a flying report of the Definitive Treaty being signed: hope it will soon be confirmed.

The *Warrior* is here. Mr C. Phillips was on board 3 or 4 days ago to see me. He is very well and seems to have no very great dislike to the climate.

I have neither been at Kingston or Spanish Town yet, indeed I don't much feel myself inclined to go, the sun being so very powerful and we can't be ashore after sunset, unless with particular permission. I have been several times ashore after dinner taking a walk, it being the most pleasant time of the day. Should I feel myself inclined to take a stroll up the country, shall have plenty of time yet as we don't expect to sail this fortnight. Fruit here is the only thing that is pretty reasonable, everything else is almost treble the price you pay in England. I hope to God our stay will be very short in this country as I long to see our native land once more.

I wrote to Mr Birch by this opportunity. I like to keep up my correspondence being so far from home as every letter must be received with some satisfaction: am almost inclined to write to Miss Gould if I thought she would answer it. It being late must lay down the pen till the morning.

13th Again I resume my pen. I altered my mind since yesterday evening about Kingston: was prevailed on to form one of a party that went up this evening. We were soon tired of the place being, I suppose, strangers. Kingston is a very large miserable town and the houses are generally pretty well built. Money is the chief object, of course: very little hospitality. I am glad my curiosity is satisfied but'll assure don't mean to pay another visit.

The Jamaica Packet is made up at London the first Wednesday in every month: must beg you'll write, if convenient, by every packet, as the greatest pleasure I can receive is in hearing of your welfare. Please to make my compliments to all enquiring friends. Accept this, my dear Sister, with the warmest affections of,

Your very loving Brother, John George.

I am anxious to know what is done for William & James. As you mentioned in your last, James was about taking his departure. Duty to Parents, &c

*

75. Miss George, Blue Boar Inn, Haverfordwest.

Bellona, Portsmouth
June 29th 1802

My dear Sister,

Agreeable to my promise I take up my pen to write again to you. We came into harbour last Friday and are nearly ready to be paid off, suppose about Friday or Saturday.

Mr Birch came on board soon after our arrival at Spithead: you can't conceive the pleasure I felt on seeing him: he looks very well, is very much obliged to you for your attention to him; begs you'll embrace an opportunity of sending to Mrs B. to say he is well and that he means to write in a few days. I spent the day with him yesterday.

I can't give you any information respecting my present situation as no appointments are come down yet: it is probable my stay may be here a month. I believe they make a custom of appointing officers to the Division they formerly belonged to. I like Plymouth.

I walked to Fareham, a village about 4 miles off, last Saturday and was very much pleased with my walk and, what makes it more, the prospect of a most plentiful harvest. The village is very pretty, quite a country place.

This place is not as gay as it used to be: not as many ships: in the course of 10 days it will be thinner as there are 4 sail-of-the-line preparing to be paid off: the seamen are very quiet, to the surprise of every body. I long to be ashore. I was at Gosport Theatre yesterday evening and such an infamous house I never saw in my life: even H'west is a Drury Lane to it. The *Fury* called here a few days ago & sailed again to the eastward: George Robbin was on board, a passenger: he sent his compliments.

I recollect you mentioning Davies our relation being at Bristol: if you know his address I'll thank you for it as I wish to see him.

Please continue to write and as the ship is likely to be paid off before your letter arrives, I think you had better address to me at No. 6 Unicorn Street, Portsea, Hants. (Mr Birch's lodgings). We are Royals[55] you know, therefore you may list us Royal Marine in your next. I fancy the Cambrians are reduced by this time: they have been here: nothing but long stories of Gibraltar I suppose. Has Colonel, now Lord K., been with you yet. I have seen his letter on being elected a Member.[56] Please to make my best compliments to Miss Gould & Miss Fields: tell them I hope to see them soon: also Mr George of Hook & family. I dare say I shall find a very great alteration in H'west since I left: do most sincerely wish I was within sight of it now. I dare say you'll agree with me in securing my commission before I apply for leave. There are several countrymen at Quarters here but don't know any of them, a Mr Phillips is one, perhaps the same that was recruiting in H'west.

My paper reminds me to conclude, therefore I remain with duty to Parents, &c., dear Sister,

Ever yours affectionately, John George.

Mr Birch's compliments to you & the family.

*

76. Miss George, Blue Boar Inn, Haverfordwest.

Royal Marine Barracks, Plymouth
Nov. 12th 1802

My dear Sister,

It is hardly to be conceived the pleasure I feel on the receipt of your very welcome letter of the 8th which I received this morning. I must confess I was kept in a state of anxiety for the last three days & intended, if I hadn't received yours at the time I did, to have written by this evening's post fearing something had happened with you or that it was possible for my letter to have miscarried: however, your reason is sufficient.

I put on the Red Coat for the first time last Sunday & between guard mounting & other duties, my time has been almost taken up since but it will be more easy for the future as officers are coming in every day from leave. George Jenkins's brig sailed before I arrived for Leith with troops, therefore 'twas lucky I had not brought his things round. I hope you will apologise to his parents for my inattention.

This place is remarkably dull since the Peace, a few guard ships, frigates, &c. are all the Naval force, and they about nothing. We embarked a few days ago 300 Royal Bucks[57] with Officers for Chatham – supposed for Woolwich. I was lucky enough to escape that duty. I find by inquiry my sea credit will keep me ashore should the Peace continue at least a twelve month, the deuce is in it if I can't get leave to see you within that time: be assured if leave is given words shan't be wanted for asking. Do most sincerely wish it to be soon.

William Bowen, Bridge End, has been here I find, but has not kept his word in calling: I should not have acted so. I saw Curgenven this evening in his shop: he has apologised fifty times to me for not calling on you in H'west: begs particularly his compliments to you & the family: he mentioned as well some of his friends, Green included. I frequently spend part of my evenings with him: he has a snug little room behind his shop and a good companion in it, a cask of good Welsh Ale, sent him, I believe from Arnold's Hill. Should you or Father see Mr Barzey, tell him he is well. I also gave Mullins & his family a call: Mary, I told you, was married before, I saw her, she is very comfortably settled indeed. The pot of butter was broached by Mrs M. I think they may look a long time for it before it comes. I heard from George yesterday about mine: I am to get it next Monday, then what a blow out of buttered rolls. Salt butter is here 1s.0d. & fresh 14d. – every thing else is as reasonable as H'west, excepting poultry.

At the bottom of George's letter, he apologises for not paying for the carriage as he didn't perceive it in your letter till he had sent it off. Why do you desire him to do such a thing? Curgenven saw Colonel Vaughan and mentioned my intention of calling upon him: he said he should be very happy to see me & tomorrow I mean to do myself the honour.

I am much obliged to the Captain (no longer Lieut. Davies) for making use of my name to Miss Brown: pray make my love to her & confirm what he has said: tell the Captn. I shall depute him as a 'Go Between', as a friend of ours, who accused me of being contemptuous has been often: make my compliments & tell him also his business with Lyne I have neglected, but mean to take it up in a few days.

I approve of Mr & Mrs Mathias's Entrée into H'west I think I should act in a similar way was I in that state. Make my compliments of congratulation to them, if you please.

Your recollect my correspondent here 'Durre', at least the name: he has contrived to marry a very pretty girl a few days ago. Miss Allen is very good in sending me her compliments: of course, let William return mine & let him tell her pretty little eyes was the principal cause of my unsteadiness in church.

If it was not for postage, I certainly would declare a Paper War with some of the folks, Miss Gould at the head.

Tell Wakelin his old ship, the *Childers*, nearly upset the other day. I breakfasted with the Captain (an old messmate) a few days ago. What's that to me? you'll ask – pardon me.

I am thinking James is about sailing now & as the wind is, am afraid I have not a chance of seeing him here: the voyage is short and pleasant, dare say he'll like it very well.

You mentioned receiving Mr Birch's letter: no, dear Mary, I have not the smallest objection to your perusing my correspondents' letters at any time but wished you had been a little more explicit of Mr Birch's, if he requested I would write [any] particular business for me to transact let me know in your next. I heard here he was gone to London. Fancy the West Indies will be his object. It is now past 10 o'clock, therefore shall lay down my pen till the morrow, first wishing you all. Good night & God bless you.

13th a.m. Again I resume my pen. Must beg you'll write, as what I have repeated before often the greatest pleasure I receive is in hearing from you. Let me have all the chit-chat that is going forward. These winter evenings by a good fire are famous for writing, therefore don't deprive yourself of the opportunity. I shan't write again till I hear from you, therefore you know what to expect. My paper is almost full; you'll say 'tis time to conclude as I am sure I have tired you in the perusal, therefore with duty to dear Parents, love to William, Grandmother & friends. I remain, dear Mary,

Your very loving Brother, John George.

I miss Lord K. very much now as I am inclined to write by every post if it was not for the postage.

Don't be angry with Thos Gibbs for I am not certain that I told him I was going. Whilst I am writing now I have a basin of hot bread & milk under my nose. I am determined not to spoil tea till I'll get the butter. Tell Davies I am determined not to have many friends shooting as he imagines, but means to make myself comfortable this winter at least as much so as being absent from friends can make me. I don't know that you can read this way of writing, but such I [know as] cross writing.[58] Let me know if you approve of it. I merely give it you as a specimen. You find I am determined for you to write long letters, whether you are inclined or not.

*

77. Miss George, Blue Boar Inn, Haverfordwest.

Royal Marine Barracks, Plymouth
Nov. 21st 1802

My dear Sister,

The first thing that saluted my eyes on being relieved from the Dock Yard Guard was your very welcome letter of the 16th. Be assured I am made extremely happy in hearing of your welfare altho' I kept my word in not writing, still it was not my intention had I not written to the Captn. a few days ago respecting Prize Money. I desired him to mention having heard from me, he being a very intelligent young man, have not a doubt of his doing it.

I received a letter from James since my last and answered it by return of post at his request. He said he had heard from you recently, expected to sail about that time but want to stop at Portsmouth. I gave him Mr Birch's address in London & desired him to call if he possibly could, as I am confident he would be very happy to see him & render him any assistance he should want.

Nothing but war but at the same time very little doing. There is a report going about of more ships about being commissioned but am thinking I'll wait some time for a confirmation. Our force here is diminishing very fast. We are going to send immediately 200 men to Portsmouth with officers. I am lucky enough to escape that duty. The pot of butter is arrived, just a week coming from Bristol & the carriage trifling. I have not had a blow out yet, not having tea things, but mean it tomorrow or next day. I do most seriously pity poor Birch having such a character as Mrs B. to deal with. I shall write to him but mean to wait a few days in hopes of hearing from James again, as I expect it he will write provided he saw Mr Birch.

I spent an evening with Curgenven & his 'companion', the cask of ale, since my last: he desires his compliments I have not called on Colonel Vaughan since but mean it in a day or two. I find by yours the Captain is enjoying himself in the country: hope he'll get my letter soon as I shall expect his answer with an order to receive his Prize Money when it is remitted to him, I shall desire he will acknowledge it to you as I fancy as his letters will be so very interesting as to require double postage: perhaps he will ask you to write them for him. You surprise me by saying George Phillips is after Miss Blethin. I thought Miss Green was the admirer. Ask the former from me whether she is partial to Pope's works as she used to be when you have an opportunity.

I am not a bit surprised at Mrs Williams's scandal, there's only one can compare with her, Mrs Bishop, both I detest.

I hope you don't make my compliments to Miss Gould with the rest, as she has accused me of contempt: I may as well enjoy the game as the name.

Your cross-writing I admire much, it being done in a master-like manner; the person who taught me is here, ordered to join a ship: I spent part of an evening with him. He told me of the *Minerva* being commissioned, in that case John Robbin will join her: as you have not mentioned it I was afraid he had made a mistake. I should have waited a long time for the *Spitfire*'s coming round, she was reported, you know, to have been waiting for a wind for this place before I left the country. George Jenkins's brig I think is not likely to go on the Milford station again as ships when once quit their station are not likely to return.

The weather has been very dull lately, particularly yesterday, raining very hard all day. I had a comfortable room certainly in the Dock Yard therefore did not feel the effects of it, excepting confinement.

Pray, has Father sown his wheat[59] yet? I recollect he was waiting for fine weather when I left home. I am sorry Wakelin exposed himself at Miss Mathews' party. Compliments to both him and Robbin. You astonish me by saying the latter & Miss Owens had broken their intimacy but seriously thinking I never had an idea of its coming to any point. Mr Levett's relation here I wrote to with his message, not having an opportunity of delivering it myself: he lives the other side of Plymouth.

Make my compliments to Mr George, Freystrop & family, Miss Brown, &c., &c., &c. Tell Miss B. I often listen to the band play 'As pensive I thought of my love', it being the favourite, but would much rather hear her sing it. My paper reminds me to conclude, with duty to Parents, love to William & Grandmother, accept this with the warmest affection of,

Your ever loving Brother, John George.

It being late, if I can pick up a subject I shall certainly resume my pen again in the morning.

Nov. 22nd a.m. Again I resume my pen. I've taken your advice respecting the new shirts: am wearing them now and in case an opportunity should offer, I think I'll embrace it of sending them round. You find I am determined to keep you employed: I would not do it if I had not that opinion of my dear Sister that she would feel herself happy in obliging her brother at all times, at least you have proved it since I left home. I mentioned my intention of calling on Colonel Vaughan since I wrote to you last. I called but the Colonel was not at home. Mrs V. received me very politely indeed and I was obliged to promise to call again; that was what I mentioned in the former part of this letter I intended doing. There is no harm in extending my acquaintance in that kind of way. My friend and old messmate is here at my elbow teasing me to conclude and as I have no particular subject further to say I believe I must please him. I have only to beg you to write as soon as you conveniently can as I am very particular in corresponding, which I hope you'll agree with me in saying. Excuse all faults. Adieu. JG.

*

78. Miss George, Blue Boar Inn, Haverfordwest.
Royal Marine Barracks, Plymouth
Dec. 1st 1802

My dear Sister,

After a silence of 12 days I at last take up my pen tho' as you mentioned in your letter, not obligated as I believe you are one in my debt now, which I looked for most anxiously to reading & shall more so tomorrow. I received some satisfaction in hearing from the Captn. yesterday, particularly so in being assured of your health. I answered his letter by this evening's post enclosing a draft on my Agent for £4.10.0 which I desired him to acknowledge the receipt of to you only. He was disposed to write an intelligent letter. He gave me no news at all, excepting his little joust to the country.

It is now seven o'clock in the evening and am almost ashamed to say not above an hour from dinner: a cold harsh westerly wind, therefore mean to devote the evening in writing to my dear Sister; at intervals I mean to take up a novel recommended by you (*Evelina*) which I perfectly agree in thinking a good one.

The wind has been very favourable for James who, I am thinking, must be sailed by this time. I was in hope of hearing from him if he called on Mr Birch, am afraid he was too busy. I am really at a loss what to do, whether write to Mr Birch or not, it is so long since he wrote that it is 20 to one if James meets him in London. Should you have an opportunity you may enquire of Mrs B. if she heard from him lately & send me his address. The Spy is out of the way now: I dare say she is not sorry for it.

I saw Curgenven yesterday: he desires his compliments.

I desired Davies to shew you my letter, which I am sure he will do. You will find there that there is nothing going forward here. The detachment of Marines going to Portsmouth have sailed: had it been five weeks ago I would have volunteered, as Birch has left it & the uncertainty of seeing James, I am much better in staying where I am, as it must attend with expense.

We established blue pantaloons and half boots for the first time today, a very convenient dress for the winter: a person can be easily [metamorphosed] now by changing coat and waistcoat.

I gave Colonel Vaughan a call a few days ago, who seemed very happy to see me. He is going to Exeter on some duty & when he returns I have promised to visit him frequently. He repeated more than once for me to particularly make his compliments to Father and the family.

Tell George Robbin it is reported that *Culloden* will go to the East Indies when ready, but advise him not to pay any attention to it till he hears from better authority. I don't credit such reports myself.

The ships on the Milford station are long coming round: I long to see some of them that I may have some news.

Davies tells me you managed to assist him and Mrs Pikes in finishing a bottle of Madeira some time ago. I commend you for it. I wish some kind person would give me a similar offer: I don't think I should refuse it. I advised him to provide more than one duck for his next party: must put him up to it on the strength of his Prize Money.

William's promised letter I shan't push for, knowing his aversion to writing: when it comes all I have to say, shall be happy in receiving it.

I am surprised I never met with Mr Cross in my walks as I generally go about a great deal. I fancy he is returned to Wales by this time.

Between this and *Evelina* I have sat up till it is late, therefore shall lay down my pen till the morning in hopes of receiving your letter & think of a fresh subject. Good night & God bless you.

2nd a.m. Again I resume my pen. Your most welcome letter of the 20th ult. I have just received: am particularly happy again to be assured of your welfare. I am sorry to find John Robbin's ship being commissioned not realised.

War is not so much talked of here as it has been some time ago. I have not seen Mullins but once since I arrived. They say they don't feel the effect of the Peace, but it is a perfect nonsense. I am confident in the prayer of the generality of the tradespeople here.

Charles Phillips will, I am sure, be happy to do any thing for you.

This country is not equal to Wales for sport & people are very particular in allowing others to shoot on their lands, indeed was it ever so agreeable there being so much parade & one thing or other that it would be useless to attempt going out.

In case I can procure next summer, which I hope to God I shall, I mean to embark on my return as it is so much more comfortable belonging to a ship than on shore, at least I think so.

Make my compliments to relations at Freystrop & all old acquaintances. With duty to Parents, love to William & G'mother and friends, I remain, dear Mary,

Your most Aff.te & loving Brother, John George.

A Post Script of course. I feel myself very unpleasant on thinking of the disagreeable disposition of William. When I was in the country, we had several disputes, which would have ended very serious if I had not given up to him. I am very thankful to you for your candid sentiments and have that firm opinion of you that you will soon act so. I mean to write to him when I am disposed to write, a moral letter which you shall have the perusal of. Don't mention a syllable of what I have written. Must beg you'll not bear animosity to him but endeavour to come to reconciliation.

You say T. Gibbs would be glad to hear from me. I should be very happy in commencing a correspondence but when once begun there is no breaking it off, and you know the expense of postage. Curgenven is going to London in January: he says he expects Grafton will pay him a visit next summer. I shall feel myself very happy to shew him the country when perhaps Curgenven will be prevented by business. Let Mr Barzey know he is well, should you have the opportunity.

I must with reluctance at last bid you adieu, it being late in the morning & also time for the post. I have still plenty of room yet to write and was I to wait till tomorrow's post most likely should be able to fill it but I won't tire your anxiety any longer for I am sure you are looking out for this. One thing more: must beg you to continue to write as early as convenient. Be assured I never part with money with as much pleasure as I do for postage of your letter. Excuse all errors. Adieu. JG.

*

79. Miss George, Blue Boar Inn, Haverfordwest.

RM Barracks, Plymouth
Dec. 12th 1802

My dear Sister,

Your most welcome letter of the 7th inst. I have just received: am extremely happy in being assured of your welfare. I must confess I was rather kept in a state of suspense in not hearing from you sooner as I calculated your letter to have arrived on Thursday last, but as the old proverb says: Better late than never.

News is very dead here. The *Escort* is in. I wrote a letter to George Jenkins and expect to see him or his answer every minute. I believe I shall trouble him to take those new shirts which I was speaking about to get altered. You see I am determined to keep you employed: indeed, I almost blush to think of it but really at the year's end to sum up every little expense, there is not much saved out of £85: in this place you can't even get a button sewn on any thing without payment: this is meant for your perusal only.

Colonel Vaughan is still at Exeter: had an hour's gossip with his brother-in-law, Mr Harris, a few days ago.

I thought my information respecting the *Minerva* being commissioned was staunch. I am very glad of it. Was she here instead of Chatham I think I should be inclined to become a messmate with John Robbin, but *terra firma* is best at the end.

Curgenven I have not seen for some days, he is very busy taking stock, if you know what that is.

I shall be very soon gratified in my writing to William but, without flattery, 'tis impossible to have a better correspondent than yourself. If I feel myself disposed shall write a few letters to some friends by George Jenkins. Miss Gould will be surprised to receive one. I think she will when she does: nothing more to say to her.

I thought the Captn. stretched a good deal respecting his Madeira: he certainly can afford to give you a good supper out of that immense sum I sent him. Make my compliments.

You may assure the Miss Maurice that Curgenven is not married, neither have I heard there is any prospect of it.

I can't see Mrs Birch has room to find fault in my not calling before I left the country: I certainly made her a great many unnecessary visits: the idea of going to her husband is all a farce as I don't think she had the smallest intention of going when I spoke to her. I do most sincerely hope he'll procure a satisfactory situation very soon. I shall certainly write to him by tomorrow's post; am sorry I neglected it so long.

I am sorry Mr Prust[60] should bear enmity with Father for such a trifling occasion: it certainly shews what a dirty mean scoundrel he is, but think it is in Father's interest a good deal to keep in with those Great Men if he can with any propriety so as to secure the House, but he knows very well what he is about.

I long to see George Jenkins: most likely he is detained on board as he sent word back to say he should answer my note in the course of an hour. Provided the shirts are sent round there is not the smallest necessity of hurrying them, sometime in the course of the next summer will do very well, and in case of a necessity they can be sent me on a very short time.

I frequently meet with the Captn. who told you he knew me, very friendly indeed but never recollect his saying of being in Wales. I have seen Mullins and family but once since I returned: it won't do to make too familiar, that you must know very well. I am sorry to find Wakelin is getting out of favour with the lasses: make my compliments to both him & George Robbin It is like a dream to me that the Insolent gun brig is here in that case most likely I shall see Wm Twyning.

Colonel Vaughan talks of going down to reside in his old house at Cartlett again, but don't pay much credit to it: they take in the Bristol Journal merely for the sake of getting Welsh news: in his last paper I saw Miss Davies's marriage, which astonished me as I really thought she had given up all idea of it. He gets another today therefore tomorrow I must enquire the news. Martha Howells is condescending indeed in sending cake to the Gentlemen: in case she was to think of me I hope she would send one sufficient to last a week or a fortnight so that I might have something to play upon.

You are indebted to my being on Picket last night at the Dock Yard for this long scroll, as I am excused from attending Church this morning by it: otherwise should have gone with the men like a good boy.

I believe you must dispense with my cross-writing this morning as it almost time for the post. Remember me to relations at Freystrop and all old acquaintances. I shall expect to hear from you again before I write to William. My paper reminds me to conclude, therefore with duty to Parents, love &c., &c., &c. I remain, dear Mary,

Ever yours most affect^{ly}, John George.

*

80. Mr Wm. George, Blue Boar Inn, Haverfordwest.

RM Barracks, Plymouth
Dec. 24th 1802

Dear W^m,

My long promised letter I at last intend writing, indeed should have wrote sooner but waited till today's post for Mary's answer to my last of the 12th inst. and as it has not arrived I fancy she expects to hear from me thro' you before she writes again as I recollect mentioning something of it in my last. My proceedings till the last fortnight you must know by my letter to Sister. George Jenkins has been here & is I believe sailed. I had not the pleasure of seeing him as he was detained on board but received two letters from him: he had an idea of the Escort being ordered to Ireland with troops which was my reason in not sending the linen to get altered agreeable to my last: trust I shall be the bearer of them myself early in the summer.

The *Nemesis* has been here, I made my brother Officer an offer to exchange, unfortunately he likes his ship and the station too well to comply with it. I don't know but I am as well off where I am provided I can procure 3 or 4 months' leave in the course of the ensuing summer as she must be paid off perhaps shortly and it would be putting me to a very great inconvenience. Two frigates have come up to harbour to be paid off, Glenmore and Ossian, and one commissioned.

I am agreeably surprised in just receiving my Sister's letter of the 19th after making the inquiry at the Office & an extremely happy in finding you all well. Nothing particular going forward.

The weather is at present very fine and I hope it will continue so for a while as I mean to take several little excursions into the neighbourhood. I was yesterday at a place called Saltash, a village about four miles off and was highly pleased with my walk: I was accompanied by a brother Red Coat. I have not a doubt in the summer of procuring leave, provided the Peace continues, therefore I beg you'll pay proper attention to the mares as I mean to be a great horseman: a ride then will be a treat as I fancy I shall not have many before [my leave]. Assure the Captain for me that I have lost the cot blocks, otherwise should be happy in sending them to him. I suppose he has given you some good treats by this time out of the money I sent him. Make my compliments.

I find the Hostler is married, nothing like it, we shall all follow his example some time or other I dare say.

I read in the newspaper of James's ship coming down the River: am pretty sure they are sailed by this time as 'tis impossible to get a better wind. I have been repeatedly solicited to embark for Officers but perfectly agree with Mary in preferring *terra firma* and hope I shall be able to enjoy it at least a twelve month yet. Let me know all the news going forward. How does Miss A. behave in church now? I dare say she would have no objections in seeing a few pretty [things] in her prayer book again. I hope you amuse the rest of the party with a few nuts sometimes. I dare say I shall find the Misses Rogers much altered. I see them as they were in a fair way of being [little] girls when I left the country: remember me to all old acquaintances I saw Curgenven a few days ago: he desires his compliments to the family.

By the time you receive this it will be the middle of Christmas: may you all enjoy it as much as it can afford is my most earnest wish: mine here will be no great things: indeed, can't expect it as I am not much acquainted with private families. I have written to Mr Birch but have received no answer: ask Mrs B. for his address & let me know in your answer to this which I hope will be as early as convenient as I shall be very happy in hearing from you.

Make my love to relations at Freystrop and all friends, with duty to Parents, love to Sister & Grandmother, accept this with the most sincere wish for your happiness from, dear William,

Yours very affect^ly, John George.

*

81. Miss George, Blue Boar Inn, Haverfordwest.

RM Barracks, Plymouth
Jan. 6th 1803

My dear Sister,

It is now upwards of a fortnight since I wrote to William and as I have received no answer mean to renew the correspondence with you again. By this time your Christmas is over. I fancy it is only the name here, no feasting or any thing else. I spent my Christmas with a brother Red Coat in the Guard Room here. We had a roast fowl & mince pies: comfortable you'll say, with a bottle of wine after, which we had.

We have as usual very little news going forward: the report was, a few days ago, and is now talked of, of a Battalion of Marines to go out to New South Wales in order to form a settlement[61] at a new discovered place, about 1000 miles from Botany Bay. I don't pay much attention to it, as I think it has originated merely from a Colonel of our Corps going out as Lieutenant Governor, but it is not very improbable: they won't find me a volunteer unless they give me some very great encouragement.

We were all very much pleased about a week ago by an account of the vacancies being filled up, as it would have kept most of us ashore much longer than it otherwise would, but were too sanguine: after the notifications were made out at the Admiralty & every thing settled, it was put a stop to for the present, for what reason is quite unknown. I was in great hopes of seeing Moore here, as he would certainly be included in the number: various opinions are given, some think a further reduction will take place but I don't think there is the least probability of it; something must be done before the summer.

Colonel Vaughan arrived at the Garrison a few days ago, from Exeter. The weather has been so very bad lately that I have not had an opportunity of giving him a call. He is going out of the Garrison and, I fancy, means to retire as the invalids are out on a very different establishment and, in that case, I suppose Cartlett will be his object, as he mentioned something of his old house to me some time past. I saw Curgenven yesterday, he desired his compliments. I have promised to form one of a party at his friend's house soon.

I can safely say we have had but one fine day to walk into the country for the last nine weeks and that I embraced in a walk to Saltash, which I mentioned in my letter to William. I did intend then taking a complete tour of the whole neighbourhood but the weather is so hard hearted that it wouldn't permit me. I wonder what reason William can have in not writing, as he must know I should be very happy in hearing from him. I have neither heard from Birch since I wrote last. The folks I think are very considerate supposing that a Lieut. of the Marines can't afford to pay the postage, this assured I never part with money with greater pleasure than in paying for letters. As I have done duty ever since I joined quarters at Mill Bay Barracks, which I will leave to the Ostler to describe, have removed over entirely within these few days, another & myself have taken two rooms adjoining, so that we breakfast together and make it very comfortable.

I mentioned in my last of making the Officer on *Nemesis* an offer to exchange but unfortunately could not effect it: in case I had I should have surprised you all now this Christmas time as she is gone round, but hope I shall before the end of six months, otherwise shall be greatly mortified.

I fancy James has sailed before this: the weather has not been very favourable lately, but not the smallest danger, tho' boisterous. He has by this time had an opportunity of judging what a seafaring life is, dare say he likes it; he is a boy of that contented disposition that will persevere I anything he enters into. You will hear from him I dare say shortly.

I beg you will write in return to this tho' William should write before as I have to expect almost three weeks' news. I think John Robbin stands a very fair chance of going to the Mediterranean again, as his Captain is a relation, or a friend, of Sir J^{as} Saumarez who is going out to take the command. I dare say he would like to go on his old station again. Make my compliments to all old acquaintances and as this is the first of the year, may you all enjoy many happy returns is the earnest prayer of, dear Mary,

Your most aff^{te} Brother, John George.

I must not forget to make my duty to Parents, love to Brother & G'mother.

*

82. Miss M. George, Blue Boar Inn, Haverfordwest.

RM Barracks, Plymouth
Jan. 15th 1803

My dear Sister,

Your kind letter of the 4th inst. I received some days ago and should have answered it sooner but waited for an answer to mine which I wrote a day or two before, as I have not received one I fancy we both wait in a similar expectation: however, I mean to begin.

I think there is little doubt but what I shall be able early in the summer to procure leave, once more to embrace my dear friends. I do most heartily wish this time had come: I have been absent from you almost three months already and in the course of another three shall certainly expect to make application.

This place, as usual, is very dead; nothing at all stirring. The report of a detachment going to Botany Bay is by some credited: I really can't say how it will terminate: however, they shan't find me a volunteer.

Tell George Robbin that Davies is promoted, I find by the newspapers, into the Calcutta, going out. I am not at all surprised at William's silence knowing

119

that he has an aversion to writing, but as he expressed a wish of corresponding, I must confess I expected his answer I don't feel the disappointment as much as if I had nobody to correspond with, having one in you who never failed in any respect of keeping it up.

So Mr Thomas & Miss Howells are at last united after a tedious courtship. I dare say Martha looks up with as anxious a countenance for the Parson. I hope she will not be disappointed, and may they all be happy, I say.

I saw Colonel Vaughan at Curgenven's a few days ago. He has taken a house in Plymouth for a short time & means to go down into Wales in the summer: both desired their compliments to the family.

I am sorry the Captain's conduct is not as you would wish. He certainly speaks in the most indifferent way respecting his wife I ever heard in my life. Tell him I found the cot blocks & shall perform my promise by the first opportunity but think it highly ridiculous in sending such a trifling thing by the way of Bristol: however, if he chooses to pay for the carriage, it is all very well. Make my compliments.

I have left the Marine Barracks entirely, except for mess time and do duty at Mill Bay. A brother officer and myself live together and are very comfortable indeed, having pleasant neighbours. You'll still continue to address my letters as usual. My acquaintance here is very much confined, all the better I think. I have had several invitations from old friends to dine on board ships in harbour, but have declined all as yet: think to commence in the course of the ensuing week.

I fancy the *Spitfire* will be here shortly: in that case, I suppose I shall see Phillips. My fellow messmate was on board the *Formidable* with Phillips (the Parson I mean): he does not speak of him as the brightest ornament of the cloth we have in the service.

The oysters, I think, may as well be deferred till I have an opportunity of enjoying them in Wales as they would soon be devoured here and, on consideration, they are no treat. I have had several supplies of them, the only difference is in the price, & quality, of course. I must give the preference to my own country. I am very much astonished in not hearing from Birch. I certainly [intended] writing sooner: remember me to his wife, as with all friends and relations. I must beg you'll continue to write, dare say there is one of yours now on the road; be assured it will be welcomely received. The times are so dull and I am so stupid that I am at a loss for a subject to pursue any cross-writing. My next, I hope, will be longer. With duty to the Parents, love to Brother & Grandmother, accept this with the warmest affections of, dear Mary,

Your very loving brother, John George.

*

83. Miss George, Blue Boar Inn, Haverfordwest.

Mill Bay Barracks
Feb. 8th 1803

My dear Sister,

Your affectionate letter of the 23rd ult. I received a few days ago with a great deal of pleasure, particularly so on being assured of your health. I should have wrote sooner but had only written a day or so before receiving yours.

The day before yesterday I was paid an unexpected visit by Mr George Jenkins of the *Escort*: be assured I was very happy to see him as he gave me late news of H'west: he expected his brig would sail about today, and promised to give me another call which I hope he'll fulfill as I then shall be able to send this round by him. Mr Davies, formerly Parson of the *Chapman*, accompanied him here. I was half-inclined of sending my trunk [round by him] as he gave me the offer but as the *Spitfire*, I find, will be here shortly, think I had better defer it.

Since my last, I paid an old messmate a visit on board the *Courageous*, the first time I trusted myself on the water since I disembarked. I am very steady, only a slight headache the next morning.

The vacancies I dare say you have heard from Moore, are being filled up but was rather disappointed in not finding him appointed to this Division, and am still in the dark which of the two he is ordered to join: if he wishes to come here I dare say he may easily effect an exchange. By these Officers joining it will be the means of keeping me ashore much longer than I otherwise should. We have eleven in addition here, all to embark before me.

I spent a very pleasant day a few days ago with Colonel & Mrs Vaughan and have promised to take a family dinner with them. They asked very kindly after the family. So you find I have not been very inactive the last week, including a whole day shooting which I had on Friday. I wished I had been near you to have presented my sport, as I knocked down a few thrushes: however you must do without them till the summer when I hope I shall be able to supply my dear Sister with every thing the season will afford.

I find by George Jenkins Mrs J. Robbin is gone after her husband: I think she is very right as she must be much more comfortable with him than in H'west.

Nothing particular is stirring here. A ship-of-the-line is under sailing orders, supposed for the West Indies: be assured, I don't envy the lads. Curgenven I saw some days ago: he is very well, desires his compliments.

In my last I mentioned something respecting Mr Bevans: of course you are anxious to be acquainted with the secret: when we meet (which I hope to

God will be soon), I'll acquaint you with the particulars, when I trust you'll feel yourself happy in being cautioned to associate with such a character.

I am rather surprised Miss Gould sends her love to me after the lecture I got from her the day before I left Wales: she surely must mistake: hope you don't make mine to her: she is one put down as an Old Maid to a certainty.

Ever since I wrote to William our correspondence have been rather confused. I should like to have received your answer before I send this: most likely you are as well waiting for mine, therefore you shan't be disappointed.

It is well for you: you can assemble as many Beaus as you mentioned on your Card: suppose you spare one to Miss Gould: I dare say she will be obliged to you. Of all the Old Maids I think her the most discontent, for if she has a one she is not content without more, for that reason I think she will remain in the state she is now in: tell her we will have some pleasant walks together in the summer. If she did but know what I have been writing it would make her the most inveterate enemy I have.

If I should have an opportunity of sending the Blocks on board the *Escort*, I mean to send them to Davies. You say he and William are at the Gail: they certainly are enjoying themselves. It will be poor James's turn and mine some time or other. The vessel must be arrived at Lisbon long ere this. Make my compliments to Mrs & Miss Brown & all relations, as well your acquaintances. My paper reminds me to conclude, therefore with duty to Parents, love to Brother & G^{mr}, I remain dear Sister,

Yours very affect^{ly}, John George.

Continue to write, if you please.

✳

84. Miss George, Blue Boar Inn, Haverfordwest.

Mill Bay Barracks Plymouth
March 9th 1803

My dear Sister,

Your kind letter of the 4th I received yesterday evening with the greatest pleasure in being assured of your welfare. I should have written sooner but waited for your answer to mine of the 21st. Yours of the 14th enclosed to George Jenkins was given me the same day & as it did not require an immediate answer, deferred writing till the present. My old companion which I mentioned in a former letter living with me, has left me, having procured leave of absence. I would follow his example but really the Spring is so backward and leaving you in the middle of the summer would be so distressing that I would much rather wait some time longer which surely you must agree with me in opinion.

The Milford ships are still here waiting for volunteers & likely to remain some time. I heard from George Jenkins about a week ago: he does not expect to sail this month yet, therefore my trunk is not likely to travel soon. I wish I had a favourable opportunity of sending it, as I then should be much more comfortable in travelling without baggage. I saw Mrs Vaughan and her brother a few days ago: they inquired as usual for the family. The Colonel has not yet arrived from London but is expected this week.

Curgenven has been gone this week past for London: when he returns I shall expect news as Davies the Druggist is to meet him. The only news that I recollect going forward is the commissioning of a ship-of-the-line, the Plantagenet, and the Captain's old ship, the *Doris*, but volunteers are so very scarce that it will be a considerable time before they are ready for sea. Respecting the report of Davies's wife which you mentioned being at Portsmouth with a surgeon, I don't pay the least credit to it: certainly when I was at Portsmouth a surgeon in the Navy lodged in the same house & seemed to be very friendly with the family but he seemed to be that quiet inoffensive fellow that would not take an advantage of the kind; besides I have a better opinion of the woman.

So, Miss Brown has given her affection to a Gauger.[62] T. Gibbs has more spirit I am sure than to allow a fellow of that kind to brow beat him. I suppose when I get among you he'll be cutting his capers the same way particularly if I pay any attention to the females. If you are acquainted with him, tell him that two can pull a 'trigger'. I had better stay away while I have my head on [my shou]lders. Tell me, am I in danger? We should put it in the paper: 'Duel between an Exciseman and a Marine Officer'. Won't it appear very conspicuous? It is very well joking, you'll say. I perfectly agree with you. Make my compliments to both mother and daughter. It is rather singular Captain Brown does not mention James in his letters: it would be very little trouble, but upon second recollection, I am not as much surprised as those kinds of Gents. are as great on board their own ships as Captains of the Navy on theirs. I am pleased that you should put off your excursion to Castlemartin till I accompany you, but why wait so long: couldn't you go now & in the summer again, or are you afraid to eat your welcome out at once? The people that side of the water are more liberal than for you to suppose a thing of the kind. The Billy horse I hope you'll endeavour to have kept in good order for me as that must be the favourite horse when you are in company. The correspondence is at last come in a regular way & hope it will be continued.

Make my compliments to all your acquaintances, relations at Tiers Cross,

&c. The weather is so very severe that my fingers are really cramped, other-wise would pursue my cross-writing. It is needless requesting you to write as I am confident you will every opportunity. With duty to Parents, love to Wm & G'mother., I conclude, dear Mary,

Ever yours affect[ly], John George.

*

85. Miss George, Blue Boar Inn, Haverfordwest.

Mill Bay Barracks
Mar. 11th 1803

My dear Sister,

I embrace the earliest opportunity of acquainting you that within this two days every thing here has a hostile appearance. The evening before last a general impress[63] took place & collected a great number of men, between 3 & 500 parties of Marines were sent out from both Barracks & collected a great many. It is also reported 5 sail-of-the-line are to be commissioned immediately & pretty much credited. Various opinions are formed: some say to complete the ships going out to relieve those in the West Indies, but the general opinion is war. We are perfectly kept in the dark; therefore, you can form just as good an opinion as we can.

They still continue pressing & it is supposed it has been general throughout the kingdom, in that case Milford has not been forgot. I am under serious apprehension for W[m.] as he is certainly liable to be laid hold of: if he wishes to remain at home, I think Father had better get him made a constable, or something, to protect him. In case of a war, most likely the Corps will be augmented to its former establishment, therefore there will 40 or 50 2nd. Lieutenants vacant & W[m.] has certainly very great claim over Lord K. However, I shall leave that for you judgement, only I don't wish to hear of his being pressed.

I wrote to you as late as three days back & should not have written as soon but thought a matter of this kind should not be kept silent.

I do most sincerely hope that hostilities will not commence, at least this twelvemonth yet as it would most likely prevent my visiting Wales as soon as I intended. We shall be able in a few days to form a better idea of it. There is a report of recruiting parties going out, but want a confirmation.

Neither Colonel Vaughan or Curgenven will come down yet: the former is expected down this evening.

Make my compliments to all acquaintances and relations. You can't expect to have this as long as I generally write as I have so latterly written. Continue to write. With duty to Parents, love to W^m & G'mo^r, I remain, dear Mary,

Ever yours affect^ly, John George.

*

86. Miss Mary George, Blue Boar Inn, Haverforwest.

Mill Bay Barracks
Mar. 19th 1803

My dear Sister,

With infinite satisfaction, I received your letter of the 14th inst. this morning & shan't lose a moment in complying with your request in acquainting you with every thing going forward here. I wrote to you on the 11th after the impress business took place, am rather surprised you had not received it before you wrote yours, hope you have long before this, as it mentioned a subject which I hope some attention was paid to respecting William's protection from the impress service.

Every thing carry a warlike aspect here, 3 ships of the line & 2 frigates have been commissioned within this last two days & two or three more are hourly expected, so that in a short time we shall have a strong naval force, sufficiently so, I trust, so as to be able to cope with the Usurper Bonaparte. Lord Keith has taken the command here & hoisted his flag on the *Culloden*. I suppose I shall see Robbin & Wakelin here shortly as his followers, of course, will flock around him. The *Escort* has sailed several days ago to the eastward, & also the *Nemesis* with dispatches, it is supposed for the West Indies, so that the Milford ships are a little dispersed The *Spitfire* & the *Insolent* are still here. I have not seen Charles Phillips yet. Mr Davies, formerly of the *Chapman*, has joined the latter; he has been good enough to make me an offer to take any thing round but under the present situation of affairs, think I had better keep my trunk while I have it. The Admiralty have stopped all leave for the present; as I am not likely to embark immediately & should this hostile business be cleared up, hope yet to spend the greater part of the summer with you.

Recruiting parties are gone out, but none into Wales. Had I the offer of one I don't think I would accept it, as the encouragement is so very little, only 3 guineas bounty and the distance so very far from Headquarters. We expect to quit these Barracks in the course of the ensuing week as we are reducing our parade very fast: 120 men & six officers embarked this morning for the different ships commissioned: there are 40 yet to go before me. All Political matters, I must refer you to the *Sun* for. The *Imogen* sloop arrived here a few days ago from the Cape of Good Hope after having been out with orders not to evacuate it & was fortunate enough not to arrive there about 6 hours before the intended evacuation. The Dutch sloops had actually disembarked & everything preparatory to taking possession, so that I fancy they were a little disappointed in being ordered to embark again. I think Providence has been greatly in our favour as we still retain the three principal places in dispute, Malta, Egypt & the Cape, and more particularly so in discovering a chest of flags that floated ashore near Brighton, as in yesterday's *Sun*, from a French vessel that stranded with 100,000 stand of arms, supposed for Ireland: the flags were Irish united with France, so you see what a pretty peace we have made of it. Of course, you have heard of the Vote for 2,500 Marines in addition to the present establishment, but an augmentation of Companies is not likely to take place immediately, unless a war, & then it must.

I advise William to be careful for once he is laid hold of, it will be a hard matter to get off & it is bad encouragement for a young man to serve 6 years now to be made a Lieutenant, & even a Clerk must serve 2 years to be made a Purser: will leave it entirely to the consideration of Parents. I am confident their good sense will instruct them what to do.

My paper tells me to conclude, therefore with duty to Parents, love to Brother & G'm^r I remain, dear Mary,

Ever yours affect^{ly}, John George.

*

87. Miss George, Blue Boar Inn, Haverfordwest.

Mill Bay, Plymouth
Apr. 16th 1803

My dear Sister,

I don't know that I have felt so much uneasiness for a long time as I have in the receipt of yours of the 11th inst. respecting William's disappointment in the situation mentioned in your last, and of James's indisposition; the only & greatest satisfaction I received was in being assured of your health.

James's arrival rather surprised me, I confess, as I thought the ship was not expected home as soon. I shall wait a post or two for his letter & then shall write. Captain Brown has acted, I think, altogether in a most unfriendly way to him, as well Parents, very different from what I thought when I met him in Wales: it was his place, & not James's, to have mentioned his ill state of health and incapability of going to sea, which he neglected in his letters more than once. His answer to your letter, I hope to God, will be satisfactory as I shall be extremely sorry to hear of poor James being let loose to the mercy of Press Gangs. I certainly must call myself fortunate in being thrown into the situation which I now fill, though think I should be much happier had I remained in some civil capacity, though perhaps not as respectable: at any rate I should have never thought of remaining dependent on my friends. Was William to exert himself yet perhaps would be fortunate but it would not be too late yet for Lord K.'s answer? He should certainly do something for him. I'll say nothing more: trust your next will be of a more pleasant nature.

War is the talk of the day here & many, I believe, wish it. We have a large squadron already in Cawsand Bay, part of which are going to Torbay in readiness for a start. Since my last there were three 3-deckers commissioned *Prince*, *Ville de Paris* & *San Joseff*, and what with the ships in harbour fitting are in a state of forwardness. We have also here a fleet of East Indiamen, with Sir Home Popham, homeward bound, waiting for a wind up Channel: they make a very fine appearance. The Custom House officers are so very strict that there is not the smallest possibility of smuggling.

There has been such demands for Marines lately that we have hardly any left, indeed not sufficient to comply with the whole: should this rupture continue much longer, I am afraid I shall be obliged to embark, which I should be very sorry, for at the moment as there are so many ships fitting out that it must be expensive & perhaps be soon paid off after. However, we must content ourselves as well as we can.

Colonel Vaughan means to leave this place in a few days for Wales, with Mrs V: the remainder of the family will go by water: they have promised to take any thing for me but under the present circumstances I am sure my dear sister will dispense with what she has a right to expect.

I had the pleasure of meeting with Mr Jones, Capt. Dobbin's relation, yesterday, who has an appointment on board the Malta as a Midshipman: he says he had seen you all lately very well, and since my last I met with Mr Ellis, the late Mr David Allen's brother-in-law, who appears to be very decent, he says he intends going into the country shortly; has been here upwards of three years. I recollect meeting him a long time ago but his appearance was such that it would not do for my associating with him. I put the question to him if he worked at his trade but he answered me in the negative – a great man, I fancy.

I am glad you enjoyed your excursion to Castlemartin; dare say I shall be highly entertained if you give me the account more fully. Who was the pretty girl you mentioned from London? Mr Gibbs, I suppose, was the Gallant.

Mr Moore has certainly been fortunate in getting the Impress service: in case of a war he is sure of keeping his head.

I fancy there is a distance in Miss Brown & Mother & you since the Captain's conduct has shewn [itself] but it is needless making any more comment on the subject. I trust every thing is satisfactorily explained on this. I shall write tomorrow if I don't receive James's promised letter. Continue to write and, as a hint, don't keep me waiting as you did the last. Make my duty to our ever dear Parents, love to Brother, G'm^r & friends & accept with the warmest affection of, dear Sister,

Your loving brother, J. George.

The papers are pacific today; God grant they may continue so.

*

88. Miss George, Blue Boar Inn, Haverfordwest.

RM Barracks, Plymouth
Apr. 25th 1803

My dear Sister,

Your kind letter of the 20th inst. I received yesterday morning & at the same time one from James. both, be assured, gave me great pleasure. James had received your letter requesting him to continue in his situation; he says was a ship sent for him to go home, he would decline it now, therefore I fancy he is a little piqued in his disappointment.

We are still in an uncertainty respecting the present rupture: things don't go on as expected in the Dock Yard as they have lately therefore it is supposed the present armament will not be exchanged unless things turn out in a more hostile way.

Mr Addington's[64] speech in the House some days ago, gave us great hopes of a speedy termination to the treaty but his second upset the whole House: I hope yet everything will be amicably settled very shortly.

Colonel & Mrs Vaughan have been gone for Wales above this week past & I fancy have arrived by this time. Mr Harries is still here waiting for the vessel's return from Guernsey which is hired to take round the furniture then he takes his leave, an enviable fellow certainly.

I saw Curgenven yesterday evening; he enquired after you all & desired his compliments. He has heard old Mr Barzey of Arnold's Hill is going to be married. Pray, is there anything in it? He also heard your name mentioned when in London in the same way. May I ask the question? It is certainly very impertinent, but you must excuse me.

I don't know any thing to suit William Phillips as well as he has in the

Impress service at H'west: therefore, I am glad he has something to employ his mind. I am rather surprised Davies has not pushed for the Lieutenancy. Pray have you heard anything further respecting his wife?

I am glad T. Moore has a frigate, in case of war he is very fortunate. My chance here is very little as there are none to be commissioned. The small vessels are generally laid up in ordinary at Portsmouth & Chatham; the largest here as the harbour is the most special, therefore, most likely, a large one will be my lot.

Mrs & Miss Brown are, I fancy, by this time, in the gay Metropolis dashing about: the latter has a fine chance now of selecting a Beau, consequently the poor Gauger will be thrown aside, I am afraid.

Mr Ellis made his advances a second time saying he was going round and if I had a letter to send I suppose you would sooner pay the postage than wait a fortnight or perhaps more for it. He will tell you most likely how distant I appeared to him: appearances must be kept up, you know.

Mr Le Sugg, who displayed his abilities in H'west last summer, is here performing wonders: as I have heard so much of him, I think I'll pay him a visit. The Players are here all the year round and at this season generally some of the Covent Garden & Drury Lane folks come down, so you see we don't want for amusements here. I very seldom go to these places.

Are G. Robbin & Wakelin still at H'west? I fancy they are otherwise I would have heard of it. Make my compliments to all acquaintances. I must beg you to continue to write and should any thing happen here, be assured I'll immediately communicate it to you. Accept this with duty, love, &c., &c, dear Sister,

Yours affect^ly, J. George.

*

89. Miss George.

Tenby
Sunday morning, ½ past 8

Dear Mary,

John & myself are just arrived: the remainder of the party I left on Arnold's Hill, not being able to keep company. I am lucky enough to meet Wm. Bowen, Bridge, and we go together to Bideford, but not to Plymouth. The vessel is now gathering under weigh.

Duty, love, compliments, &c., Adieu dear Mary.

Ever yours affect^ly, John George.

*

90. Miss George, Blue Boar Inn, Haverfordwest.

Tenby

June 29th 1803. 5 p.m.

My dear Sister,

I am just this moment returned from Saundersfoot[65] much disappointed in not being able to go to sea as the vessel did not float at high water & God knows if she will next tide, which will be at 2 o'clock in the morning: it is very provoking indeed as the wind just came fair at the time we were expected to have sailed. I almost deserve it for my own stupidity in not abiding by Davies's advice: if I had I should now have been at H'west & should not have left it before the morning. I hope Tom George & W^m got home safe, it must have been late as it was 9 o'clock before they left. W^m was much inclined to stay and I wish he had, as the mare would have been of the greatest use to me now. I have walked already today to Saundersfoot & back & must return again: one comfort is I shall have the cool of the evening presently. Wright has made it rather pleasant in having his company: he is out at present, therefore I have resumed the correspondence. On my return here I met with Lewis of Grondre, Mr Thomas in Bridge Street, & a party. I was in hope Thomas intended returning as I should have given a message for Davies, or somebody, to have taken a ride out in case of my not going to sea next tide, just to have passed the dull hour away: indeed, Wright is remarkably pleasant but you know he must attend to his business. Had I kept the mare it would have been pleasant & then I could have rode out, even to Hwest between the tides, but it is now quite out of the question as I hope to be at sea before you receive this. In case of our not sailing next tide I shall forward an official letter to Plymouth as my leave will expire tomorrow.

Since writing the above I called on Miss Roberts, formerly of Wiston, who lives here. She particularly desires her compliments to the family and should any of you come here, begs that you'll call. I heard the intelligence of her being here at Hean Castle where I was induced to go this morning owing to William mentioning her being Housekeeper there.

Adieu my dear Sister, first remembering me with duty to Parents, love to W^m & G'm^r,

Yours very affect^{ly}, John George.

*

91. Miss George, Blue Boar Inn, Haverfordwest.

Royal Marine Barracks, Plymouth
July 3rd 1803

My dear Sister,

I arrived here yesterday evening in health and safety after a pretty tolerable journey. My letter from Tenby, of course, you received. I was fortunate enough to find the following tide the vessel had floated and after a tedious passage of 36 hours, we arrived safe in Bideford. After stopping about two hours to take some refreshment, I left my trunk and proceeded in company with the old Veteran, as I had planned out to you, on foot to Tavistock, a distance of 40 miles: this was about 4 in the evening and after travelling all night (the pleasantest part of the 24 hours) arrived at our journey's end by seven the following morning. I then took the coach for this place. It certainly is the first, and I think will be the last, of travelling on foot again, for I was cursedly fatigued and nothing but perseverance obliged me to go through with it.

The folks in the Barracks are quite elated with the idea of an immediate augmentation about taking place in the Corps, of 43 Companies: it will be the means of making & promoting a great many: how far it will affect me, can't say; of course, put me well up the list. I dare say there will be 80 2nd Lieutenancies to be completed. My sea duty is approaching very fast, only about 4 or 5 now before me and there are vacancies for twice the number. I don't mind how soon the time arrives for I dislike being kept in suspense. I waited on the General this morning. He says nothing but a scarcity of men keeps us ashore. The prospect of getting a frigate is very distant indeed. One will be commissioned in a few days and who knows the luck of a lousy calf (as the old proverb says), perhaps I may be as fortunate as a few of my brother officers.

I was fortunate enough to meet with Mr Mends[66] this morning, of the *Impatience*, and delivered the packet from his mother. There is no alteration in his dress. I promised to go on board in a few days, as there is a very old messmate of mine on board who was on board the *Bellona* all the time with me. I shall forward Mrs Summers's letter, and one from myself, to George Robbin the very first opportunity.

Tell the Captain there are several ships fitting out, but very short of men & show this to him as I promised I would write and, having nothing particular to say, think 11d. saved is better than thrown away. Tell Tom George of Freystrop and William they shall hear from me in due course of time. Lt. Jones, who I wrote to on board the *Malta* about Evans, is here, left behind his ship. I saw him this morning and he was saying that nothing can possibly be done for him without his friends would wish to push him forward in the

Navy which I would most certainly recommend them to do, for to procure his discharge now is beyond reason.

I received a letter of the 28th ult. from James just now: he is very well: they wait at Spithead only for the convoy to sail, which will be very shortly. I mean to write tomorrow; two other letters came with James's: one was yours of the first May, which had been detained here, and the other from an acquaintance from off Brest. No news at all.

4th I have written to James and mentioned my taking a short trip to Wales before I embarked, therefore he'll be a little surprised: it can be of no consequence now as I am returned. I said it was at my request you did not mention it in your letter as I wished to surprise him myself.

Tell Sally Mathias the country looks charming, & compliments to her. Miss Gould will now have a free scope for her chase, and so will her neighbour Miss Beynon: one consolation, I don't care for either. Remember me particularly to all acquaintance: be assured nothing will give me more pleasure than in hearing from you, therefore don't fail gratifying my wish.

Accept this with duty to Parents, love to W- & G'm^r,

Your aff^{te} & loving Brother, John George.

*

92. Miss George, Blue Boar Inn, Haverfordwest.

RM Barracks, Plymouth
July 15th 1803

My dear Sister,

Your kind letter of the 8th which I received the day before yesterday gave me great pleasure in being assured once again of your welfare. I would have written immediately to ease your anxiety respecting my embarking but waited to make a few enquiries which I wished to communicate.

A scarcity of men still prevents any embarkation: indeed, the number of prizes which are constantly coming in induces me to wish I was on board something as I then should be enabled to make a little or I should be very unfortunate indeed. Two frigates will be commissioned very shortly and should I procure one, will think myself fortunate, as the odds are so much against me. I spent yesterday on board the *Impatience* and had the pleasure of seeing Mr Mends and his brother: the junior one expects an appointment in the Marines which I dare say he'll be able to procure as there are so many to be given away at this moment: both asked kindly after the family.

The *Culloden* is in but George Robbin has left her with the Admiral to join the *Canopus*, and has left the Channel Fleet with a small squadron destined it is supposed to the Mediterranean. The letters I sent seemed not to have reached him before they parted company, therefore they must be soon off. Barsh, an officer of the *Culloden*, has promised me he will either send them back or find out their address and forward them. Robbin must be very uncomfortable in not getting his things, as I have enquired and find his trunks are now in a warehouse at Plymouth, and how he will get them, God knows, as ships in that secret way that they don't know themselves where they are going to. Mention it to Mrs Summers and assure him that I will see & get his things secured.

John Robbin will feel the loss of the *Minerva* very considerably; Pursers lose more than anybody else, which I am certainly sorry for.

I went out a-fishing last Monday and Tuesday with a friend in the country: you must suppose as sportsmen we walked before we began: our success did not answer our expectation at all: as the weather was so very fine and the novelty of the country and the little adventure we met with made up for our bad sport and in the course of next week intend making a second treat.

If you recollect, I mentioned to you Miss Gould would endeavour to bring matters about after I left the country which, by your letter it appears she has: you of course may do as you please, but I can never have the friendship for her I formerly had, for had she attempted to have shewn any [as good an] opportunity offered respecting the Preacher & in which I think she acted quite the reverse. I am glad you enjoyed your little excursion to Crowhill still particularly with the Captain, as I am unable to accompany you.

Mrs Charles, I think a very pleasant woman and a good companion: make my compliments to her & her husband. The brother of the Captain which I mentioned to W^m, lives with me: he says his brother is in the country and has no idea of being employed, therefore it is needless placing any dependence there for Charles's situation, was he employed. I am confident he would be happy to take him but really think, between you and I, a Compter would be much more preferable: mention this to William and let it go no further. Through the brother I have a pressing invitation into Cornwall, about twenty miles off, and if I am here much longer was [meaning] to go down for a few days, as it will be some change, particularly for me.

You have been kept so long without practice of cross-writing that I'm afraid you'll not be able to peruse this; if you cannot, my next will be more clearly written: however, to prevent difficulty I will number the pages. Curgenven's compliments. Make mine to Miss Llewellin of Rudbaxton and all those whom you think worthy of friendship. Tell the oldest Miss Llewellin I am very sorry I had not known till it was too late of her being at Newhouse when we passed it as I took the sporting bag by it.

By this time you are heartily tired of this scroll, therefore I'll bring things to a conclusion as fast as I can. Accept this with the warmest assurance of affection, duty to Parents, love to W^m & G'm^rr dear Mary,

Your ever loving brother, John George.

*

93. Miss George, Blue Boar Inn, Haverfordwest.

RM Barracks, Plymouth
Aug. 14th 1803

My dear Sister,

I embrace the earliest opportunity of acknowledging the receipt of your kind letter of the 7th inst. which has given me infinite satisfaction in being assured of your welfare. Since my last, a few embarkations have taken place and I am now second to go but in the present aspect of things: don't think it probable I shall embark for some time to come as we still labour under the old complaint: 'No men'.

Several young officers have joined lately: I wish I'd have seen William in the number, but it is of no use repining, only had Lord K. fulfilled his repeated promises, it would have been the case. Mr James, who you mentioned in your last, is here. I think him a fine young man: he made himself known by being in your company at Llanunwas lately and being a school-fellow of James's. Captain Howard is mistaken, I fancy, respecting the person he mentioned in being a messmate of mine for I never had one of the name of Jones, nor do I know of any that is likely to be now in Ireland. Prizes come in now very seldom indeed; therefore, all chance that way is at an end. The chief topic here is a court martial on Captain Barlow of the Dragoon Guards. I felt much interested from him being a fine young man and have little doubt myself that he will meet with an honourable acquittal. I trust those Heroes of H'west will succeed in their gay Corps of Volunteers. T. Gibbs will certainly charm the hearts of the fair sex with his martial appearance. I pity those that should drop in his way, as it will be impossible to resist him.

If you should have an opportunity at any time, inquire, & let me know, if Mrs Birch has discharged her lodgings at Cole's yet and what is become of the furniture as I forgot to inquire before I left the county, and her husband wishes to know as she is perfectly silent on the subject. In some of the late papers I saw there is a man detained of a suspicious appearance in London of the name of Carty: I wonder if it is the person you know? It strikes me it is as there is something very mysterious in his conduct.

I approve of Tom George's sentiments respecting soldiery for it is certainly much better to ride than walk, particularly when a person can march his own horse, and as the country is to be under arms, agree with you in opinion respecting William, for it would attend with little expense and at the same time a protection against the Militia, and should he procure at any time another situation I fancy it would be an easy matter to relinquish the first: however, as I am not totally acquainted with the subject, must leave it to your judgement.

I think Mrs Flemming is fortunate in meeting with a man that sports his coach and four: it is certainly a very unusual thing for Davies and the first I have heard of dash in that way. I fancy he has been some thing in Ireland receiving his education.

Make my compliments to Davies and all friends and as I have nothing more particularly to say, shall defer my cross-writing to another opportunity. With duty to Parents, love to W^m & G'm^r,

Yours very affect^{ly}, John George.

Tell Mrs George of Freystrop that this is not the season for the Tongues & Sounds, therefore she must wait with patience a little longer as I have been making inquires without success.

*

94. Miss George, Kensington Place, Haverfordwest.
Royal Marine Barracks, Plymouth
Aug. 25th 1803

My dear Sister,

Your kind letter of the 18th inst. I have just received and am made particularly happy again on hearing of your welfare. Respecting Lord K., I don't see the smallest impropriety in speaking to him (I mean William) in order to remind him of his repeated promises: indeed, I wish he would as he then may form some idea of the result.

All the intelligence I can give Mrs Summers respecting her son is that Admiral Campbell has a squadron cruising off the coast of Spain and that he has sent in to Gibraltar some valuable prizes. My letters, I fancy were forwarded to him and I have not heard anything of them since. I won't expect to hear from Robbin soon: when I do I will let you know: his stockings shall be left with Curgenven when I embark as it is uncertain when I may go and perhaps his ship may come in here to refit.

My embarkation approaches very fast: I am now the first to go and it is

135

very probable my next you'll find addressed from some ship: patience is requisite as it is uncertain what I may have. I hope you have not given Mrs Birch an opportunity of finding out you have been making enquiries respecting her as I should be very sorry to offend: you would then be the spy.

The harvest in this part of the country is very forward, being more than half in: surely, the farmers will not complain this season as they have had such a run of beautiful weather. The only little excursion I have taken lately is with a family of my acquaintance to see an encampment a few days ago, it being the first I had seen, of course, I was highly gratified.

Prizes come in very seldom now, only two or three since my last. The intended invasion is at present the principal topic. I wish Pembrokeshire was in as good a state of defence as this country: you would then have little to fear, but I think you are pretty safe, as those Gentlemen that invaded us last went home with a determination not to make a second, at least we should suppose so from the treatment they received.

I am sorry Davies is prevented visiting you thro' a trifling dispute with William. I hope you'll turn mediator and settle it: tell him there are a great many Lieutenants here want employ as well as himself. Callis, I fancy, is happy in his inactive situation, as it is a pleasant thing for a married man to procure such a thing. Pray is the Brother still in H'west as he expected some time ago an appointment as chaplain in the Navy.

In your next you will be able to give me some account of your gay races[67] the last sickened me & had I been in the county now I don't know that I should have even gone out as it is an amusement that affords me none.

Continue to write and when I embark you shall know. Remember me to all friends. How do the loving pair of Rudbaxton & Freystrop get on? Tom's martial appearance I fancy will completely captivate the heart of the fair one now. My paper reminds me to conclude, with duty to Parents, love to W[m] & G'm[r], I remain, dear Mary,

Ever yours affect[ly], John George.

I shall make you great by addressing this 'Kensington Place'[68] agreeable to promise: let me know if you approve of it.

*

95. Miss Mary George, Blue Boar Inn, Haverfordwest.

RM Barracks, Plymouth

Sept. 6th 1803

My dear Sister,

Your unexpected, tho' welcome, letter of the 26th ult. I have received and embrace the earliest opportunity of answering it in order to ease your anxiety respecting my fate. You are a little surprised, I fancy, to find me still here after informing you in my last of my expected embarkation that then I certainly did expect it as we had a few men to spare, but a ship-of-the-line mad a demand to complete her party and took all the men we could spare so that at present I have very little prospect of being off soon.

A Spanish war is much spoken of: I hope it will be confirmed as it can be of little injury to the country & the chance of prize money will be much greater: there are several ships in a state of readiness for sea in the harbour, but without seamen or Marines & as long as the Army reserves are embodied will remain so.

I feel very thankful for your information respecting Mrs Birch but hope she has left H'west long ere this as I must call the visit on my account and feel for the inconvenience she must have occasioned: it was not my intention for you ever to have thrown a hint to her but merely to gain such intelligence you could collect; however, as things have gone thus far, it is useless recalling them.

Mr James is going on very well; I don't think him proud by any means but merely a degree of modest reserve, which I like: perhaps he is altered since you saw him but I can assure he has often spoke in very respectful terms of you since Llanunwas.

I am sorry Lord Kensington's offer of raising a Corps of Volunteers[69] was refused: a man of that consequence should have a command: indeed, I think it would raise the ardour of the people much higher than being commanded by Mr Mathias. I hope William has embraced an opportunity of speaking to him as I have been well informed his memory requires refreshing.

The Oporto ships are arrived, therefore I suppose you have heard from James by this time. A dreadful accident happened her a few days ago. Colonel Brown of the Montgomery Militia riding through a street, his horse startled and he fell which occasioned a fractured skull, poor man, he lived about five minutes and then expired. He was buried with military honours. How uncertain life is.

I feel thankful for the compliments of the Rudbaxton family: pray make mine in return, as well Davies and friends. Martha Howells has completely proved herself a gift to more than one: had I any influence with the young men of H'west I would not take the smallest notice of her.

Mr Phillips is in a critical situation for somebody may pop in & throw him aside again. Mr Mends is gone to sea in the *Impatience*.

Remember me to the Freystrop family, as well as those you think proper. I would beg you to continue to write and as I have mentioned everything my ideas have collected, must draw to a conclusion, therefore with duty, love, &c., &c. I remain, with the warmest affection,

Your truly loving brother, John George.

*

96. Miss George, Blue Boar Inn, Haverfordwest.

HM Ship *Fisgard*,[70] Plymouth
Sept 13th 1803

My dear Sister

I fancy you are a little surprised on finding me address this from one of the most desirable ships here. I embarked this morning with a detachment and am happy to say the little I have been able to judge, find her a very pleasant ship. We expect to sail tomorrow or next day; the Captain being a man of good interest, hope to have a favourable cruise. Thus far I am fortunate and in case of a Spanish war, we shall be very unlucky indeed if we don't make something. I was in great hopes of hearing from you today. Hope I shall not meet with disappointment tomorrow. My party consists of 1 Serjeant, 1 Corporal 1 Drummer & 20 Privates so that I shall be able to manage them very well. Our complement is more but that is all we could get. News as usual is very dead; nothing at all doing. I saw Curgenven yesterday; he desires his compliments. I have written two letters since the receipt of your last, consequently you must be indebted to me. You may continue to write and address 'Plymouth Dock', as letters will be forwarded to us if possible: be assured I shall not lose an opportunity in writing. I addressed one of your letters agreeable to promise Kensington Place. I wonder if it arrived safe?

George Robbin is gone up the Mediterranean; part of the squadron is arrived, but have not heard from him. One consolation in this ship is she is not likely to go abroad so that in a short time we shall be coming in again, I hope with some Prizes. I think it is rather apropos in my embarking in the ship that landed the troops in the neighbourhood of Fishguard & taking her name from it afterwards, and being on the spot at the time myself.

Remember me to all friends particularly the Freystrop family. As I wish to save this evening's post, you'll excuse this short letter. Should we remain here some days longer, shall write again. Accept this with the warmest assurance of affection from, dear Mary,

Your very loving Brother, John George.

*

97. Miss George, Blue Boar Inn,
    Haverfordwest.

HM Ship *Fisgard*, Plymouth
Sept. 20th 1803

Dear Mary,

I am now about commencing a long letter in answer to yours of the 16th inst. which I received yesterday evening. I should have answered it immediately after I had an opportunity offered, but at that time, we were under sailing orders. And had no communication with the shore afterwards. I wrote only 4 days ago, on my appointment to the ship, which hope you have received.

We left Plymouth this morning on our way to Portsmouth and if any success attends us hope to arrive tomorrow: our destination from there on is entirely unknown, several conjectures of course are formed: some think to take charge of a convoy, others again to receive orders for the Mediterranean. I have only to say the Captain has such powerful interest that we are sure of being satisfactorily taken care of. I am glad to find George Robbin is promoted to the *Canopus*. He is certainly fortunate in [his relationship] with the Admiral as he must in course of time arise to greater rank. Had your letter arrived in time I would have endeavoured to have his things sent round, but they are perfectly secured where they are as the man who has charge of them assured me they should be so.

Whilst I have as good a correspondent as you, I can't think of soliciting any more. George Robbin is, perhaps, not so fortunate consequently gets those he is intimate with to write: had I an inclination to keep an intensive one, dare say there are many that would write but I don't see the utility of it as the postage would amount high in time and a correspondence with indifferent people would not suit my inclination at all.

I hope Lord Kensington will exert himself for William: should he not I would advise Father by all means to remind him again as I am well informed that he is a man whose memory requires refreshing. I think Davies has acted extremely ill in not accepting Mr Peregrine's kind offer. A Lieut. of a Tender is no bad thing particularly when he can get no other employ; however he knows best how to act if Mrs Davies is at Portsmouth; perhaps [we can] have a little conversation respecting him. I shall neglect fully opening my sentiments to her as I am afraid there is some misunderstanding between them. The Oporto fleet arrived about a week ago therefore suppose you have heard from James ere this.

Spithead. Sept. 21st a.m. We are just arrived after a boisterous passage, tho' a good one. Two small men-o'-war have already put themselves under our command and as a Mediterranean convoy is collected here, it is supposed that we are going out with them. I am glad of it, as it is the pleasantest station I know of and in case of a Spanish war, stand a good chance for prize money. It would have been incurring a great risk had I taken George Robbin's things on board even should we go under any uncertainty: his Prize Money will enable him to purchase new things as I am told they have taken one or two valuable ones.

The *Malta* is expected at Plymouth hourly therefore it will be a good chance for Mrs Evans if she wishes to get her son made Midshipman. I am sorry I had not an opportunity of seeing Mr Doyle at Plymouth before I left it: be assured I should feel myself happy on meeting with any of my sister's friends.

When I know to a certainty our destination, you shall hear, and tho' a greater distance from each other, hope the correspondence will be carried on with as much spirit as hitherto. Make my compliments to all friends, and with duty to Parents, love to W^m & G'mother, I remain, dear Mary,

Your affec^{te} & loving Brother, John George.

*

98. Miss George, Blue Boar Inn, Haverfordwest.

HMS *Fisgard*, Lisbon
Nov. 23rd 1803

My dear Sister,

A considerable time has elapsed since I felt as great a satisfaction as I do now in addressing this to you: be assured I should not have omitted writing so long but expected when the last Packet sailed to have been in England almost as soon as her.

My last was addressed from Spithead at the time of our sailing and in order to give you an account of our proceedings since, I must turn back to that period. Our passage out was particularly tedious, having a number of heavy sailing ships in company & blowing weather almost the whole of the three weeks we were out. After seeing the convoy safe in and remaining here two days, we proceeded agreeable to orders on a 14 days' cruise but owing to the calmness of the weather we did not meet with the smallest success. I hope such luck don't mean to continue with us. We then returned and have been waiting for the convoy back this fortnight past & not only for a wind. A man-o'-war brig going home alone has induced me to embrace the opportunity of writing as she must arrive long before us, consequently it will ease your anxiety respecting me and afford me the pleasure of hearing from you on our arrival in The Downs.

Lisbon is well worth visiting for a stranger, once, but afterwards it must appear insipid, the buildings being in general very circular, the streets badly paved & nothing but filth and dirt to be met with. I have gratified my curiosity, I believe, in visiting every thing that is worth seeing. The churches certainly are very fine, as well as some other public buildings, but what must strike disgust in the heart of every British subject is the number of convents that is to be met with, more like gaols, with grated windows & in short worse than any thing you would conceive. A messmate & myself collected a little impudence & went to the only English convent here to enquire for God knows who, merely for an introduction: one of the nuns through the grate conversed with us for a long time & related what we imagine the mysteries of a convent. She said she had been 19 years in it & that there are 17 English nuns together (no other but English being admitted) and that they are under no restraint but may leave it when they like but being so truly happy that they had not the smallest inclination in so doing. I could give you a very different account of those belonging to the Portuguese but my paper will not allow me to be too prolix on one subject . . .

I had an opportunity of seeing the Opera twice & think the scenery, &c., very fine, also went to the Ball but won't say much in its favour, being a selfish kind of people throughout.

I had almost forgot to tell you I met Bloss & had an opportunity of thanking him for his civility to James. I promised to give him a call but it blowing hard for the last 8 days prevented my going ashore & as it is now pretty moderate & preparing for sea, am afraid I shall not be able to see him as he is some distance from where our boats land. I made him an offer of taking any thing for him home which he declined as somebody had promised to take things for him by the last Packet, which sailed a day or two after.

My paper has completely filled & as cross-writing may make this unintelligible, I will draw to a conclusion, but request you will write to me all the time and address to The Downs as your letters are ordered to be sent there. With duty to Parents, love to G'mother & William & compliments to friends, I remain, dear Mary,

Yours very affect^{ly}, John George.

P.S. Don't fail writing very soon as the wind is now fair & most likely we shall be in The Downs before your letter arrives.

Dec. 13th Off Plymouth. I had an opportunity of sending this from Lisbon but embraced the present. Write immediately to The Downs. JG.

*

99. Miss George, Kensington Place, Haverfordwest.

HMS *Fisgard*, St Helens.[71]

Dec. 27th 1803

My dear Sister,

I can't lose a moment in acknowledging the receipt of your two very kind letters of the 19th & 22nd inst. which arrived late yesterday evening: the unusual long silence and the idea of being once more assured of your welfare has given me indescribable satisfaction, but reflecting for a moment on our dear Father's situation has dampened that ardour I just felt. I hope to God ere this his leg is much better & that he may be restored to his former good health shall be my most earnest prayer: the last account you gave me from appearances seemed to be favourable as a discharge must take place before the pain is abated, but there's your good management & his perseverance. I flatter myself you will give me a very agreeable account in your next.

We arrived at Spithead a day or two after my last and after remaining there about four days were very unexpectedly ordered down here with several other ships to be ready, it is conjectured, to meet the Usurper & his flotilla mid-channel should he hazard an attempt to invade. However, if he fully intends it I [must] make haste as it will be much better in having a good prize in view than lying here [on board] ship. Someone says the flotilla are in motion: I hope they are as it must be the wish of every British subject being [so] perfectly prepared both by land & sea to face them.

The weather has been very bad indeed lately: on Sunday it blew a perfect hurricane, but am happy to say without sustaining any damage to the Squadron: as the weather still continues bad, I don't know a more satisfactory way of passing time than in writing a very long letter to my dear Mary: if I test your patience, do pardon me as it is merely the dictate of affection. As we must be in port but a very short time, I am determined to give you every opportunity of hearing from me. A few days ago I wrote to Davies & requested him to communicate it to you; if he is at all intelligent, he will write me [a letter] in return as I have a right to expect a good many for the last three months [from him].

I am extremely sorry to hear of William's disappointment respecting a situation in the Marines: indeed, I often thought before our arrival that from the flattering promises of Lord Kensington, which had been made him that he had procured William a Lieutenancy. I assure you I felt the disappointment as much as himself, but hope yet he will find some success through Mr Mathias's interest, but if Mr M. wishes to count himself for the family, why not write to Lord Cawdor? He may procure a situation as well as if His Lordship had been in Wales.

I am really ashamed to acknowledge the expense & trouble I caused my dear Parents in fitting me out, particularly in being prevented in compens[ate]ing them for the attention: however I am now in a situation, should fortune favour me, to make something & rest assured (should fortune smile) my friends' independence should be considered before my own. In fitting out William, it may be done with less expense than me because, in the first place, he has no business to remain in London after the appointment is made out & travelling may be effected in a much more reasonable plan: if his prospects are favourable, I can write to my Agent to assist him, as well letters of introduction to Head-quarters; however, I shall wait for your next respecting that: the pay certainly is sufficient and no more if economy is strictly adhered to, but if not, I defy any person to live upon it. More lucrative situation, I think, would suit his position much better; however that must be left to your serious consideration.

I am very happy to find William Phillips promoted. Pray what ship has he? As you have not mentioned Wakelin in yours, I suppose he is still in H'west: being a young man, I fancy he would be much better had he some action in play: however, he knows best. Being at Lisbon consequently would not have it without procuring some trifling thing as a token of affection. Should a couple of [working baskets] be acceptable? Should they reach you, present one of them to Martha George from me as I have long wished to send something to her for the particular attention I have received at all times from the family. Assure Mrs George I have not had an opportunity [to send] her any Tongues & Sounds which I have so long promised since I have seen her, but I shall be happy the first opportunity. Remember me faithfully to the family.

I am pleased to find my dear Mother has an opportunity of visiting the town sometimes, tho' I am prevented from accompanying her. Still, I hope William Davies has fulfilled his promise: say everything you properly can for me as I am not able to express my feeling, how much I love & revere both Father and Mother: tell them their welfare shall be my constant study and should it be ever in my power to promote it, how happy it would make me, God knows. Say I have a frail of figs for them, but should not an immediate opportunity offer of sending them am afraid they will not keep, and their carriage by hand would amount to more than the value of them.

Miss Gould, I find, still wishes reconciliation, poor girl. I certainly pity her sincerely that a peculiar disposition should cause that difference which, otherwise conducted might be [led] into friendship.

I shall leave it entirely to you in remembering me to those you should think fit and as I have written till I have completely filled my paper, the longest you will have ever received, I shall draw to a conclusion, first requesting you'll write as early as convenient.

Accept this with the warmest assurance of duty to Parents, love to Brother, Grandmother & friends from, dear Mary,

Your most aff^te Bro., John George

I have just room to wish a Merry Christmas to you all, with many returns.

*

100. Miss George, Kensington Place, Haverfordwest.

HM Ship *Fisgard*, St Helens
Jan. 9th 1804

My dear Sister,

I am now peaceably & quietly seated in my cabin in order to answer your two kind letters of the 25th ult. and 2nd inst., the latter I received this evening with much satisfaction in being assured of your welfare and Father's good state of health after his indisposition. Nothing particular has happened since my last: rumour says a few of the enemy's gunboats are taken and destroyed by our cruisers, the particulars of which I must refer you to the papers for. Here we are a fine active frigate lying guard ship & how long we are to remain God knows: at present it is uncommonly stupid, therefore hope sincerely to be active on some station as it would then answer two ends in intercepting the enemy & getting something for a future day. William Davies sent me a sheet full, some parts very entertaining. I find Miss Gould is still sneaking about, foolish girl or rather old maid. Now Miss Green has left H'west I fancy she will use every effort to get into your notice but really her conduct hitherto has been such as not to deserve it. While you & your friends were celebrating the New Year under the word of God, the Surgeon and myself were over our glasses determined to see it in: at the approach we drank many, many happy returns to our dear friends: be assured it afforded me infinite satisfaction at that late hour in taking the opportunity of pledging those we dearly love. Indeed, I am much surprised Mr Gibbs allows his daughter with a young man in Stephen Davies, which I should disapprove in your doing: he maybe a fine pleasant fellow but really in my appearance there is something disgusting about him. I am so confident of the propriety of your conduct that you would scorn to associate with those dashing heroes, but why not select a few chosen friends & make it pleasant to each other without scandal & other infamous proceedings, but H'west is such a place that it is absolutely impossible. You may easily presume that I am not very partial to my native place really – were my friends comfortably out of it I don't know if I ever should feel inclined to visit it again for in most places you meet with some civility except the proud haughty town I have just mentioned. I certainly must differ with my dear Mother respecting your visits to Llanunwas, idleness surely cannot be called for after being penn'd up ¾ of a year in a confined town and most of that time in the house, a little jaunting is very requisite for the health; another thing, I thought a respectable society was my Mother's object in that kind family she cannot be displeased with for they have ever proved themselves friendly to you. However, I will say no more.

I have still George Robbin's stockings on board, not having had a safe opportunity of sending them, as the climate he is in don't require them much, he cannot miss them a great deal. Assure Mrs Summers they shall be carefully kept and sent by the first convenient opportunity.

Tell William Davies I have not been on shore since we anchored here & no prospect of going: when I go I will certainly comply with his request. Your letters certainly come cheap enough: had I an opportunity for writing under cover it would be very pleasant & I then could oftener. I believe at present I have little more to say only to request a continuance of the correspondence.

Accept this with the warmest assurance of duty to Parents, love to Brothers & Grandmother & compliments to those few you think proper, from, dear Mary,

Your truly aff^te & loving Brother, John George.

Monday, Jan. 9th. a.m. Our signal was made last evening, after I wrote the within, to proceed here & we have just this moment anchored for what reason is not yet known. I am happy I did not send this before our arrival. Adieu. JG. Spithead.

*

101. Miss George, Kensington Place, Haverfordwest.

HM Ship *Fisgard*, Spithead
Feb. 3rd 1804

My dear Sister,

Your kind letter of the 27th ult. gave me infinite satisfaction in being assured once more, before we sail, of your welfare. At last the wind and weather seem to be favourable for sea & should it continue an hour or two we shall be off, as we are now unmooring. I shall have many opportunities of writing by homeward bound vessels, therefore don't despair of hearing from me . . .

Davies did not wish me to answer his letter unless I had something particular to communicate and as I have not he could not expect it. I have certainly been in Mrs Davies's company often but I'll assure you I know no more than you do of the difference between them & thought it of a too delicate nature to put the question. She has written to Davies four or five days ago, an agreeable letter, I hope.

I have seen Phillips of the Bonetta, he looks remarkably well & begs his compliments. Make mine to those friends you think proper and [be assured] tho' I am to make a short letter, there shall be no opportunity allowed to pass unnoticed without writing. Accept this with duty to Parents, love to Brother & G'mo^r, dear Mary,

Yours very affect^{ly}, John George.

James is not arrived here otherwise I must have seen him ere this. The Lisbon convoy are preparing for sailing but don't think they go immediately.

*

102. Miss George, Kensington Place, Haverfordwest.

Fisgard, Falmouth
Feb. 8th 1804

My dear Sister,

In consequence of a change of wind we did not leave Spithead for two days after my last and on our arrival off here an unfavourable wind obliged us to come in this morning: how long we are likely to remain here, God knows: a change of weather only can determine it.

As we are likely to be absent from England for five months I could not deprive myself of the satisfaction in writing, the idea of postage you must blot out as it may be a long time before you possibly can hear from me again & I think in that instance the later the news the more satisfaction it affords. I had an opportunity of hearing before we sailed from my old friend Birch but not a syllable of his wife: pray what has become of that creature now – for really I can call her nothing else. He begged his compliments to the family.

I have never been here before and as every strange place affords some novelty, think of going on shore in the morning, therefore you shall have my opinion of the place in my next. I have two or three houses in Cornwall where I am welcome at, but the uncertainty of our stay & the distance, will not allow me taking the jaunt.

A Mediterranean convoy left Spithead the time we did, therefore I fancy Captain Brown has lost his chance. I am certainly rather surprised I have neither seen James nor has he answered my letter as I particularly requested one of him in my last.

Pray make my compliments to the Freystrop family & those few you think proper, and with duty to Parents, love to &c., &c., &c, I remain, dear Mary,

Yours most affect^{ly}, John George.

Pray write: address – Falmouth, Cornwall.

*

103. Miss George, Kensington Place, Haverfordwest.

HMS *Fisgard*, Falmouth
Feb. 12th 1804

My dear Sister,

The wind is now fair & we go to sea this morning, therefore before you receive this we shall be many miles distant. I have been on shore & like the appearance of the country much: a few of us went to a ball the same evening & met with every civility we would wish for. As I know two officers of the Cornwall Militia, it would have made it very pleasant having received an invitation to a private Coterie next week, but there is no accounting for wind & weather.

It is hinted, and pretty well believed, that we return to Lisbon after our provisions, &c., are out, and as we expect that will be about the latter end of June, or beginning of July, must be you'll make a kind of a journal & send it in the course of five or 6 weeks & at the same time have the goodness to enquire & let me know if Mr Adams, hair dresser, has received the amount of a Note which a Mr Howells, farmer, of Pembroke, gave to Bloss, or how far he has succeeded in it. Have the goodness to be as explicit as you can as I promised Bloss I would make every inquiry & should I not, perhaps he may draw unpleasant allusions from it.

Make my compliments to all friends & believe me I remain with duty to Parents, love to Brother & G'mo., dear Mary,

Ever yours affect^{ly}, John George.

*

104. Miss George, Kensington Place, Haverfordwest.

Fisgard, Spithead
June 21st 1804

My dear Sister,

Your kind letter of the 14th inst., gave me infinite pleasure in being assured once more of your welfare, indeed, I should have answered it sooner, but my mind for some time past has been kept in a perplexed state in consequence of a Court Martial taking place between two messmates: fortunately I had nothing to do with it except as an evidence and as long as I adhere to truth, of course, they cannot hurt me. Another is to take place tomorrow which I hope to God will be the last, as harmony on board ship is the only comfort we have to look for.

I have frequently seen Mrs Davies who is very well & desires her compliments. Pray what has become of the husband, as you have not mentioned a syllable about him. As you felt sorry in being confined in your last for room why not take a larger sheet? as I expect a great chat of news yet. I have not yet wrote to James but will in a few days. You must excuse the shortness of this. I am assured you will after the reason I have before stated.

Make my compliments to friends and believe me, I am, with duty, love, &c., &c., dear Mary,

Yours very affectionately, John George.

We expect to sail in the course of a fortnight but our destination is not yet known. Do write soon.

*

105. Miss George, Kensington Place, Haverfordwest.

Fisgard, Spithead
June 25th 1804

My dear Sister,

I have the mortifying intelligence of communicating to you our being ordered to complete immediately for foreign service; our destination is not known but suppose the Mediterranean. We shall have this on Thursday and as we have no convoy to take, expect dispatches. I wrote a few days ago and hope to receive your last before we sail. Tho' I date this from the *Fisgard* I am now seated in Mrs Davies's parlour writing and talking the same time, therefore it is very probable you may see a few blunders in the perusal. She begs her compliments. I forgot in my last to inform you of young Peregrine's embarkation in the *Fisgard*; he joined as Second Officer accidentally about a fortnight ago. I think him a fine young man & dare say we shall agree very well. I have nothing very particular to say: Courts Martial are at last over, thank God, and as we have several new Officers, consequently have new dispositions to study. Most likely I shall see George Robbin, therefore shall deliver his stockings to him myself As I have not heard any thing particular respecting the family, therefore must conclude they are well and shall make this report accordingly.

Remember me affectionately to all friends and rest assured I shall ever remain with duty, &c., &c, dear Sister,

Yours very affect^{ly}, John George.

I have wrote to James but have received no answer. Since writing the within, I have heard we sail with a convoy to the Mediterranean on Saturday and it is possible that we may be on Sunday or Monday. I beg you to write. JG.

*

106. Miss George, Kensington Place, Haverfordwest.

Portsmouth
July 1st 1804

My dear Sister,

I wrote a few days ago mentioning our going to the Mediterranean and as we expect to sail today, I could not deprive myself once more the satisfaction of writing to you. I received your friend's letter two days ago, as well one from James, which afforded me infinite pleasure in being assured of your welfare.

As it is very probable we may continue in that station some time I beg you will write to me under cover to 'Messrs I. & I. Westmore, Grocers, Portsmouth,' which will be forwarded every opportunity to me. You may write by frank once a month, or oftener if you are inclined and rest assured I'll embrace every opportunity of answering them.

Since writing the above I hear we are to sail at daylight tomorrow. Have the satisfaction of acknowledging yours of the 28th, ult. which I have this instant received. Respecting the Freystrop family, I am sorry there should be a difference between you, but as it seems it did not originate with you I think the loss of their society cannot be much missed.

Poor Davies I am sorry for: would wish you to pay some little attention to him. I saw his wife yesterday, who desired her compliments. Curgenven of Plymouth is married but I don't know the person, so that Jane Morrice is completely cut out. Remember me to them all.

We go to Malta first, thence to Lord Nelson to put ourselves under his orders.

My paper reminds me to conclude, therefore, with duty, love, &c., &c., I remain, dear Mary,

Yours very affect^{ly}, John George.

Peregrine is very well. I shall certainly expect letters by the next convoy. JG.

*

107. Miss George, Kensington Place, Haverfordwest.

Fisgard, off Toulon
Aug. 16th 1804

My dear Sister,

I cannot neglect the opportunity which now offers of writing, it being the first since we left Portsmouth and perhaps another may not occur for a considerable time to come.

Our passage out was very pleasant: after waiting 3 days at Gibraltar, we proceeded here to join Lord Nelson who we had not seen until this morning, after looking out three weeks for him, having left the station in consequence of bad weather. We have 10 sail-of-the-line & a great number of frigates. The French have an equal force but don't seem at all inclined to face us, tho' we have seen since we arrived several under weigh, knowing their superiority in number, some future time we may possibly surprise them. We must give up all idea of Prize Money unless in the event of a Spanish war, then I think we stand a chance. George Robbin is very well: I have not seen him but only heard verbally. Your letters I hope to receive some time or other: the latest news received before our arrival was four months old, therefore I have a great distance to look forward but hope you'll continue to write as they may possibly afford a happy moment some future time. Mr Peregrine embraces this opportunity of writing; he was fortunately prepared before, therefore I dare say he has written a long letter to his friends. Duty, &c., attracted my attention until the moment the signal was made & as I am now pressed for mine, you must excuse me saying more than I am, with duty, love, &c., &c., dear Mary,

Yours very affect^{ly} John George.

Pray excuse all errors you may see.

*

[Letter from D. J. McCarthy].

108. Lieutenant George RM, HMS *Fisgard*, off Toulon.

HMS *Argo* off The Texel[72]
September 4th 1804

Dear George,

Some time ago I directed for you, care of Mr West, Portsmouth, understanding that one of your Mess was left behind and waiting there for a passage to join the *Fisgard*. I now embrace with pleasure this opportunity that offers of writing to you by Lieut. Touch who leaves this ship to go first Lieut. of the *Le Tigre* and is a very worthy man and a very pleasant messmate. Should you meet I am convinced you will like him much. I have heard from my old friend Captain Durham to whom I wrote an account of the Court Martial. He very properly remarks that whatever censure, or cause for it, the Court Martial may find in my conduct, it is evident that the Commissioners by giving me an appointment so specially and to so good a ship, did not think I acted improperly. Some well meaning friends of mine advised that I would let the affair drop but I have determined otherwise and hope it will be over this month I shall send a copy to you if I can meet with any safe hands, if not I will send one to Captain Kempster to be kept till your return. The *Argo* does not remain in this station and possibly may go up in the convoy as I rather think she will be disposed of in that manner. I shall use every effort to get into a snug berth in harbour when we go in to refit. Should I succeed I then will take care and have a cot ready slung for my friend George and some good old cheese and salad and a welcome I presume he doubts not receiving.

My sight, which is truly getting worse, will insure me when I have an opportunity to learn music by note before I get quite blind as in that case the flute will be my only amusement. Should matters go very hard with me you know I may trump up a good story about losing my sight in the Court and get an old dog to lead me about and pray for the thoughtless unthinking men of the world, however a truce with this fun as enow Folly. Whenever I may sit down with my household gods, there my friend George will ever find a true Irish welcome and every endeavour on my and Mrs. MaC part to induce him to prolong his visit and every thing in my humble but contented cottage will be at his service, excepting my wife and woman servants. In truth, my dear fellow, when this Cursed Scourge of Mankind, Bonaparte, is no more and peace becomes the order of the day and you can sense the busy scenes of life for the tranquillity of the humble cot of a half pay Surgeon and put up with his [eccentricties and] assure yourself of a cordial reception, with my sincerest thanks for pleasures your society will afford me.

Tell Maxwell, to whom I desire to be kindly remembered, that the Vestas is arrived from the West Indies but whether his brother is come in her the papers don't mention but should suppose he is. Remember me also to Taylor Gelwin Scott and young Pickles. I shall expect to have a long letter from you soon with any news the *Fisgard* affords. How does Iago go on? When you come home, if you have any spare cash bring me a few pots of Naples soap for shaving and I owe you a good tanning for not letting me have the song you promised.

Believe me, dear George, unchangeably yours,

D. J. McCarthy.

*

[Letter from George Robbin].

109. Lieutenant George, RM, HM Ship *Fisgard*.

HM Ship *Canopus*

Oct. 15th 1804

My dear George,

Having heard from the Victory that you or Peregrine have not been fortunate enough to be classed among those who have heard from their friends by the last conveyance, I hasten to give you a little Welsh news, tho' as far back as 25th July. In the first place our friends are all well and in daily expectation of a long threatened visit from our friends on the opposite shore. . . .

Captain John Mathias of the Bridge married to that amiable girl Betty Levy much against the consent of his Aunt who is so averse to the match that she (Mrs M.) is now living in Cardigan. So much for a run away excursion: would you have expected so much news from Haverfordwest?

Every thing at Milford is in a state of stagnation. Building completely stopped and some [persons in arms]. The fair ones seem to have great confidence in the Naval Department: so much for males. You, of course, see great alteration in our Squadron. *Tigre* and *Conqueror* joined us two days after our parting from you; at least the former ship. The latter being charged with some victuallers, which parted yesterday with the Active, supposed for Madaline where we (I believe) are bound.

The *Ryder* is gone to Malta with a convoy. The Admiral obtained a paper as late as 15th, September which arrived in the *John Bute* (Cutter) which vessel sailed from England 21st charged with dispatches for Lord Nelson. The dispatches came from Town and were instantly shipped on to the *John Bute*, the

152

Dreadnought being in Cawsand Bay at the time, a Lieutenant from that ship was ordered into the Cutter, and sailed immediately with no other rigging than a jacket, trousers, boots, etc., and dined with his lordship in that apparel.

Yours, George Robbin.

*

110. Miss George, Kensington Place, Haverfordwest.

Fisgard off Toulon
Nov. 4th 1804

My dear Sister,

Your kind letter of the 16th August I received two days ago, tho' such an old date, it afforded me much pleasure in being assured of your welfare. I immediately forwarded Mr Robbin's which I dare say he has received before this: he was very well three days ago.

My last was the 22nd September: since that time we have been constantly cruising off this place without success, except sending a neutral Brig with oil to Malta for examination in company with the *Amazon* which, should she be condemned, a few Pounds in the course of a year or two will be acceptable. You say Mr James mentioned to his father his intention of remitting cash home: pray has he made anything, for his last letter informed me he had received only two or three Pounds, if he has not, have the goodness thro' his friends to ask him in what manner he is able, out of his pay, to remit any, in order that I may follow his good example, for at present I am really at loss. My last year's Mess amounted alone to £65, besides clothes, &c., out of 4s.8d. per day, therefore you must suppose that I have not a great deal to spare – perhaps my Mess the next year may be less, sincerely hope it will – but at the same time must assure you, I do not look for assistance, but merely to convince you of the impossibility of a thing you at present suppose.

I have seen the Cornish Militia[73] at Plymouth: they have a very good character of being a set of steady & orderly men, which I dare say they will prove to the H'west people. Peregrine received his letter & intends writing by this opportunity to his friends. I would wish you to continue the same method of addressing my letters as Mr Westmore is a very attentive & obliging man & would be happy to do anything for me: you may thank him in one of the covers for his attention. I rejoice to find William Davies is at last employed but fear he is with a man, in the Captain, who will not agree very well, being one of the smartest Commanders in the Navy and Davies, I know very well, is a man not over stocked with brilliancy: he has my warmest wishes for his welfare and hope I may be deceived.

George Robbin mentioned in a note to me he had embraced an opportunity of writing when we were absent from the fleet, stating we were very well; should he not write, you may say both he & C. Phillips are well. Remember me kindly to all friends and be assured your letters at all times will afford me infinite pleasure. With duty to Parents, love &c., &c., I remain,

Ever yours affect^ly, John George.

A Spanish war is much talked of. The unfortunate state of Gibraltar, of course, you have heard. We have received no late account.

*

111. Miss George, Kensington Place, Haverfordwest.

Fisgard off Cape St Vincent
Nov. 29th 1804

My dear Sister,

We are now on our way to Lisbon and am happy to say we captured, about two hours ago, a valuable ship (Spanish) from Rio de la Plata to Cadiz. I have just time to write to you by her to inform you with our success which, should she arrive safe in an English port, may possibly give me one or two hundred pounds, in the course of time. She would indicate more but another frigate partakes with us. Since we heard of war with Spain we captured a few other vessels in company with a line of battleships & frigates, which are sent home, their arrival of course you will hear, should the rascally French privateers not meet with them.

We are now going to refit being ordered down to cruise by Lord Nelson, but finding Sir John Orde[74] Commander in Chief of the Cadiz station on our return probably he may order us back, then adieu Spaniards for the Mediterranean will produce none. I wrote some time since, which I hope is received. Peregrine is very well and as he has not time to write begs you will inform his friends of it.

I have no particular news. The state of Gibraltar is still awful – several people are dead which I knew very well: we passed close to it on our way down but had no communication with it.

Make my compliments to friends and, believe me, I am with duty to Parents, love to Bro^s, &c., dear Mary,

Yours very affect^ly, John George.

At Lisbon we have no chance of going on shore as they will complete us with every needful in a state of quarantine.

*

[Letter from Lieutenant William Davies, RN, to Mary George]

112. Miss George, Kensington Place, Haverfordwest.[75]

HMS *Spartiate,* Hamoaze

Dec. 26th 1804

Dear Cousin,

Yours of the 15th inst. I received last Friday: the one dated the 17th of November has been at sea I suppose, I received this evening & I am very glad to hear that you are all well. I am sorry to hear that your nearest relations are so shy: I suppose they thought you expected a fairing from them. Our ship was only one day in dock: we are alongside the Medway hulk a-fitting out for sea: the ship's company was at work all day yesterday (Christmas Day). There is no account when the ship is going as yet, but I think we are to join the Channel Fleet again. If you have the stockings ready to send me, the best way I think will be to send them to Bristol by the coach, directed to Mr George Mathias. You can send a letter to him & tell him to forward them to me at Dock, directed to be left at Mr Griggs, Grocer, Fore Street, [Plymouth] Dock. I will send you a money letter from the Post Office; that will be safest way, better than the risk of a bill in the letter. You mentioned about Mrs Davies in your last letter. I do assure you that if she would return from Portsea and go down to Wales to live that I would think nothing of what has happened and I would allow her 40£ a year to maintain her and whatever more I could spare. Give my love to all the family and compliments to all our relations and acquaintances in town & country. Let me know all the news in your next letter and believe me to be, dear Cousin,

Yours affectionately, W[m] Davies.

P.S. I will send you the price of a gown and gloves against Easter Sunday; let me know how Mr Green come on. Mr Llewhellin, our surgeon, is going to leave the ship, I am sorry for it. I wish you a Merry Christmas.

*

113. Miss George, Kensington Place, Haverfordwest.

Fisgard off Carthagena
Dec 31st 1804

My dear Sister,

After a five weeks silence I again resume my pen to assure you of my welfare which I am convinced will afford you some satisfaction; indeed in writing to my dearest sister is the greatest pleasure I receive in this part of the world, though lament much in not receiving hers in return. My last went home in a valuable detained Spaniard from Cape St Vincent. We were then on our way to Lisbon where we arrived two or three days after and immediately put in quarantine. The arrival of James's ship[76] I heard of soon after she came in but unfortunately was not able to approach her within 100 yards. I got on board & passed within hail. James appeared very well and assured me of the welfare of the family. It was certainly very distressing, two brothers who had not seen much of each other for the last six years to be deprived of that comfort. I received one letter and expected another with some of yours enclosed, but was disappointed. The *Britannia* went up the Tagus the day I saw him; we were then about three miles from Lisbon, the place ships generally ride quarantine. About four days afterwards we sailed without being released from the unfortunate state we were in.

On our way to Gibraltar we had the good luck to capture a French Letter of Marque[77] of 18 guns (formerly a Guineaman) from Cayenne bound for Cadiz (*L'Tigre*) which we left there and proceeded here to reconnoitre, now we are satisfied; we returned immediately to complete with stores, &c., &c. I must tell you first, in consequence of an order from Sir John Orde to return to the Mediterranean, we have the sole command under Lord Nelson from this place to Gibraltar, a range of three hundred miles, and I shall proceed on a topic relative to the Spanish war.[81] Our detaining a number of vessels under the Spanish flag I mentioned in my last, since that we have not had the pleasure of saluting one. War, I am sorry to say, was not declared before the 15th inst, consequently all those we supposed prizes will become droits of Admiralty[78] the proportion to the captors, I am informed, will be very small, therefore we have our fortunes to begin again, indeed in this country we have very little prospect of success in consequence of the dreadful malady which has visited the principal mercantile ports in Spain, however we will hope 'all is for the best'. Gibraltar I am happy to say was very healthy when we left it, tho' am sorry several unfortunate people I knew fell victims to the malady. A convoy had arrived with troops, &c., but the port not being proclaimed free had no communication with the shore. Tomorrow is the day appointed for that purpose.

I have not heard from George Robbin since we left the Fleet, therefore can say nothing of him. Admiral Campbell is gone home.

Jan'y 1st 1805. Dear Mary, you must pardon the abrupt way I dropt my pen last night. Now I begin with a new year wishing you all compliments of the season and many happy returns. The day commenced very pleasant with us in releasing our French prisoners to a Neutral, going to Spain, poor fellows! They were really happy in going, though national enemies, I believe a few among them possessed the warmest friendship for us. We have at present a fair wind for Gibraltar where we expect to arrive tomorrow; in compliment to the day we all dine with the Captain; a bumper to my dear friends, of course, I shall fill, being the only satisfaction I can at present expect, tho' candidly confiding I detest the generality of any neighbours but those dear to me I shall now revere.

Mr Peregrine is very well; he wrote home from Lisbon. I hope James did also, as he promised me he would. I have certainly shewn you a good example in long letters, hope you will continue to write thro' the same channel; as usual remember me to those friends you think proper and when you write collect all the news you can; what you suppose as out of date probably may afford me much pleasure. What is William about? Is Wm Davies still in the *Spartiate*? And are the marriageable ladies in Bridge Street still single? Tell them I hope to have a *tête-à-tête* with them yet. I could ask you a thousand questions more but as you will, I dare say, be able to fill a sheet of paper, I will drop the subject. Your friends at Llanunwas remember me to, if you think proper. I have lately written to Mr James.

Make my most affectionate remembrance to dear Parents: say I wish them many happy returns of the season, as well Wm & G'mother. I shall conclude this but have room for our arrival at Gibraltar on the other side – with wishing you all every happiness, I remain, Dear Mary,

Yours very affectly, John George.

Jan'y 3rd, p.m. We are just arrived at Gibraltar. The port is not yet proclaimed free but expect it will in two or three days. We sail about that time. JG.

*

114. Miss George, Kensington Place, Haverfordwest.

Fisgard, Gibraltar
Mar. 14th 1805

My dear Sister,

I am again disappointed in the expectation of receiving your letters; can account for it no other way but supposing them lost in the *Raven* a few weeks ago near Cadiz. We arrived here this morning after a wild goose chase of five weeks without success in pursuit of the French frigates which captured & dispersed the Malta convoy up the Mediterranean, the particulars it is needless entering into, as you must have perused it in the public papers long ere this. I should have written when we were here before but want of time prevented me. Mr Peregrine did, I believe, to his parents and informed them of a serious affray we met with in our boats on boarding a Greek armed vessel near Cartagena some time ago: of course you have also heard the unfortunate account, therefore I'll be mute on the subject except that I must thank my good luck, I escaped without being hurt, the loss of a valuable & faithful servant I still lament but, you know, 'tis all the fortune of war.

By the newspapers at home you have a right to suppose we have all made independencies but am concerned to say, you are very much misled; to be sure, we have sent home a ship and schooner which are accounted pretty valuable (the Imogen sharing) and also a few here which we share with other ships, but of no great consequence to us; in being droits of Admiralty must give us a very small proportion. However, when I receive prize money, I acquaint you with it – the only prize we called our own was a French Letter of Marque which was totally lost in a gale of wind here: am sorry to say we have just heard of the loss of another, a valuable brig from the Rio de la Plata going home. Some of the ships have been very fortunate, indeed we expected to have been one, but Sir John Orde ordering us here damped our spirits. We expect to be here some time, being in great want of repair, afterwards resume our station between this place & Cartagena, but there is nothing whatever to be picked there, I fancy, in consequence of the late exchange along the coast. The Rock at present is in a perfect state of health but the inhabitants fear much a relapse the ensuing summer.

Since writing the above we were informed a leak, which has been discovered some time since, is of that nature as to oblige us to go home. I sincerely wish it, being heartily sick of the station.

I have not heard from the Fleet for some time so that I can say nothing of my townsmen – we hear they have made several captures. James ere this must be in England: his letters, which I expect, are not yet arrived. I wonder if our dear parents think at all of his situation? – as his apprenticeship is now drawing to a conclusion, if they can reconcile themselves to his being [in] the Navy as Midshipman, sooner the better, as protection of some kind is highly necessary before his time expires, otherwise 'tis about a hundred chances to one he is pressed & tossed about without allowing an opportunity of providing for him: this is certainly a critical moment which should not be lost sight of. Our dear friends' good sense, I am satisfied, will direct them how to act, therefore must pardon me for dictating, indeed there is no necessity for you mentioning it, unless you really think it advisable.

Write your next 'by the way of Lisbon' to Gibraltar, paying postage, if not too expensive, and recollect as I have not heard from you since August last, shall expect the heads of a great deal of information. Should we go home, your letter will be easily forwarded. Pray what is William about? I could ask you a thousand questions, but as you have sufficient to fill a sheet of paper, will spare you the trouble.

Let Mr Peregrine's friends know he is well. We are so close to the shore that there is a plank from the ship to it. You may be assured I shall enjoy my walks, not being above 6 days ashore since we left England. The only inconvenience we suffer is a plentiful scarcity of live stock in the Garrison. Spanish privateers, &c., intercepting every thing.

My last was early in January which hope is received. Remember me to those few you think proper & with duty to Parents, love, &c., &c., &c., I remain, dear Mary,

Yours most affect^{ly}, John George.

*

115. Miss George, Kensington Place, Haverfordwest.

Fisgard, off Cork
Apr. 23rd 1805

My dear Sister,

To your great astonishment, I fancy, you again find us near *terra firma*. To me it has been almost a dream, having orders to proceed to Lord Nelson.[79]

However, to the subject. We left Gibraltar the 9th inst. in consequence of the Toulon Fleet of 11 sail-of-the-line & 7 frigates passing the Gut. We had our powder, &c., &c., out at the time but was enabled to make sail three or four hours after they passed: too late, I am sorry to say, to keep sight of them. They attempted to sail about six weeks ago but were driven back in consequence of bad weather: at that time they had 10,000 troops embarked, therefore we conjecture they having that force now & destined to Ireland: how far we are right, time will decide. One thing in our favour is the probability of being kept in the home station. The Mediterranean I detest. An officer is gone to the Commanding Officer at Cork: on his return, we shall know something more. It would be a charity to give us a run on the Sod for, correctly speaking, we have not known what a good dinner is since December last, nothing whatever to be got at Gibraltar except fish, without paying an enormous price for it.

It distresses me a little to think of being so near and prevented hearing from you after such a silence. I would not advise you to write here because our stay is so very uncertain. We have some distant idea of going to Plymouth or Portsmouth, the ship being deficient of a number of things & also in course of pay. We will hope for the best and when I request a letter, I am convinced my dear Mary will not deprive me of the satisfaction.

Pray have you thought any thing of James's situation yet? His time must be nearly out and if he is left on board the *Britannia*, pressed he will be to a certainty & altogether disagreeable to come over again: I would have you to consider seriously his situation.

I shall expect, one of these days, quite a journal from you of all the things which has transpired in H'west and its vicinity. I hope all our good friends are well: remember me to those you think proper. Mr Peregrine's son is very well: pray do they send up when they hear from him? My last letter was March 14th from Gibraltar.

Apr. 27th off Brest. We are now joining the Fleet, having received orders from Cork to proceed here: in a short time we shall know if we are to return to Gibraltar or go to England – the latter I earnestly hope: however, I prepare myself for the worst.

Plymouth 28th p.m.

We are just come to on anchor but unfortunately in quarantine, in which state we expect to remain 8 days. Write by return of post. Believe me, I remain, with duty to Parents, Love, &c., &c., dear Mary,

Yours most affect^{ly}, John George.

*

116. The M. Officer of the *Ariadne*.

Fisgard, Plymouth Sound
May 7th 1805

Sir,

A Brother Officer addresses you on a subject, which he trusts will be pardoned when made acquainted with it. About the latter end of March a young man and a brother of mine of the name of George was pressed [80] in The Downs from the *Britannia* of London by the boats of the *Ariadne* and am concerned to state has since entered for that ship – his friends, intending him for the Mercantile line and not the Navy, are much distressed about it and are exciting themselves to bring him forward either as Midshipman or Clerk – the latter they wish, himself the former – therefore it is not decidedly determined which. Any attention you can pay, or cause to help him in his present situation, and should I be favoured with a line, will be ever considered a lasting obligation conferred on.

Sir, Yours &c., J.G.

Miss George, Kensington Place, Haverfordwest.

My dear Sister,
    The above is a letter forwarded this day to the Ariadne in consequence of James's being pressed – it is what I have long looked for therefore am not much surprised. As Captain's clerk he might leave the service with consent at any time, on 2 years servitude be made a Purser – Midshipman 6 years before promoted and as for Master's Mate he has not any right to expect; indeed, a mated Midshipman at first is difficult to procure. If Mr Morgan is going to do any thing let be done instantly, otherwise write & let me try what I can do.
    Captain King is not known in the *Fisgard*. As for expense I have received no prize money but certainly expect some and am so deep with my Agent in consequence of his ensuring my proportion of the Dido for forty guineas that I am not enabled to draw. I will give a note of hand with interest for 20, 30 or 40£ to any of our friends on payment of prize money to fit him out – reflect seriously and let be done before the ship sails.
    Part of your letter gave me much pleasure: remember me to friends: believe me, I am,

Most affect^{ly} yours, John George.

Write immediately. Birch is Master Attendant at Sheerness. I would write to him but am at a loss to act. I will write again on receipt of your promised letter.

*

117. Miss George, Kensington Place, Haverfordwest.

Fisgard, Madeira
June 16th 1805

My dear Sister,
    An opportunity offering of sending this via Lisbon and not being able to

apprise you of our destination before our departure from Plymouth induces me to resume my pen. We arrived here about six days ago after a very pleasant passage and intend sailing tomorrow morning, God knows where: one thing I can say, we call here again and expect to be at Plymouth in the course of eight weeks from this, therefore request you send me every information to No. 17, Cumberland Street, Dock, particularly respecting James. Birch, I trust, has done something for him ere this – by the by, I received a letter from James as the ship was getting under weigh, too late for its being answered. He mentioned Mr Lewis's promise of patronising him, which I think a most handsome thing done. Should he do any thing, on arrival at Plymouth, will thank him. I know an officer of the same name: it cannot be him, otherwise would have mentioned it. James wishes much to be Mid. in this ship, which might be easily accomplished so far as the 'name', but the 'rating' is what I could not immediately expect unless wishing his Lordship to slight several of his own followers, which would not be pleasant. If Birch has done nothing, write him.

We have been treated in the most hospitable manner by the English merchants since our arrival – large party every day. I won't be more particular in my account; it would take up too much room, therefore will leave it for a future day to relate of a winter's evening by a good fire.

I would pay postage on this from Lisbon had I an opportunity, but not: trust you'll not think much of 2/- or 2/6 thrown away. I'll promise you you shan't hear from me for some weeks to come again. Adieu and, believe me, I am, with duty to Parents, love to W^m, & G'^{mr} & friends, dear Mary,

Yours most affect^{ly}, John G.

*

[Letter from K. Lupton].

118. Lieut. John George, R.M., HMS *Fisgard*, Plymouth.

Stamford
13th Aug. 1805

Dear George,

I received your welcome epistle this morning: am happy to hear that you and the rest of our friends are well. Your late cruise seems to have been a very barren one indeed, considering the favourable track you have been in.

I suppose we shall hear something of our prizes soon. Mr Halford seemed very anxious to make a payment before you sailed and I am convinced would have done it had the business been settled on the part of the merchants who may have claims on the Spaniards.

I touched my friend Jemmy Sykes with a lawyer's letter concerning my demand on him for prize money due to me while in the Iris about six years back. When he found me in earnest he, without further ceremony paid me 180 pounds in part, with promise of the remainder as soon as the business could be settled. You may see by this case what villainy there is in agency.

I am sorry to say that I have enjoyed but a poor state of health till within these three weeks, I am better. My ill health has kept me backward in prosecuting the business relative to my estate. Had I been tolerably well, the business would have been settled these last assizes at Lincoln, but was obliged to be put off on account of my not being able to attend. Since I have been better, have employed a good deal of my time in angling, an art in which I flatter myself, am a tolerable proficient considering the short time I have been at it. At other times, I take a little exercise on horseback. Indeed, I have a great deal of amusement only wanting my health to be thoroughly re-established to make me very comfortable.

Should the old ship come to Portsmouth, would send you a basket of game. if I can only manage to shoot straight. I mean to take out a licence soon as the season comes in.

Pray make my kind remembrance to Sproule, Taylor, Peacock & Taylor's wife, father, sisters, &c., &c. Please to say to Sproule that I have been under Dr Dalby's care ever since I came home; the family are well. Their eldest daughter thought to be the finest girl in Stamford or within a many miles of it.

Your account of the Patriotic Fund really astonishes me. That of the Bear does not, having had some knowledge of it prior to my quitting. By the by, you don't say who you have got in lieu of Maxwell, nor do you mention Peregrine, please to make my respects to him. And if you think it would be agreeable for his Lordship to hear from me, will thank you to make my respects to him, and say that in consequence of his very handsome letter & certificate, I was told at the Navy Office the Commissioners was disposed to do anything for me in my line.

I hope you will write me again before you go to sea & give me all the news you can collect: rest assured there is no one in existence whom I shall be happier to see or hear from than yourself.

Believe me ever yours sincerely, K. Lupton.

I think of being in London in the course of next week but am not certain when my health was recovered to enable me to serve again. Provided I made application for a situation through his Lordship. Poor Miss Ham and me had a dreadful fall out the second day I was at their house – in consequence went & lodged in Hawk Street where McCarthy lodged.

*

119. Miss George, Kensington Place, Haverfordwest.

Port Royal, Jamaica
Jan. 9th 1806

My dearest Sister,

No doubt, you will be glad to hear from me after an elapse of four weeks from Barbados. We arrived 6 days ago and thank God am able to say in good health. Your letters not reaching me by the last packet annoyed me a little, however disappointment we must put up with: to partly avoid it for the future you had better address your letters direct here instead of trusting to friends as many things may occur to prevent them from being forwarded which we are unable to account for: the Mail is made up in London the first Wednesday in every month, therefore if you embrace an earlier opportunity I shall be certain of hearing from you by every Packet. We look forward to you for news being here quite out of the way. Part of the Brest fleet we know are at sea & are prepared to give them a warm reception should they attempt to pay us a visit: as it is very improbable their coming it is needless saying more of the despicable race of beings.

Peregrine & myself had an unexpected visit two days ago from David Bevan, formerly of Marloes Court,[81] who is Master in the *Petherel*. I had not an idea of his being in His Majesty's Service otherwise, of course, should have been on the look out. However, I felt much satisfaction in the meeting as the greater part of his relations have ever proved very friendly. Write to Mr Gilbert Bevan, should you not see him, say he is very well & had received a late letter from him, make my best remembrance to both himself & wife for whom I have ever had the highest esteem.

I sincerely wish some time or other to be able to blot the obligation[82] I labour under: God grant it soon.

We sail tomorrow or the next day on a cruise and shall return in 10 or 12 weeks when I expect to receive your letter. Every thing is extravagantly high in this place. Having the honourable post of Caterer[83] to fill occasioned my going to Kingston market: turkeys are 4 dollar a piece, geese the same, small fowls 2, in short every piece of stock in proportion. European articles cent per cent more than at home: indeed, our principal wish to leave the country is the enormous expense we must live at here if tolerably decent.

I gave my brother officer in the *Seahorse* going to the Mediterranean an offer of exchange but could not succeed. I wrote George Robbin and William Davies, for the latter, I fancy, will be a surprise to hear from me, not having wrote him but once since leaving Wales. Have you heard of Mrs D. lately? I received a letter from her when last at Plymouth. What a pity there should be a misunderstanding between husband & wife: she is a charming little woman certainly and the son a very amiable boy: as to her affection for the Surgeon, I know nothing of, or I should not write in the manner I do. He is a person I should think very few women would be fond of, being very plain & his manner not at all prepossessing: people are very fond of scandal, you know. Did Mrs D. merit the character given her in Wales, I am sure the company she met at Portsmouth would soon have shunned her. I may be mistaken in my opinion: if so, am much deceived in the woman: time will bring all things to light, therefore will change the subject.

Do you know such a person a native of H'west of the name of Owens? He is Master Attendant here &, it seems, a townsman. I don't recollect him, therefore shall not make myself known, unless he is a relation of Owens the tailor or shopkeeper.

Since commencing this, we have received intelligence of the arrival of a French squadron at Martinique from Europe & of Sir John Duckworth[88] blockading them with an equal force from Gibraltar. It seems the *Canopus* is one, therefore George Robbin will experience a great difference between the blockade of a West India port and the Mediterranean. Mr Peregrine is very well: embrace an early opportunity of mentioning it to his friends, as he does not write by this packet.

Should you still be on terms of intimacy with Mr & Mrs Harries of Llanunwas, make my kind remembrance to them: say I shall be very happy to execute any command they might have in this part of the world. Indeed, remember me kindly to all friends and relations – the Freystrop family in particular. I fear much my absence will be much longer from Wales than any hitherto. It is already 2¾ years since I left you and think it probable it will be that time yet before I have the extreme satisfaction of again embracing my dear Mary. I have only to say that I look forward to that happiness. Write me all the news – believe me I will not lose sight of an opportunity in answering your invaluable letters.

I have attempted to peruse this but finding so many blunders that I am afraid to go on: excuse errors & rest assured I remain, with duty to Parents, love &c., &c., &c., dear Mary,

Most affectionately yours, John George.

*

[Letter from J. Moull].

120. Lieut. George, R.M., HMS *Surveillante*.[84]

Port Royal
June 21st 5 o'clock

My dear George,

I enclose (not exactly within this but call it an accompaniment) a letter or two in a considerable hurry fearing to lose the opportunity of the vessel – it has been raining very hard all day, therefore was obliged to delay.

Bless you, my dear boy, wherever you go. I shall not readily forget you. Taylor has searched his cabin for my letter but could not find it. I have scribbled a few lines. If you have it in your power, my dear boy, see me. I know you will for the love you bear me, if possible. Therefore, I shall not put it further.

Taylor is gone to Kingston. I requested him to use his interest to get your letters as the packet is just arrived. If he should not before the *Imperieux* sails, write and say where they shall be sent. I can write no more now. Drop a line or two when you can and let me know your address.

I am, Sincerely yours,
J. Moull.

All hands (our Friends) desire their compliments

*

[Letter from Lieutenant James George].

121. Lieut. John George, RM, on board HMS *Surveillante*,
      Deptford, River Thames.
      (To be forwarded)

HMS *Lucifer*, Spithead
Sept 17th 1806

Dear Brother,

I received your kind letter of the 5th inst. last Sunday which gave me great pleasure in being assured of your health being in a more forward state of recovery. I should have answered it long ere this but unfortunately having the convoy signal flying for the westward and the wind coming fair so that we sailed on Monday at 6 a.m. and did not arrive here until 1 o'clock today, when I take the first opportunity of writing this. Dear Brother, you desired me to let you know how I liked my situation: to tell you the truth I can't say I like it, for I ardently wish for to get in to a more active ship when I shall see some service to what there is here but the old thing over again in boats all day long.

The Captain behaves very well to me. I believe I told you in my last that I was rated mate so, dear John, if an opportunity offers you know what to apply for. Indeed, John, I can't inform you a word of family affairs, no more than if I had been out of the land.

My dear Brother, excuse my intrusion but I am really short, so must beg of you, can you spare a trifle until I am able to repay which I hope we will be in a short time. So, I must conclude, dear Brother,

Yours truly & affectionately, James George.

P.S. Write by return of Post and direct to The Downs for we shall sail from here in a day or two. Adieu. J.

*

[Letter from B. L. Taylor].[85]

122. Lieut. Jno. George, Haverfordwest.

HMS Fisgard, off Cape Maisi
15th October 1806

My dear George,

I cannot allow this opportunity to pass without [response]. I received your very kind letter to the Superiors on the 8th inst. wherein I, with pleasure [feel] you had a right, from appearance, to expect still more than your most sanguine hope could have imagined when you quitted Port Royal. Your kindness in writing Simpson & forwarding those trifles committed to your care is exactly like Jno. George, that solid old major that charged the last crab. I trust that you will put your threat into execution, if passing my draught and insisting on her taking Trot with you, tho' I doubt Mary Ancilla will be of the party. It struck me she is become a part of Dr. Ferris: whether or not, remember me kindly to her and all her friends. I shall write you every [spare] opportunity that may present itself. As you requested Sproule I think it would be as well if I direct you to No. 30: also when, indeed, I hope to see you and [take] many a jovial glass together accompanied by our friend J.M., who will enliven the scene. I feel rejoiced, my dear George to find you are so comfortable. I have sent two letters to you under cover to Miss Ann Thomas.

I am very happy to note your resignation to the Divine will. The last letter I received from my better half has made me very happy. She seems to be drawing towards that path which promises a safe journey & an eternal rest when she will surely shine one of the brightest jewels in the Redeemer's crown. Forgive me, George, my dear friend, when I reflect on her whole life: it astonishes me to think she could unite her fate with mine. I look forward to that happy day when I shall walk with her & my dear friend Jno. to the house of God. Our days are fast passing.

Why Taylor (I think at this moment I hear a sound exclaim): Do you know you are writing to a Marine officer? Yes I do, and he will pardon my rhapsody. Since you left Port Royal we have had a cruise in the Mona Passage.[86] I was rapidly drifting when they had declared they would not help the boat as I advised. You may rely I did not spare their feelings if they possessed any. Within five minutes after they bore up, they were washed over board & the next sea took all the rest except your faithful friend, the boat at this time running at the rate of five miles an hour on the reef on the larboard gunnel, a very pretty situation, my dear fellow, wasn't it? I stood on the gunnel and looked over the starboard, by which I was holding, when I observed an enormous sea about to break on his starboard quarter (at this time Robt. Wardle was holding on by the starboard bow). I instantly jumped over board towards the larboard quarter, by what means I escaped for the boat by that sea was overset. On my gaining the surface I observed four men on the boat's bottom; immediately after I was carried with great velocity towards the reef: between the shelves, your friend's head was fastened, nor could I extricate myself from this perilous situation, or could any but an Almighty arm have saved me.

I had been so long under water, even our friend Rennie who was on the shore said he entertained little hope for again taking me by the hand. I was a little cut & bruised & almost breathless & was supported to the shore. We only lost one man from Robt. Kaller: we buried him on the Beach. I then settled for the Baltock and accompanied Rennie on board. Next day we made sail and have been cruising in the Mona Passage. Rennie was away fifteen days. he took a Spanish schooner, tho' not very rich. Yet it made us all happy to see him again in safety. The barge, with eight men, separated from him and we found her [capsized]. We captured all together seven small vessels, which ought to pay my Mess. I have purchased 11,500 lb. of beef this cruise and have given Vouchers for it to Grant. The Capt. has signed them saying he would allow me twelve per cent on the money that might arise thereon. The overplus, I mean what was killed by ourselves he would be so generous as to allow

12 per cent for my trouble, but this day he sent for me to ask me for a statement of what I had received & what it cost me, to enable 'him' to give me 12 per cent for my trouble & place the remainder in a general fund, to be shared when it amounts to any thing worth sharing. I informed him that I considered it an emolument of my own & that the ship's company and nothing to do with it: he says that he will bring me before Capt. Ross of the *Regina* who allows his Parson so much. I said very well. I was certainly right, and if Parsons are so far by interested motives led to act thus, I have no other opportunity of making a farthing. You, my dear fellow, knew my great expenses. I am happy to say this has enabled me to pay all my debts here: so he'll find very little cash paid in this mean manner by Taylor. I'll rather risk a Court Martial than give up a single farthing. [As for] Court Martial he cannot bring me for he has collected [   ] a share himself & I am not surprised at anything you mentioned of him. I cannot forget Lucian where I was branded with the epithet of a Niggard. I cannot forget or forgive him he ha in this and in many other respects proved himself the meanest wretch I ever knew. The alligator [hangs] in the mainstay still. Sproule, Perry and Rennie desire to be affectionately remembered to you, and Mr Macracott desires his compliments. Remember me to all friends, Mrs Latham, Mrs Bank: tell them I have wrote them long letters: Mrs Thomas, Mrs Bevan and her Sponsor and my affectionate remembrance to my beloved [   ]: tell her I am in tolerable spirits & expect to be home shortly. Believe me, my dear George, your very [   ],

B. L. Taylor.

*

123. Mr William George, Kensington Place, Haverfordwest.

Swansea
April 6th 1807

My dear William,

Thus early I commence a correspondence which hope will be punctually continued, tho' shall generally keep it up with Mary[87] – her attention to the little girl and the domestic concerns will, of course, attract a part of her attention, consequently cannot expect she will or ought to devote so much of her time as she has hitherto done to me. To my dear & revered Parents I shall often address but, as yours, I shall consider public: hope they will be received as such.

I arrived after a jolting day's journey about 7 o'clock last evening: to express myself would have been impossible as to my feelings at parting would be impossible. Mary's presence at the moment added much to it: she must have known my reason for not taking leave: surely, she could not have doubted my affection: a tear I observed force itself into my Father's eye has endeared me, if possible, stronger than ever to him. My dear Mother also – but enough – if it is boyish to feel at parting, I am completely so.

I called on Williams last evening to inquire for Tom Childs who informed me he was in Neath with his wife. I stopt a short time and took ale, but did not observe any thing very cordial in the reception: perhaps I am deceived, however it is a matter of no object. I shall leave T. Childs at Neath uninterrupted and proceed on my journey either this evening's tide, or the morning's, therefore by the time you receive this you may almost to a certainty place me in some part of Devon.

3 a.m. The Packet is not in, fortunately a collier is just going to sea, by which I take a passage – you shall hear from me soon after my arrival at Plymouth. God bless you – believe me to remain with duty to Parents, love &c., &c.

Most affect^{ly} yours, John George.

*

124. Mr Stephen George, Blue Boar Inn, Haverfordwest.

Royal Marine Barracks
Apr. 10th 1807

My dear & hon^d Parents,

No doubt your anxiety for my safe arrival is great therefore have thus early resumed my pen. I came in about 5 last evening and was received in the most cordial manner by Curgenven where I slept. This morning I made my appearance at headquarters and shall commence soldier in 2 or 3 days. Two of Mary's letters soon after her marriage were taken up for me by a friend, had been in the West Indies and back so that the postage amounted to something considerable. I should not have taken them up myself neither shall I, should there be any old ones as the occurrences of H'west are well known after my long stay with my very dear friends. Believe me, neither distance nor absence will lessen the affection so truly grafted. Hope in course of time to be again enabled to meet your embraces.

At Swansea I met with unexpected attention from Mr Edmonds, who I met at the Tavern the coach stopped at. He took me to his house for breakfast and appeared uncommonly friendly: such conduct should not be forgot: indeed, I should be extremely glad to meet him here should he at any time come.

Mr Hill called on Curgenven yesterday morning but has not yet sent the things on shore: should he not this evening, shall call on board in the morning.

Tell William to call on Golding and desire him to send half a dozen views when they are finished and to wait for farther directions respecting the others. Curgenven has requested me to say so.

Remember me affectionately to Mary and her husband: in short, all friends: to the former, my next shall be: hope very soon to hear from you. You must excuse the shortness of this as my time is a good deal taken up in preparing my apartments for to reside in. Believe me to conclude with my prayers for your health and happiness, my dearest Parents,

Most affect^{ly} & dutifully yours, John George.

*

125. Mrs Green, Bridge Street,[88] Haverfordwest.

RM Barracks
Apr 18th 1807

My dearest Sister,

Tho' last, believe me, not the least in my affection since that never to be forgot parting under the Kilns. I have wrote two letters: the first to William, and the second to our dear Parents.

Here I am pretty comfortably settled having tolerable good apartments. Mr Harries is a close neighbour: we have already agreed to join breakfasts which will make it pleasant for each other. My old friends at Plymouth & Dock have very politely received me. The last evening I spent with a musical party through Mrs Taylor's introduction at Miss Somerville's, daughter of Captain S. of the *Nemesis*, who was on the Milford station in the Peace. We parted at an early hour : it is a rational way of spending an hour or two, much pleasanter than sitting down at a card table, or making too frequent use of the bottle, which is too frequently made use of here.

In my rambles, three days ago, I was really surprised in meeting Wm Davies's wife; she would have avoided me I believe if she could but we were so situated that it was impossible. What she is doing here, God knows. I never had so much cause to suspect the rectitude of her conduct before, She stopped and merely put & answered general questions, and bid me good morning; if her proceedings were just, she would have at least said where she resided and the cause of her being here, but not a word. I am really sorry for Davies, unless she has given him some satisfactory account of herself; she knows of him being in Wales, however. I'll say no more: you had better inform him of it. Tell him I have not yet had an opportunity of calling with his letters.

Remember me kindly to Mr & Mrs Davies: inform the latter I have seen her brother, who asked much for her: her sister's letter I forwarded to the former, say. Mr Pleace regretted much the shortness of the letter, but rejoiced much his doing well in business.

My embarkation is quite uncertain: suppose not before the fall of the year, therefore think it probable I may be down again some part of the summer. Mr Hill has sent my things on shore but has not called himself. I sent a servant on board with a note two or three days ago to ask him but did not receive an answer.

Curgenev is gone to London. I have promised to substitute him should John Mathias and his wife call in his absence, a task I can't very well dispense with. I hardly think Mr & Mrs Crimes are arrived or should have seen them, being a good deal in the neighbourhood where the mother resided, the Mathias's in Short Row.[89] Remember me to Cousin Sally and make my best regards to our Cardiganshire friends.

April 19th William's most welcome letter I received on going into Plymouth last evening. The welfare of my dear friends you must allow afforded me the greatest pleasure. For the future you had better address for me here as the one yesterday was at Curgenven's & which I should have had much sooner.

I am glad to find William's charger is sold, indeed for more than he could have expected. I know him to have been a great eyesore to Mother: the two mares are quite sufficient for the house, therefore useless beasts are always best disposed of. To William I give great praise for his letter: it far exceeded my expectation. Tell him my next shall be for him.

Mrs Whitham's conduct has been highly insulting throughout, therefore her passing in triumph by our [   ] she must confess from infancy [   ] I am not surprised at proceedings at Hook [   ]

My knee is quite recovered [   ] from which I suffer no inconvenience [   ] pain me a little bit, but nothing to speak [   ] exactly. Do write me an answer to this as soon as convenient. To Green remember me affectionately – to his mother & sister also: the latter's health hope in this is perfectly restored. My dear Parents duty, William, Grandmother & friends love,

John George.

I mustn't forget little Mary: tell me if she is grown much since I saw her.

*

126. Mrs Green, Bridge Street, Haverfordwest.

Royal Marine Barracks, Plymouth
June 9th 1807

My dear Sister,

An unusual long silence occasions my taking up my pen, not having heard from Wales since the beginning of last month. Since that period have wrote I believe by two opportunities, the last by Captain Mathias whom I met here a fortnight ago with his wife: as I entrusted them with two or three letters with a small parcel for Mother: hope he or she availed themselves of an opportunity of calling.

The Cambrian has informed me of Lord Milford[90] again succeeding to the County. I shall neither express my regret or joy, not knowing the sentiments of our friends. Harries is still with me but expects shortly to embark, as well myself, how soon or what ships we may be appointed to is uncertain: a future day will explain when you will soon hear of it. By Capt. M. I had an opportunity of sending Sally Mathias (I hate the formal 'Miss') a favourite piece of musick which I hope she will make herself perfect in by the time I see her: tho' not acquainted with the Pianoforte hope she will get Miss Jane Jones or some friend to instruct her.

Tell Davies I have seen nothing of Mrs Davies since my first, therefore suppose she has left this: I fear much a prison will be his fate unless he can, thro' her, compromise with the creditors. Pray how did his love affair at Newport luminate,[96] has he advanced or what? to preserve silence.

I have been fortunate enough in getting a very friendly introduction to the wife and daughter of a Captain Thomas who lived not long since, I believe, in Pembroke: he is at present absent abroad: was brought up under Captain Tasker of Upton: they reside in a very elegant house about a mile out where I have an opportunity of taking a pleasant stroll when inclined.

My dear little Mary I hope is well: I long for a confirmation, do write me soon and pray don't let your nursing deprive me of a long letter. I really fancied myself yesterday in Bridge Street being in a friend's house who had just made her appearance after her confinement with a crib (the only one I had seen) exactly like yours. I hope you enjoy much of Greenhill,[91] it is a delightful situation and am convinced would promote health. Bridge Street, you must be fully aware, is in a very unwholesome situation, therefore take my advice and embrace as much of the former as possible.

Remember me affectionately to Green, his mother and sister. Mr Davies, his wife, & friends, my best regards.

I have wrote a second letter to George Robbin requesting his assistance to James which I have not a doubt it will be readily complied with. I had not time to write to James but hope you have by the last Malta Packet which sails the first Wednesday in every month: it will be most advisable to post pay the letters.

My worthy friend the Surgeon of the *Fisgard* is coming home having been invalided after severe indisposition. A dreadful mortality have taken place in the ship by fever. Peregrine was unwell late in April – you had better not mention the sickness to his friends as it may distress them.

Excuse me adding more: except the arrival of Sir Sydney Smith yesterday from the Mediterranean, I have no news whatever Believe to remain with duty, love, £c., £c., my dear Sister,

Most affectionately yours, John George.

Mr Harries's remembrances to you, having met you at St David's.

*

127. Mr Wm George Kensington Place, Haverfordwest.

RM Barracks, Plymouth
July 14th 1807

My dear Brother,

Your two kind letters I have received; in reply, have to assure you I shall take every proper step to procure leave once more to approach the embraces of my dear friends. I am almost certain it will be 3 or 4 months before it comes to my turn foe sea duty. I hardly entertain a doubt the General will refuse to forward my application, tomorrow shall determine it. Though the weather at present has set in unfavourable for travelling, should I succeed, shall go to Bideford and take the chance of a vessel crossing for limestone.[92]

It affords me great satisfaction to find I possess still the goodwill of our Penlan friends: Miss Jane is certainly a character that must gain admiration as being destitute of pride and affectation, so much attached to girls of her situation in life. Was I blessed with a good fortune, I don't know a person I'd sooner tender it to than her, but, alas! I fear it is not ordained so, we must content ourselves with the situation we are appointed to and hope 'All's for the best'. You find that I am inclined to philosophise this morning, indeed it is so wet & gloomy that it invited me to proceed. Writing, you know, I am fond of: had I an opportunity of sending my letters free, should very often.

Remember me kindly to our upper country friends thro' the medium of

174

S.M.[93] – probably they may be down to the races but the society they, of course, will mix with, will prevent you speaking with them. Harries is now with me, he intends giving me letters for his friends which of course I shall forward – an introduction I don't look for, indeed don't want – he expects to sail almost every day, it is believed for the Baltic. You astonish me by saying Father has made an addition to his stud for I thought it was his intention of reducing it by selling his last – pray where is the little mare? Is she not to be rode this summer? I shall avoid Somerset for the future: the Penguin one has completely sickened me tho' I have not the smallest pain from either my shoulders or knee, the latter has made me knock-knee'd by having a large lump upon it, but of no inconvenience whatever.

Our Cousins not fifty miles from Tom Davies's I fancy will be well attended during the race week, a difficult matter to speak to them: you must if possible engage them for a walk in order to establish our fame. I shall long to see the stranger, as she must be very beautiful indeed from your account. Keep W Davies from the house, as there is no resisting him, being such a fascinating fellow.

July 15th This morning's paper has damped my prospects of yesterday in consequence of the almost certainty of a Danish war, no doubt every exertion will be made to hasten ships for sea: in consequence, fear the Admiralty will refuse to grant leave, indeed was there a prospect of my soon embarking would not relinquish my chance or any consideration: a few days long must determine it, when you shall immediately know the result. Surely, I could never have raised expectations to such a pitch as you mentioned in your last for I requested you in all my letters not to be sanguine: believe me, if I can with credit to myself obtain leave, I will.

We are making great preparations for the reception of our Commandant who is expected here in a few days from London. Both old and young are out every morning a 6 o'clock: as for myself, the very important duty I am appointed to at the Hospital precludes me from every other.

I long much to pay a second visit to the Danes, tho' hope the Commander will be a man of greater abilities than the last, in Sir Hyde Parker, or it will be very bad indeed. No doubt the Russians & Prussians will be necessitated to stop their supplies by and by, which will occasion hostilities to commence, in that case we shall require a most formidable force.

Remember me dutifully to Parents, love to Mary, her husband, &c., &c., &c., and believe me to remain,

Most affectly yours, John George.

Write me almost immediately and let me know the news from both the upper and lower country. Has Mrs M. finished her snuff?

*

128. Mr Wm George, Kensington Place, Haverfordwest.

Royal M Barracks, Plymouth
Aug. 4th 1807

My dear Brother,

To remove suspense I thus early resume my pen: disappointment we must admit to, but to the point, I have this morning withdrawn my application for leave in consequence of the General sending for me saying that having had five months so very lately, he should subject himself to the censure of the Admiralty in forwarding my letter; that he won't be extremely happy to accommodate me in any other way. What could I say? I thanked him for his politeness and rather than subject himself to censure I would submit to any thing, so here I am having relinquished every thought of a visit to Wales for the present. Indeed I must confess I've been much indulged, more so than any at Quarters, therefore ought not to grieve at the disappointment: resignation is absolutely necessary, but enough. Assure our dear Parents that I have used every means to see them: sincerely hope I shall yet ere long. The budget of news you had for me, I shall expect very soon.

I fancy Mr Mends will leave this next week: I shall entrust him with a few letters: he has not seen his friends for five years, therefore it is natural to expect that he will succeed in his application.

I met Charles Phillips a few days ago who gave me a very pressing invitation to dine on the Phoebe: I partly promised but shall not, as the person who turns his back on my friends I conceive do so to me. I expected a long account in *The Cambrian* of the news, &c., but it was very laconic indeed. By the by, there is a quarter due for the paper, desire Potter to let it go on and I will settle with him half yearly.

I answered Mary's letter about ten days ago, which I hope she has received. Pray, who is Miss Green's favourite at the moment? I might add the plural number for she generally has more than one.

We have had our Commandant to inspect us, who passed very high encomiums on the Division. He dined with us last Saturday, having prepared a most sumptuous entertainment for his reception: of course, it is needless saying it caused a few headaches the following morning: for my own part I can assure you I was very steady, having left the table very early. The band attended in full uniform: in short, every thing passed off very well.

I have had two or three conversations with Captain Phillips respecting Penlan, &c. He spoke very highly of Miss Jane. I fancy he is little aware I am acquainted with his proceedings when in the county. Miss Betsy Hassall, I am told, is going to be married: pray have you heard any thing of it?

Where is the Captain, and how does he get on? I should not be much surprised if he was called for again, as they are getting every thing ready for sea in a state of forwardness. I fancy my embarkation will not be this 3 months therefore shall have frequent opportunities of hearing from you: do write me soon: believe I feel the greatest pleasure in parting with my money for postage. With duty, love, &c., &c., &c., I remain, dear William,

Most affect^{ly} y^{rs}, John George.

*

129. Mr Wm George, Kensington Place, Haverforwest.

RM Barracks, Plymouth
Aug. 26th 1807

My dear Brother,

Yours of the 13th I have received in consequence of an unexpected change. I embarked yesterday on board the *Garland*, a very fine new ship rated 22 guns but mounting 34, the Captain and officers seemingly pleasant, the former is mentioned in the highest terms as an officer who would do his utmost to promote the welfare of those subordinate to him, therefore I am fortunate so far, and should there be a rupture with America, I think we shall do well.

I should be glad to know what Plymouth news Davies expects? Had he given me 'Mary Martain's' address perhaps I might have collected some, but most likely this beautiful girl is nothing more or less than some old bag not worth the trouble of enquiring after. My compliment. Tell the Captain as we are close to Torpoint I shall endeavour to see the beautiful Miss Jackson but most likely I shall be disappointed. I must confess you astonish me much in saying Davies had not dined with Green since his arrival in the county: I think he ought to have asked him merely out of compliment to the family but probably they had other reasons for doing so. It appears strange certainly but I hope he is not much hurt at the seemingly inattention.

Should we go abroad I shall discontinue taking up *The Cambrian* as it will be a difficult matter to get them forwarded. I long for Sally Mathias's tough story respecting Penlan, &c, &c: pray is her neck as stiff as it used to be? If so, would advise her to consult some professional character in order to render it more agreeable, particularly to strangers. I would wish you to mention it to her, as I would not like to conceal what is so much to her advantage.

Mr Rees's letter enclosing 3 for the Mediterranean I have just received which I shall forward agreeable to his request – his frank cost me 3s. 8d. as being over weight which of course he will refund you as he cannot suppose I would be at the expense: you may mention my paying the postage which I suppose he would immediately pay, but would not wish you to demand it.

Tell Tom Davies Mrs Hawkins's letter was sent immediately I received it to Mr Curgenven to be forwarded: make my best regards both to him and his wife, indeed as well to those few you can class as friends and acquaintances.

Our destination is unknown, but from the Captain's very great interest expect something good, most likely a foreign station as those class of ships are not well adapted for Channel service. I would not advise Davies to apply for employ, as he is much better on half pay.

Address your next which hope soon to receive 'HM Ship *Garland*, Plymouth Dock'. Believe me to remain, with duty, love, &c., &c., dear William,

Most truly & affect^{ly}, John George.

The *Fisgard* is expected home in 3 weeks but expect Peregrine will be left at Caracas.

*

130. Mr Wm George, Kensington Place, Haverfordwest.

HMS *Garland*, Plymouth Sound
Sept. 18th 1807

My dear Brother,

Your kind letter I should have answered long ere this but waited from day to day with the expectation of knowing our destination, still we are kept in suspense the ready for sea. We dropt into the Sound five or six days ago and fancy our leaving it will be very sudden as it is very probable we will sail with dispatches. The surrender of Copenhagen, as well our unfortunate transactions in the Rio de la Plata, of course you are acquainted with therefore shall say nothing on those points. Another expedition is shortly expected to sail, supposed for Madeira: some Artillery, &c. embark here and people have so far conjectured that we accompany them: time alone will reveal it.

Pray who is Captain Hunt Davies alluded to for his Prize Money? Tell him if he gives me the address with power to receive any he may be entitled to, I will call, otherwise it will be fruitless. You had better discontinue *The Cambrian* at the expiration of the half year as it will be quite uncertain my getting them regular and you may have frequent opportunities of sending some old ones to

Curgenven. By the by, a thought has struck me: pray where are the views Golding was to have sent here? As they have not been received and no account sent of them, be particular and let me know soon in answer to this in order to [reassure] any supposed inattention on my part. I have frequently put the question without getting a reply and as you mentioned in a former letter your sending a chart of Pencaer[94] in the box for me I am still astonished. I shall write today or tomorrow to London and shall suggest the tailor to send you the leather breeches but are puzzled what to say as to size but shall endeavour to describe it as a size or two larger than mine.

I hope George Robbin has paid James some little attention ere this. I cannot agree with Mr Moore in wishing him to run, as it would be the worse thing he could do. We may go to the Mediterranean, which should, even would, enable me to interest myself a little for him. I sincerely hope I may have it in my power, as he must think it strange my not writing for such a length of time.

Tell Mary her letter afforded me much satisfaction and shall soon answer it.

Watson, Mr Peregrine's son-in-law, is here: I am told he wishes to join the ship. I hope he may, as we want a person of some stability as 2nd Lieutenant.

Remember me dutifully. Mr Rees's letters are forwarded agreeable to his wishes.

Affectionately, &c., to relatives and believe me to remain, my dear Brother,

Faithfully yours, John George.

*

131. Mrs Green, Bridge Street, Haverfordwest.

Garland, Plymouth Sound
Oct. 13th 1807

My dear Sister,

Accept my warmest acknowledgement for your affectionate letter which I received some days ago. We are ordered to prepare for sea immediately but our destination is yet unknown, suppose the Mediterranean, in that case shall endeavour to get James here, indeed I have hardly a doubt that I shall succeed as the Captain appears to be a most pleasant man. Your last mentioned you having packed good butter this season: pray did you receive a letter on that subject from Mrs Curgenven as she speaks much of disappointment in not getting your answer, indeed I must, knowing your punctuality on those occasions, request you will write to her informing her if you can, or cannot, supply her wants: surely it can't mean any thing to Green as payment will be just as good as sending it to Bristol and Peregrine will, I am convinced, at all times be happy to forward it. I must beg you will write immediately to remove any unpleasant remarks which I must confess I have been obliged to listen to, but enough.

Your dear little Mary's health ere this I hope is completely restored. I long to see her but fear it will be some time before I shall: resignation is necessary for every class in life, particularly for a sailor & as I give myself the credit of possessing a good stock, we will hope to meet each other's embraces yet some future day. You must know well your letters at all times afford me infinite pleasure, therefore any leisure moment you might have, hope you will devote a part in assuring me of your welfare. Tell William he shall hear from me when we know our destination which I expect will be in a few days.

John Mathias, I hear, is Mayor for the ensuing year. What a change. It reminds me of a little story of Whittington & the cat which I dare say you recollect. Mrs M. is a good creature but those honours I fear will cause a change.

You must excuse the shortness of this as I am much engaged at present with Mess concerns preparatory to sailing. Remember me dutifully to Parents, love to William, Green, &c., &c.,. and believe me to remain,

Affect^{ly} yours, John George.

Address your next to the care of Mr Taylor, No. 29 Durnford Street, Plymouth. Best regards to Mr & Mrs Green.

*

132. Mrs Green, Bridge Street, Haverfordwest.

Garland, Cove[95]
Nov. 10th 1807

My dear Sister,

We are now getting under weigh with a fine wind for Jamaica. I regret now leaving the *Fisgard* as it is a station I am convinced will agree with my constitution: of course, debility must at first take place going into so warm a climate but I can assure you since I left I have not been clear of an oppression on my breast which in the country I was perfectly rid of. A continuation of our correspondence, believe me, will be gladly looked for, therefore beg you will write me by the next Packet addressed 'Port Royal, Jamaica'.

I heard today from Mr Peregrine: I cannot but express my astonishment at not hearing from William in reply to mine prior to my leaving Plymouth. I hope he has received the box containing leather breeches, as I write by this post requesting my Agent to settle with the tailor.

Let Mrs Summers know I heard lately from George Robbin that he is very well and is surprised he has not heard from his friends for a considerable time past.

Remember me affectionately to Green, his Mother & Sister, dutifully to Parents, love to William, &c., &c. Believe me to remain, my dear Mary,

Most affect^{ly} yours, John George.

*

133. Mr Wm George, Kensington Place, Haverfordwest.

Garland, off St Domingo
Feb 14th 1808

My dear William,

To remove any uneasing relative to my safety, I avail myself of an opportunity of sending this to Port Royal to be forwarded by the first packet: indeed, I should have written prior to my having it five weeks ago but having had occasion to write to Mr Peregrine relative to his son and requesting him to say I was well, an unnecessary expense of postage, I thought acidly.

The present cruise will expire about the latter end of April when I hope to receive your letters: I long much for the time, as I have not heard a syllable from Wales since the beginning of November. You will hear long ere this the Americans having laid an embargo on their shipping; how it will luminate is at present a doubt; so far it is certain they intend taking a part in the common contest. Jefferson is inclined to favour the French but the general voices are for us – a few days or weeks must determine this. We have already this cruise captured a Spanish schooner, recaptured a small English one and detained an American, but as the expenses are so very extravagant in this country, prize money is not to be considered, as it is received and expended the same moment. I share with my brother officers in the *Phoenix*, therefore trust to hear some good news from him on my arrival, having two things to my bow might not agree with the general opinion, but as it is done there is no retracting. The *Phoenix* is one of the finest frigates in the Navy, therefore the chances are equal.

My dear sister, when you receive this, is perfectly recovered from her confinement and that I may shortly have to congratulate myself on a second relation. Remember me affectionately to her & to Green; to my dear Parents say everything for me, that I enjoy good health, & to our Cardiganshire friends, &c., &c., remember me kindly. Should James be in England advise him (should he have an opportunity) to pass at the Trinity Board for a Master, let me know by first packet as I will solicit Sir T. Thompson to forward his proposition. Believe me to remain, my dear William,

Affect^{ly} yours, John George.

I saw Billy Howells' son, the writer (John) at Kingston: time would not permit me to be in his company. Should my letter to Mr Peregrine have miscarried, say Hugh is in the Bachante on this station.

*

134. Mrs Green, Bridge Street, Haverfordwest.

Garland, Port Royal, Jamaica
Apr. 26th 1808

My dearest Sister

The convoy leaving this for Europe tomorrow, I avail myself of the opportunity of assuring you I am still in being and, thank God, in tolerable health. We have had only one cruise, on our first arrival, and mean to commence another in a few days. The packet arrived yesterday & not a line from my friends, not even since the middle of October last. Pray what am I to conclude from it? I have only to assure you the welfare of my dear friends at all times, a confirmation of afforded me the greatest pleasure – indeed, I mistake, it was in September I received your last, but as I am not much inclined to write from your 'supposed' silence, I will conclude with duty, love & affection, my dearest Sister,

Faithfully yours, John George.

Peregrine is well.

*

135. Mr Wm George, Kensington Place, Haverfordwest.

Garland, off St Domingo
July 16th 1808

My dearest brother,

We left Port Royal four days ago with the Packet to convoy her clear of the

Islands: by her I avail myself of the opportunity of assuring you I am still in existence and, thank God, enjoy tolerable health. I can't assign any reason whatever but silence that your letters should not reach me, as I have received answers to others from another quarter and indeed sorry should I be to tax you with inattention, or even allowing that I did so, that I should retaliate, for I well know the dread the people of Europe entertain of the climate that it would be the extreme of cruelty in my doing so, I hope, indeed flatter myself with the certainty of all doubts being cleared up by the perusal of your long expected & long wished for letter on my arrival in post from our present cruise.

Lately I have met with three or four neighbours, one a boy belonging to this ship of the name of Jones, who used to work on the farm with John Anthony: his father, a Militiaman, and his mother, lived in the house next to George Bevan's, on the Back: he is a quiet boy, in consequence have got the Captain to take him as assistant to his steward. The next is Wm Owens, (formerly of the Packet house), who is out on promotion: he begged his kind wishes to you and requests you will let his friends know he is well. A Captain John Thomas of Brawdy (master of the Diana from Bristol) I also met with and was much entertained by his company: indeed, I feel gratified at all times in having a little conversation with a neighbour relative to the county: as it's most likely you will see him you will have an opportunity of sending me a pile of *Cambrians* as he comes out again soon: address for me to the care of Messrs. Harper & Conway, King Street, Kingston.

I want much to know where James is: if in England I would advise him to pass at the Trinity Board for a master which would be the best thing he could do at the moment: between you & I. I intend assisting him as far as I can when in a way for promotion but as midshipman, those little things would be uselessly thrown away. Let me request you will write to me by first packet after you receive this: say what ships the Evanses of Mabws[96] belong to as I should like to see them on the family's account.

Tell Sally Mathias (to whom & family remember me to) when she writes to the upper country to make my sincere regards to our friends. About next [summer] I hope that I shall be leaving this country: indeed it would be very improper my doing so before, for at the best time, you know I am not of the strongest constitution and to arrive in England in the winter would be the almost certainty of bringing on my old complaint.

My dear sister, with her little family, I hope are well; her last confinement, I trust, turned out favourably: remember me affectionately to them with Green, his mother, sister, &c. If the Captain is still with you tell him his mahogany colour friends in this part of the globe say he ought not to neglect the little ones. Miss Sophy is grown a very fine girl and very soon likely to have 'Man for true'. We must quiz the old boy: make up a good story for him.

To my adored and affectionate Parents, say every thing for me; a short time yet and I hope to meet their warm embraces: indeed, all friends include in my regards, tho' very few you will find of that description in our neighbourhood, but I will not croak. Believe me to remain, my dear William,

Affectionately yours, John George.

You have no occasion to pay postage for my letters as they come out [by packet]. Mr Peregrine's son is well: he expects his ship will shortly go home. Captn Thomas is well acquainted at Mr Attwood's;[99] should he not pay Wales a visit, his address is No. 56, Queen Square. He goes home with this month's convoy.[98]

Appendix I

𝔇r. 2nd. Lieut. 𝔍no. George in Account with George Kempster:

				£ s d
1800	May	To paid your Bill J[no] Birch	12 Apr	21.
	Jun 30	To do. purchase 2 eighths Irish Lott. Ticket	" "	2. 6. 0
	Oct	To do. your Bill J. McArthur	3 Sept	30.
	"	To do. " " J[no] Birch	29 "	10.
	Dec	To do. " " " "	25 Nov	15.
1801	Feb	To do. " " W[m] Turner	27 Jan	15.
	Mar	To do. " " J[no] Birch	19 Feb	12.
	Jul	To do. " " 1st. Ex Alex Hogg	7 Jun	20.
	Sep	To do. " " 1 Ex " "	29 Jul	10.
	Oct	To do. " " 1 Ex " "	24 Oct	10.
	Dec	To do. " " 1 Ex " "	16 Nov	15.
	"	To Agency £4. 4. 0. Postage 13/11.		<u>4.17.11</u>
				171.18. 8
1802	Jan 13	To paid subscription two prints Battle of Copenhagen		1. 1. 0
	Feb	To do. your Bill 1st. Ex A. Hogg	17 Dec	10.
	Mar	To do. " " 1 Ex " "	20 Jan	10.
		To Agency £1.1.0. Postage 2/11.		<u>1. 3.11</u>
				22. 4.11
		To Balance		<u>26.14. 6</u>
				£<u>48.19. 5</u>

185

1800	Mar 31	By balance from	4. 9. 6
		Mr Coombe's Books	
	June 3	By draft on Dosset & Co.	10.
	" 13	By Prize Money for 3 Frigates	8. 2. 6
		& 3 Brigs taken 1799	
		By 275 days' Pay for 1st April	64. 3. 4
		to 31st December	
1801		By 365 do. for 1st January	85. 3. 4
		to 31st December	
			171.18. 8
1802		By Balance of Account	6.14. 9
		By 181 days' Pay for 1st January	42. 4. 8
		to 30th June	
			£48.19. 5

Errors excepted
  G. Kempster

No. 3 Marlborough Street. 3 July 1802

Sir,

In compliance with your request, above you have a statement of your account from 1st. of April 1800 to 30th June 1802. The only Prize Money received in your account is £8.2.6 and I have not heard of any other payment.

I am,
Your very humble servant,
G. Kempster.

Appendix II

REMARKS made on Board His Majesty's Ship *Bellona*, 1799:

April 24th 1799. Embarked on board HMS *Bellona* together with Lt Watson, 2 Serjeants, 1 Drummer and 20 Privates in Hamoaze – nothing material till the 30th at 2 a.m. – received orders to prepare for sea immediately, all hands being turned up began bending sails and by daybreak got all bent, sent to the Gun Wharf for our guns and by 8 a.m. got the Lower Deckers in. At noon cast off from the moorings and warped towards the Lower Buoy. The pilot came on board. Received 100 men from HMS *Cambridge* to assist: employed warping down the ship, hoisting in the guns, setting up the lower and top-most rigging, bringing on board stores, &c. p.m. the wind setting in against us, took in the moorings again: heard the French Fleet were out, 19 sail-of-the-line.

May 1st a.m. Light airs, made the Signal for Assistance, employed getting in stores and preparing for sea. Noon: light airs favourable, slipt the Bridles and ran out into the Sound – from thence into Cawsand Bay, found riding there the *Robust, Ramillies, Saturn, Canada, Atlass* and *Triumph* moored. Nothing material happened 'till the 6th when Admiral Sir Allen Gardiner arrived, and the *Repulse* and *Captain*. On the morning we received 40 empty casks from the *Atlass*; no good sign, everything secret. At 11 the Capt. went on shore, but no other person permitted. We had the good fortune of getting off, thro' Mr Birch, a sheep and two small pigs for the price of £5. 1. 0. At 11 a ship appeared off the Bolt Head, every glass looking at her when she made the signal to weigh, which was repeated by Sir Allen Gardiner in the *Royal Sovereign* with the *Bellona, Captain, Defiance* and *Repulse*'s pendants, also the *Phoenix* frigate, therefore instead of preparing to dinner it was all hands unmoor ship and at 1.30 we weighed with a light air at SE and got out of the Bay and joined HMS *Queen Charlotte* – Rear Admiral Whitehead. Cheered Dº as did every ship – every Capt. went on board agreeable to form. At 4 made sail down Channel, 5 sail of very smart ships and noble Admiral; light breezes and favourable weather. On the 11th made Cape Ortegall [   ] variable winds and weather, nothing material till 16th off L[isbon] after making the *Phoenix*'s signal to weigh, the Admiral made [the fleet] steer S.

till 8 p.m. and prepare for close action and repair which made us conclude he had some information from [the way] he spoke and the *Phoenix* being off her station continued till [   ] making the best of our way for Gibraltar and at 8 a.m. [   ] the Bay found from information that the French Fleet had [   ] days 19 sail-of-the-line and the Spaniards 6 days with 23 sail [   ] Fleet between both with only 13 sail. At 10 we bore up to join Lord St Vincent's or any person having the command. 21st spoke [to the frigate] *Caroline* and her convoy from Minorca who informed us [that the] Spanish Fleet of 10 sail were off Algiers part of which were [partly] disabled in a heavy gale of wind. Nothing of consequence till the 27th when we spoke a Privateer belonging to Gibraltar who [   ] as Lord St Vincent had then 26 sail-of-the-line and was at Mahòn. 30th Off Mahòn. Admiral sent on shore for intelligence. At 6 p.m. [   ] the Admiral having information that the Fleet were off St Sebastian or Roso Bay.

On the 1st June joined Admiral Lord St Vincent and his fleet. 2nd a.m. Light airs. The *Ville de Paris* parted company 3rd Off Toulon and on the Heiris Islands is a bold coast with every opening fortified & large Batteries. 4th Light airs. 7 p.m. abreast of Nice several volleys were fired at our brigs and small vessels passing.

Nice has [a] battery on the south side before you come to the town. The town [is on the] water's edge and, at sea, appears to have 2 gates on the north entrance [   ] & Ville Francoes is a grove of trees appearing as an island [with] batteries also a tower on the E side and a battery on the point. It being unfavourable in the evening, tacked. 5-8 a.m. Close in and observed Remo on our landward bow, a larger town on a point apparently, seen with glasses near the point & between C. Francoes & Remo there is a lighthouse nearly like the Eddystone. The land abounds with points and hills, [   ] are in every bay & villages innumerable every hill having a town, the next is St Leorenza, a large town seemingly unfortified having many churches and cathedrals and a number of houses along the seaside and on the declivity of a hill next to which for information is Orsilla, a large looking town which at present appears very pleasant. There is a large place near the Point, Milan, having a number of churches and houses. Milan makes in a bluff & you, in going to the eastward lose sight of the land without you are very near inshore. 6th 5 a.m. Light airs. Pt Meline Nd nearly 4 leagues observed the land trend to the northward we steering E all well set. At 10 the wind came to the eastward blowing fresh. Admiral made the signal to bear up for Minorca on steer SW and at noon dispatched the *Bellerophon* and *Powerful*, the Fleet steering SW and a fresh gale. At 7 p.m. the *Centaur* spoke a Swedish brig & immediately made the signal of having intelligence to communicate: the fleet brought to: made sail.

7 a.m. Light airs & hazy [sun] to look out. At 12 light airs & variable. 3 p.m. Bore up: very squally. 5 a.m. The Admiral spoke a merchant ship which continued with the fleet. Noon. 24 sail in company, 18 of the line. 10. Very light airs employed airing the people's bedding. Master on a survey on board HMS *Edgar*: gained information that 10 sail-of-the-line & 4 frigates were round C Melline at anchor when we were off that point. Fleet very well collected. a.m. Light airs. Calm. Sent on board the Admiral's a Petty Officer. Received orders to have our men in readiness for landing in case of a signal being made and proper Officers with them. 8 p.m. The high lands of Minorca SW 10 leagues: received 30 hogsheads of wine (Prize) from St *Theresa* per Launch,: made sail. Men employed stowing wine away, hoist in the Launch. 12th. a.m. Light airs from the northern^{d,} at 12 off Port Malone. Delivered 400 hammocks to 4 different ships, nothing material. 13th a.m. Sent an Officer on board the Admiral's for orders, &c. At noon, 3 transports came out with stores, &c. A general chase. 3.30. The *Centaur* made the signals Friends, they proved 7 Prizes to the *Ethalion* and *Phoenix*, laid on with stock. Hauled our wind again and stood for Minorca. 14th Had information that the French fleet were off C. Melline as before mentioned when we bore up. Lord Keith & Admiral Whitehead changed ships. p.m. Variable winds: Lord Keith went up to Mahòn in the *Thetis* lugger with the *Triton*. 15th a.m. Fresh breezes with drizzling rain. Fleet very compact, heard of Admirals Cotton & Collingwood coming to join with 12 sail-of-the-line. Our stock begins to run low, a plentiful scarcity of fresh stock in the Fleet. Paper has risen 20 per cent & mutton 2000, how we shall do in future God knows. It is truly ridiculous to see how absurd we are in nature & our fashions: was I to ask a friend to dinner and give him sheep's head and the neck made palatable with the liver, &c. fried, also a shoulder roasted with anything you please, it would astonish you to hear every person crying out for a sheep's head and I will thank you for the fry: this I have seen many times and out of 13 members, have heard 12 call for the head or fry preparatory to taking in stores for the several ships appointed. 17th Light winds, made sail from P^t Mahone, 19 sail-of-the-line & 6 frigates stood at anchor. 18th 4 a.m. Admiral made signal, a general chase, very light airs & variable, all vessels a long way astern except the *Centaur, Bellona, Captain* & *Defiance*. The St *Theresa* at 7.30 made the signal of an enemy NE&N, 5 sail very [   ] times. At 8 perceived them very plain at intervals. 9. The St *Theresa* led them & us; out boats to keep ship's head the right way. At noon, light air, the Fleet a long way astern, *Centaur* and us nearly close together. At 1.20 p.m. the breeze freshened from the wester^d all sail set, found enemy gained on them fast 3 ships & 2 brigs. 3. 1 brig tacked, fine breeze [   ] *Centaur* fired a shot at one and we fired at another & they both struck: the

Centaur made our signal to take possession of the Prizes and proceeded after the other frigates which she brought to: the *Triton* and *Captain* after [   ] brigs, the remainder of the Fleet scarce in sight. Employed shifting the prisoners; found the Prize to be *L'Junon* 44, *L'Courageux* 36 and *L'Alces* [   ] 36, frigates & the *L'Salamine* & *L'Alerte* of 14 guns each from the Bonaparte Army in Alexandria with 1 Admiral or General (Perry) they having very little provisions on board & bound to Toulon and was within 10 hours sail of it when captured; lay'd to shifting prisoners & securing prizes. 19th 6 a.m. The Fleet appeared on the lee quarter, bore up & joined them; sent an officer on board the Admiral per signal. Captain went on board Do 10. The Captain returned & sent the French Admiral on board the Commander in Chief's. Employed sending the prisoners on board the different ships per signal. It appears from the information of the prisoners that the army left were in a cold situation & that they had not heard from home near 15 months, know nothing respecting Ireland or any defeat the French had met with in Italy. They have let their beards grow to an amazing length and wore amazing whiskers truly frightful, and what with their natural dirt, truly disagreeable to every person: the ships and brigs have gone for Minorca. We hear that the Genereux and 2 more is in Toulon disabled. Our last pig is killed, therefore short commons. Nothing very material happened between the 20th and 24th. We were then joined by the *L'Espoer* and *St Theresa*, also the *Vancage*. The news from them was the French Fleet had returned to Toulon. 25th Off Genoa; sent a frigate with flag of truce but they fired on her. 26th Laying to off Do 27th 6 or 7 cartels came out for our prisoners to land them at Antibes as the French fleet had taken from Genoa 700 men and they expected the Austrians every day in the town therefore would have no French land.

Made sail to the westerd, a continual westerly wind till the 3rd July when we spoke to Russians who saluted the Admiral, got the length of Nice, information that the F. Fleet had been joined by 2 sail-of-the-line and were off St Sebastian; a foul wind – westerly and NW winds to the 6th when we made Minorca. 7th July, a.m. Was joined by Rear Admiral Sir C. Cotton in the *Prince*, of 98 guns and 11 more making us now complete 31 sail-of-the-line. Noon. *Queen Charlotte* anchored off Mahòn, the remainder laying on. 8th. We anchored being calm in 5 fathoms. Fort St Phillipe NW & W. 2 fathoms fine sandy ground about 2 miles from the shore. The Fleet employed watering and getting various stores and provisions from the different transports. The watering place at Mahòn is a long way up the harbour and the water very bad and difficult to get at for so large a fleet every one striving to complete his ship first and every exertion surely was made that could be in the small space of time. 8th About 10 o'clock weighed per signal. The Admiral with the *Van* and *Centaur* ran into Mahòn. 9th We anchored again. The *Phoenix* joined with information of the French & Spaniards having found a junction in Cartagena. The Admiral made the signal for the Fleet to come out but the wind being against them they could not till the 11th when they all got out but 3 sail: continued watering and getting provisions. During our stay here we endeavoured to get some stock but sheep and pigs were very dear and they very poor. Cabbages 6 for 5s 0d and onions in proportion, but as they knew we must have them they rose the market accordingly; there is a very good vegetable market when there is few shipping but so large a fleet made everything very dear; it affords plenty of stock for the inhabitants. There is a very good dockyard, with shears for dismasting any ship, and water plenty for her along side the wharf. I saw 27 sail-of-the-line in harbour at one time and I suppose a 100 merchantmen and transports. The forts, &c. are very strong, the harbour rather narrow and the entrance well defended against the attack of an enemy. The are plenty of headlands and heights to see the approach of an enemy. 14th The whole fleet weighed and made sail, 31 sail-of-the-line of which 12 are three deckers, under the command of Lord Keith. 15th Boarded a Brig: Prize to HMS *Ethalion* who informed us the French and Spaniards were sailed from Cartagena towards the Gut; nothing material till the 21st when the Admiral spoke to HMS *Argo*: the intelligence gained by her was that the French and Spanish fleet had passed the Gut 4 days before. 22nd Spoke HMS *Beaulieu* which confirmed the above account. 23rd Finding the wind still blowing strong into the Gut the Admiral stood over for Tetuan Bay and anchored with his fleet to water except the Rear Division. Rear Admirals Frederick and Collingwood which anchored in Mazareen Bay in 15 fathoms water, good ground; sent the launch a-watering, plenty of water for watering a fleet close to the boats in a small river; every ship had a Marine guard and carried 2 cartridges as a present before they would allow us to water. The Plague raging along the coast with great violence, we were not permitted to purchase any stock tho' there was plenty and we much in want, continued watering all night as did every other ship. 24th Light air; continued watering. 25th Weighed and made sail; received a quantity of bread and wine from various transports, as did every other ship that could come near enough to the transports which had come over from Gibraltar. 27th a.m. The Admiral stood over with the fleet for Centa Bay making the Montague's signal to lead and anchor: stood on in frustration and sounded from Tetuan Bay to Centa Bay from 15 to 10, 11, 12 fathoms about 1½ miles from the shore; very fine sand and clear. At 11 o'clock anchored per signal and out launch as did the fleet. At 12 the Admiral made the signal for 7 or 8 sail to weigh and run into Mazareen Bay and anchored again with the *Queen Charlotte* and 16 more and immediately began watering.

27th Employed watering and getting provisions from different transports. Weighed. Nothing material till the 30th, when we got a gale from the eastward & passed the Gut. 31st A flag of truce passed thro' the Fleet which was spoke by some of the frigates.

August 1st Passed Cadiz. No fleet there. 3rd The Impeleux saw an 80 gun ship under a battery with her main mast gone near Largos. 4th The Admiral formed a flying squadron of the *Triumph*, Admiral Collingwood, *Impeleux*, *Dragon*, *Centaur*, *Bellona* and *Beaulieu*. 6th Board a brig from St Lawrence for Lisbon laden with fish, £1.1.0 per hundred. No intelligence. On the 5th, about ½ after 5 p.m. when we were beating to quarters a very melancholy accident happened. Capt. E. Betty of Marines went to the 2nd Gallery and remained some time longer than usual; the door being opened he was found in an apoplectic fit; every means was used to recover him that ever was known by the Surgeon but to no effect; the next day he was opened and nothing appeared that could have occasioned his death either from decay of liver or any other apparent complaint. 9th 6 p.m. He was buried with the Honours of War. Being off C. Turiñan spoke HMS *Stag*, Capt. York, who gave information to the Admiral of having passed thro' the French and Spanish fleets on the night of Sunday (4th): being very dark they did not see him; they were at that time steering NE and a fine gale at SW, a very large fleet but had no opportunity of counting their force on account of the darkness of the night. 10th 11 a.m. The Admiral altered the code of signals for the fleet. Noon. A light air springing up from the westward, made sail. We are in hopes that the Channel Fleet will fall in with us, then they may be sure they will have very few to moor either in Brest or Cadiz. 11th Died Thos Wellinford, a seaman, of a decline; exercised guns, [muskets] & small arms & prepared everything for the formidable foe. Fearless English mastiffs will fight for their food, how much more would we who were fighting for peace & plenty. Nothing very material till the 15th, hearing with sorrow that the French fleet with that of the Spaniards had got into Brest. HMS *Impeleux* joined having counted 46 sail-of-the-line in Brest harbour. 15th continued blowing very heavy obliged the Fleet to bear up, some proving very leaky. 16th at 10 a.m. anchored in Torbay after a severe gale of wind which damaged many of the ships, especially the 3 decker *Princess Royal*, *London*, *Hector*, &c: found riding here Lord Bridport in HMS *Royal George*, Admiral & Commander-in-Chief, with [2] sail-of-the-line. Moored ship; prepared to water. HM Ships *Defence*, *Princess Royal*, *Hector* & *Prince George* weighed and ran for Portsmouth in consequence of their bad state: had an action commenced I must leave the reader to judge the consequences which must have attended so serious an undertaking in such crazy ships; found our bowsprit sprung in three places, also the naval piece of the hawse gone. 19th 10 a.m.

The *Marlborough* and *Edgar* parted company for Plymouth. 22nd Went on shore, purchased 4 sheep, 6 pigs, 16 geese and sugar & tea in proportion, the looking forward to prevent our starving at sea again. At 4 p.m. received orders to proceed to Plymouth to refit and get a bowsprit, unmoored and hove short. 5 a.m. Weighed and made sail, working down Channel; at 11 passed HMS *Marlborough* and made the signal for a pilot. Noon. Anchored in Cawsand Bay in 10 fathoms water. Found riding here HMS *Triumph*, Rear Admiral Collingwood, *Windsor Castle*, *Namur*, *Gibraltar*, *Edgar*, *Warrior* & *Dean* and moored ship.

This finished the cruise from April 24th to Aug. 19th, the ship never having put into any port or anchored but to water off Mahòn & Tetuan. Captured 3 frigates, 2 brigs & 9 sail merchant ships & entitled to £10 Prize Money, besides being starved in order to be in readiness to live on our half-pay. Should we outlive the War may our next be a better & of a more valuable nature.

Appendix III

LETTERS FROM JAMES GEORGE

A. Mr William George, Blue Boar Inn, Haverfordwest.

> Her Majesty's Ship *Lucifer* off Southwold.
>
> Dec. 6th 1805.

Dear William,

With pleasure I take my pen in hand to write you these few lines in hopes that you may have forgave me for not writing before. I received Mary's kind letter of the 25th of November, the day we were ordered to hoist a signal for convoy to the eastward and I was as busy all that day giving instructions to the Swedish ships, for they are all foreigners in our convoy, and sailed the next day, or else I would have acknowledged the receipt of it before. We are going to Yarmouth first and then we shall know if we proceed to Gottenborough, with them or not. We are now about 20 miles from the port will be there about 2 o'clock when I shall send this on shore. Dear William, you mentioned of my having time to write to both you and Mary, but you are very much mistaken in that for when we are in harbour I am always in the boats, but I think you have plenty time nevertheless I miss one of yours

I received a letter from John [from] Cork, 14th November, by Mr Charles Phillips of *L. Argus*, Sub-lieutenant. He invited me to dine with him that day but being busy had not time, but I called. He was very well. Desired his compliments to you all & all friends in H'west. John was well likewise but sailed before *L. Argus* left Cork. Dear William, we have excellent weather & fine moon light nights We shall be soon in The Downs again so answer this in two or three days after you receive it and direct to The Downs. Mary asked me in her letter how much pay I received: tell her I thought she knew better than that, for I shan't have any until I am here a twelve month. Neither did I receive any from Captain Brown's. My pay here is £1. 14s. per month, so dear Brother, I must conclude with blessings to Parents, love Sister & Grandmother and, dear Wm, believe to be one of

> Your most affectte Brother, J[ames] George.

P.S. W. Davies desires his compliments to family.

B. Mr Stephen George,
     Blue Boar Inn, Kensington Place, Haverfordwest.

HMS *Lucifer*, Spithead
Dec. 10th 1806

Most Hond Parents,

With the greatest of pleasure I, this morning, received your kind letter of the 26th Nov. & 2 Dec., which both came to hand the same time. It gave me great pleasure in being assured of your welfare as this leaves me at present.

I return my poor Mary joy of her daughter [90] and hope if ever I should return to H'west to have the pleasure of embracing my niece. I begin to think myself a man, now Uncle.

My dear Parents, you are unwilling to believe that our destination is foreign but you might take my word we shall not be in England in a month's time. You talk about the ship being so small: she is as large again as the *Britannia*. Some say Buenos Ayres, others going with the *St George* to bombard the Havanah on the island of Cuba, others say that Sir Sidney Smith[99] have sent for us up the Straits & some says that we are going to the east with Sir Samuel Hood.[100] I can't tell you whether the Captain speaks authentic or not but he yesterday told the Doctor on the Quarter Deck that the *Meteor* & our-selves were ordered to Buenos Ayres. I would prefer going to the southward than northward.

I shall require to have a good deal of clothes, for I don't think we shall be home in less than two years at least. I got but £12.7.0 to receive, which will be very little to buy clothes for two years. Most hond Parents, I think I am one of your most unfortunate sons: it grieves me to the heart to think I am here away most of my life and can't do without troubling my friends: that one thing makes me very unhappy. Dear Father, I will allot half my pay home as we are going out of the land and then you will be able to receive it monthly £1.6.0 which will, if we are out any time, in a manner pay you. I can't see how John can be angry with me, for the last letter I had from him desired me not to wait till I heard from him again and I have not heard from him since. The *Triumph* is here. I wrote to William Davies yesterday: have not had an answer yet. All that I have got to wish for is that our Master gets appointed to another vessel before we leave the land. Then I should stand a good chance to win his buttons.

So I must conclude, with love to Mother & Sister & Grandmother, and all friends, and accept this, Most Hond Parents, from

Your affectionate & dutiful son, J[ames] George.

P.S. Write by return of post. Tell John I shall write to him in a couple of days & to Mary before we sail. Thanks for enclosure.

Dear Parents, we this morning received orders for to go with the *St. George* which is going convoy to the West Indies into a [   ] and then to go with the *Sabrina* up the Straits, so I hope you will let me have what I requested by return of post. For we shall sail the first opportunity.

C. Mrs Mary Green, Bridge Street, Haverfordwest.

Her Majesty's Sloop *Barracouta*
at anchor in Mera Bay, Straits of Sunda
29th September 1812.

My dear Sister,

I received your letter after arriving from a cruise off the east end of the Island of Batavia, the first person I met on landing was Mr Cobb who gave me the most gratifying information of having letters for me. Went on board with him; he is the 2nd mate of the *Marquess of Huntly*, Indiaman, and also a letter from my dear Mary and another from Green the first word I had of my friends since I left England, which is now near 3 years. I certainly was surprised at not finding one from Wm particularly as he knew they were coming out with a friend of mine. I hope little quarrels did not prevent you telling him of the opportunity, if not, I should think Wm. has more love for his brother than to slip such a chance considering the distance we are from each other. I wish you had told me what he does with himself, for since my Father has given up keeping House he can have no home and I sincerely wish he was married to some girl: this would take care of him, although I have pity for her for his temper. Do not show him this or he will be offended with me.

My dear Mary, what pleasure it gave me to find that our Father was with you and happy . I think I can draw his picture after dinner: there is my dear Father in the corner of the little parlour with a paper and a glass of warm Gin Toddy, little Mary and Jane, with the other little one, playing about his knee. I hope to be in Bridge Street to enjoy this scene before long. I hope my dear Father, nor any friend, can accuse me of neglect of writing for I assure you I have scarce missed an opportunity during in India and I always thought [to myself] that writing to one was writing to all but however I shall now know how to please you. I had the opportunity the other day of going to England but as I was not confirmed I joined this Brig with an old messmate of mine that is Captain. I am first Lieutenant of her: very comfortable and in good health, thank God, altho' this coast is reckoned the grave for all English men, but I think I shall disappoint them this time as our [tour] will be out in 2 months more.

I sent you by a Mr Reynolds, from near H'west, a few cornelians, likewise some for Wm's sponsor, supposing him married at the time I sent them. I do not think [I'll write] to any of the Haverfordwest Bucks [until I] return for not sending me the news.

Captn. Wm. Bowen who, if you recollect I mentioned in my letter from the Isle of France, died about a fortnight since at Batavia: he was a very fine young man and much regarded by all the Officers on this Island.

My dear Mary, I am very much obliged to your Green for his uniting his interest with my Father's for me & it is my most ardent wish that I might have an opportunity of showing him that I am not ungrateful. There is no news in this country. We are anxiously looking out for an American War that we might bring a few shiners home in our Packets. I have no doubt but my last appointment will be confirmed on arrival in England, it being a Death Vacancy. If I have a vote, give it to whom you please. Green gave me a hint about a little Parsell, I hope she will be disposed of to advantage for I have almost made my mind up to being an Old Bachelor. I do not know what the sight of pretty faces might do as to a change for we see nothing but black ones here.

Doctor George Phillips's son is Commandant at Macassar, and another Welshman, a Colonel Adams, is Commandant at Sourabaya, but they are 'the quality' and perhaps would think themselves above me was I to make myself known, so I will not for now. I meet them at publick places and my rank entitles me to all societies I have a mind to go to.

I have sent Wm. Howell letters to Bombay for him. Give my compliments to Miss Morris, to your friend Mrs Harries, Miss Green and all females that will condescend so far as to ask after Old George, as they call me in this country.

Nov. 5th, Augen Roads.

We arrived here this morning on our way to Batavia and from there shall go to Sourabaya to refit. I hope at Batavia to have an opportunity to send this, likewise one for Green and Father. From what you mentioned in yours, I suppose there is a good many letters kicking about for me: that is the worst of a foreign station: you cannot get your letters for yourselves but I am in hopes to get a few letters every year. [I] must not trust, only to my friend Bob. My best respects to Mr Morgan.

Love to your little family and duty to Father. I shall write to William by the opportunity likewise, and conclude, dear Mary,

Your affectionate Brother, J[ames] George.

D. Mrs John Green, Bridge Street, Haverfordwest.

HMS *Barracouta*, Simons Bay, Cape of Good Hope

June 20th 1814

My dear Mary,

We left Calcutta on the 11th of March in expectation of arriving in England in August but on our arrival at this place which, by the by, was after a very tedious and tempestuous passage of 95 days we are detained until the arrival of Troops from the *Isle of France* that is going home and our convoy, which cannot be until the middle of August in consequence of which our arrival in England will be November & I am afraid very cold weather it will be for us Indians: this is winter here and I assure you so cold that the thermometer stands at 54°. I am now shaking altho' in a close place that I can scarcely hold my pen. The merchant ship arrived from Batavia two days back and sails immediately with dispatches. I take advantage to let you know what is become of me for I really think you must be at a loss from my letters. This last eighteen months, my dear Mary, I am returning from India with the same charge against you on returning from the Mediterranean: only one letter this five years nearly, but my dear Sister I am confident when we meet you will be fully able to clear yourself of that charge: the fault must be in the conveyance as there are no regular packets for India.

I had several letters from John Napier while at Bengal and altho' in the same town together for three weeks never met nor did either of us know it until I had left town for the ship which was a hundred miles down the river. I have a letter for Mrs Napier which I shall send on my arrival in England or deliver myself giving my compliments to them & say that John was very well in health and likewise in a fair way of making a handsome fortune in a short time.

Capt. Pavin at Bombay was very kind to me: was he my father he could not have been more so. If you see any of his family say that he is very well and about leaving India.

My dear Mary, I only want one thing, that is to fall in with the *Hornet*, American sloop of war. I have no doubt as to the result. I should then, should the Almighty once more spare my life, return to my friends as a Captain. However, I must conclude hoping for the best, with duty to my dear Father, love to Brother, Green and family with whòm, I hope, next Christmas Day to eat a family dinner is the wish, my dear Mary, of

Your affectionate Brother, J[ames]George.

P.S. Excuse the scrawl for I really am so cold that I cannot steady my hand.

NOTES

1. The Reverend William Cleaveland, was rector of St Thomas á Becket Church, Haverfordwest, from 18 December 1777 until his death in 1799. That he was a man of influence is indicated by his ability to obtain a commission in the Marines for John George and, had he lived, no doubt, he would have helped the other sons, William and James, who found difficulty in obtaining sponsors to enter the Royal Navy. Cleaveland Row, now Upper Market Street, was named after him.

2. The Board of Admiralty comprised the First Lord of the Admiralty and a Civil Lord, both of whom were political appointments, together with a number of Sea Lords, who were naval officers: Admiral Sir William Young (1751-1821) had been appointed a Sea Lord in 1795.

3. Captain Wier, RN, appears to have had a connection with Haverfordwest: families of that name lived in the town. He was a friend of the Rev. Cleaveland, news of whose death George conveyed to him. George states that he was 'old and infirm' and suffering from the gout, and that he had two plain daughters. (11) He advised John George on the purchase of clothes, some items of which he was able to buy from the Captain's brother.

4. Stephen George, landlord of the Blue Boar Inn, was born in 1741. He was sheriff of the Town and County of Haverfordwest in 1791 and died in 1821. He married Jane Mathias in 1778 by whom he had three sons, John born in 1780, William, born in 1782, who served in the Royal Navy, and James, born in 1786, who entered the Merchant Navy and was press-ganged into the Royal Navy and was later a Lieutenant serving on HMS *Lucifer*. Mary, the only daughter, was born in 1781 and, in 1806, she married John Green, only son of John Green, sheriff of the town in 1781, of whom it was said that he presented his back to John Wesley, preaching in the street on his last visit to Haverfordwest in 1790, so that he could use it as a lectern. Descendants of the marriage include the founders of Greens Motors Ltd., and, in our time Colonel John Green, OBE, TD, DL, mayor of Haverfordwest in 1955, sheriff of the town in 1958 and sheriff of the county of Pembroke in 1970, and Malcolm Green, sheriff of the county of Dyfed in 1995.

5. The Blue Boar Inn stood 'near the West gate at the bottom of Dew Street', close to the junction of that street and Tower Hill, on or near the site of the present Registry Office. It appears to have been patronised by people of quality. A previous, less popular, landlord had requested a local rhymester to compose a verse to place on the sign, of which several versions exist: the following appeared in April 1752 under 'The Sign of the Blue Boar Inn':

> Our Landlord here,
> And sign, I swear,
> Are very near akin;
> An ill-shaped Boar
> Hangs at the door,
> And a grumpish Hog's within.

6. A Marine officer wore a smart scarlet tail-coat with elaborate cuffs, lapels and epaulettes, tight white breeches, low shoes and white silk stockings. Powell had misled George in his 'discourse' as to the cost of the initial equipment and of providing for himself in the Marines so that he was in a permanent state of financial embarrassment and having to borrow money to meet his commitments. His pay of £85.3s.4d (£85.17) per annum, or 4s.7d (23p) per day, was little more than enough to pay his Mess bill (Appendix I). His only hope for additional funds, he reckoned, lay in the Prize Money, namely, the net proceeds of the sale of enemy shipping and property captured at sea in time of war. His account shows only the prize money taken in 1799, amounting to £8. 2s.6d (£8.12), but this does not represent his total takings from that source. Aware of the sacrifice of his parents in getting him his commission, George was most anxious to convince them of his non-extravagance and he strongly refuted rumours circulating in Haverfordwest that he was living other than a straight life (15).

7. The Davieses lived at No. 6 Pall Mall.

8. Franking was the right to send a letter through the post, free of postage, by having its cover signed by an officer or a person in authority. George stated that one 'could get 2 or 3 franks or more if they are wanted,' (4) but there was a limit to the number obtainable. He had to pay 11d. for his postage. (91)

9. Billy was his brother William who was sixteen years of age and proving to be a difficult boy. He was showing signs of wanting to go to sea but George thought that it would be better for him to find a job ashore. Earlier letters refer to Price as though he were a member of the family but his identity is not discernible.

10. George would have bought China tea which had reached this country in about 1620 but only became fashionable with the advent of Catherine de Braganza on her marriage to Charles II in 1662. It was not until 1823 that it was discovered that tea was indigenous to Assam.

11. Lord K. was Lord Kensington, William Edwardes (1711-1801), the son of Francis Edwardes of Haylet, MP for Haverfordwest (1722-25), and his wife, Lady Elizabeth Rich. Lady Rich was the only daughter of Robert Rich 5th Earl of Warwick and 2nd Earl of Holland, by his wife, Anne, daughter of the Earl of Manchester, and was said to have fallen on hard times and had moved to live in Wales. On the death of the 7th Earl of Warwick and 4th Earl of Holland, unmarried in 1721, his estates passed to his cousin, William Edwardes, while his titles reverted to his kinsman, Edward Rich.

    Sir Henry Rich had married the daughter and heir of Sir William Cope, Chancellor of the Exchequer, who brought with her the manor of Kensington and Holland House, and he was elevated to the peerage as Baron Kensington in 1622 and granted an earldom, as Earl of Holland, two years later. Edwardes sold Holland House to Henry Fox.

    Charlotte, widow of the 6th. Earl of Warwick and 3rd Earl Holland, became the wife of the essayist Joseph Addison in 1715 whom she had met, it is said, when they were both at Haroldston, on a visit to Sir Herbert Perrot who, it is claimed, was the inspiration for Addison's eccentric character Sir Roger de Coverley in his contributions to *The Spectator*.

William Edwardes was returned unopposed as MP for Haverfordwest, from 1747 to 1784 and from 1786 to 1801. In 1776 he was granted an Irish peerage and took the title of Baron Kensington, of the second creation. He married, in 1762, Elizabeth, daughter and co-heiress of William Warren, formerly of Trewern, by his wife Jane, daughter and heiress of William Skyrme of Longridge, in the parish of Bletherston. He lived at Johnston Hall, purchased by his father in 1703, which he failed to maintain properly in his latter years. A contemporary commentator noted that 'his lordship seems an uncommon sloven if the traveller may judge from the appearance of the house and garden' and upon inquiry, 'found his lordship to be a miser and her ladyship a spendthrift.' He had a town house, Kensington House, on Tower Hill, now demolished, which stood near the Blue Boar. He was described as 'a mighty hunter', able to vault into the saddle when he was eighty-six years of age. He was aged ninety when he died in 1801.

12. Colonel William Edwardes (1776-1852) appears to have had rapid promotion as he was the 'Captain the Hon. William Edwardes' who rode off to Fishguard with Colonel Colby when the French landed, to assess the situation, and Lord Cawdor sent him, as one of his ADCs, to round up the surrendering French troops.

13. John Potter was a particular friend, whom George wished would be successful in his application to join the Marines, and understood that he had asked Lord Kensington to be his sponsor (30), but his application 'proved fruitless' (33) and he became an innkeeper (34). A reference to his 'reformation' (40) is intriguing. Potter was the son of Theophilus John Potter, an Irishman, who came to Haverfordwest with a company of Tragedians, settled and set up as a stationer, printer and bookbinder. In 1779, he married Elizabeth Edwards at St Martin's Church and in 1790 he was elected sheriff of Haverfordwest. Another son, Joseph, followed his father in the business and founded the Haverfordwest Literary and Scientific Society in Victoria Place, which was later transferred to High Street, on the site of the Imperial Buildings, where Potter's Library and Reading Room was established. The Reading Room was 'only open to the élite of the town'. He published *Potter's Electric News* in 1855, which was incorporated in the *Pembrokeshire Herald*, of which he also was proprietor. He was sheriff of Haverfordwest on four occasions, and mayor in 1843.

14. An early complaint about having to pay Income Tax. Tax on income was introduced by William Pitt in January 1799 when he remodelled the fiscal system in order to pay for the war against France. It was abolished by Henry Addington in 1802 following the Peace of Amiens, but he had to restore it in 1803 when war broke out again.

15. HMS *Lavinia* was a 44-gun frigate that was being built at Milford at the time but was not launched until March 1806. It was named after Lavinia, daughter of the Earl of Lucan, who had married Earl Spencer, First Lord of the Admiralty

1794-1801. The Countess Lavinia was known in naval circles as 'the Lady of the Navy'.

16. Mr Birch is mentioned more often than any other person, outside of the family, and yet he remains a mysterious figure. He first appears on April 19th, 1799 (16) when George abandoned the idea of dining with him and decided to reply to a letter he had just received from his sister. He constantly 'desires his compliments' to the George family in the letters up to 1803, when he no longer served on HMS *Bellona* and he often requested that his love be given to his wife as he was 'very busy doing the duty of the ship, otherwise would write', and would shortly do so. She appeared to be a wayward person who had no desire to remain in contact with her husband and was the object of concern to George who asked his sister to keep an eye on her and to help her find lodgings in Haverfordwest. Birch was obviously from Haverfordwest, and was known to the family. George describes him as 'my old friend': when *Bellona* returned from the West Indies, Birch came aboard at Spithead and took him to his lodgings in Portsea, which George used as his postal address (75). Birch was in London in December 1802 but George seems to have lost touch with him for a time and was glad to hear from him again in February 1804 (102).

   Birch's position and rank are never clear: in one place he is described as 'the Cater', in charge of the catering for the *Bellona*. He was promoted Surveying Master early in 1801 (65) and appears again in 1805 as Master Attendant at Sheerness (116) when George expects him to help his brother James, recently press-ganged, and instructs his sister 'if Birch has done nothing, write to him.' (117). He had already asked him to help William, while he was in London. In George's account with his agent, Captain George Kempster, for April 1800 to June 1802 (Appendix I), the item 'To paid your bill J^{no} Birch' appears four times for sums varying from £10 to £21.

17. HMS *Bellona* was built at Chatham in 1760 and had recently been refitted at Plymouth when George joined her on April 24th 1799. She sailed down the Hamoaze, the stretch of water between Torpoint and Plymouth, to join the Channel fleet on the 30th. George kept an account of his first voyage, to the Mediterranean, as 'Remarks made on Board HMS *Bellona*' (Appendix II). *Bellona* was with Lord Bridport's fleet off Brest early in 1800 On March 3rd 1801 she sailed in Lord Nelson's squadron to join Admiral Sir Hyde Parker in Yarmouth Roads from where they sailed on March 12th and anchored at the entrance to the Sound, leading to the Baltic Sea, on the 21st. On April 2nd, the ships weighed and took up their stations across Copenhagen harbour, where there are shallows. *Bellona*'s pilot led the ship too far to starboard and ran her aground near the rear of the Danish line, and Russell also ran aground with her bowsprit almost overlapping *Bellona*'s taffrail. The two ships were able to use their guns, although they were within range of the Danish fire. Some of *Bellona*'s guns burst, killing two marines and nine seamen, and injuring others, while the Captain Sir Thomas Thompson lost a leg. After refitting, *Bellona* joined the Channel fleet off Brest. In January 1802 she sailed to the West Indies

and returned from Jamaica on June 24th to Portsmouth where, early in July, she was paid off and laid up in ordinary.

18. Lord Bridport (Admiral Alexander Hood: 1727-1814) was Commander-in-Chief of the Channel Fleet from 1797 to 1800 during which time he maintained a continuous blockade of Brest. He was raised to the peerage in 1794 and advanced to the dignity of a Viscount in 1800 by which time he had been appointed General of Marines.

19. A ship-of-the-line was a man-of-war with sufficient gun-power to take a place in the line of battle. The ships were rated according to their gun-power: the first rate had a hundred or more guns, second rate had over ninety guns, and the third rate had seventy-four or up to eighty. Frigates were fully-rigged ships with up to forty guns on one complete gun-deck. A three-decker had three-gun decks. Below sixth rate ships were sloops, brigs, bombs, schooners and cutters. A bomb vessel was a floating siege engine, a broad ship with the foremast removed, carrying huge shell-firing mortars, mounted on reinforced beams, for bombarding stationary targets such as towns, fortifications and harbour installations.

20. Sir Thomas Boulden Thompson was in command of HMS *Bellona* at the Battle of Copenhagen, where he lost a leg.

21. Admiral Sir John Jervis (1735-1823), Commander-in-Chief, Mediterranean, and Commodore Nelson, with fifteen sail-of-the-line, defeated the Spanish fleet of twenty seven warships off Cape St Vincent in 1797. Jervis took command of the Channel Fleet in 1799 and, in 1801, he was made First Lord of the Admiralty and was raised to the peerage as Earl of St. Vincent. To George's great delight, he hoisted his flag on HMS *Bellona* in November 1800, having bought a house at Torbay for the winter, but disappointment was to follow when he removed it to the *Ville de Paris*. (58)

22. Admiral Sir Charles Cotton (1753-1812). When the French fleet escaped from Brest in 1799, Cotton followed it to the Mediterranean, whence he returned in company with Lord Keith. In 1807 he was appointed commander-in-chief in the Tagus and in 1810 to command the Mediterranean fleet in succession to Lord Collingwood; in the following year he was recalled to take command of the Channel Fleet.

23. Cartels were ships used to convey prisoners in war-time.

24. Admiral George Keith Elphinstone, Viscount Keith, (1746-1823), succeeded Lord St Vincent as Commander-in-Chief Mediterranean and blockaded the Italian ports.

25. Admiral Adam Duncan (1731-1804) was Commander-in-Chief North Sea from 1795 to 1801. On 11 October 1797, a French force of 15,000 men, having been assembled to attack Ireland and sailing out of The Texel, convoyed by a Dutch fleet, was destroyed by a British squadron under Duncan at the battle of Camperdown, a coastal village in Holland. This victory put an end to the danger of an invasion of England by the French and the Dutch. He was raised to the peerage as Viscount Duncan of Camperdown.

26. Mr Fortune's 'rash exit' was the result of a duel that had taken place ten days before he wrote this letter, on September 16th 1799. Samuel Fortune and his friend, John James, to whose sister he was engaged to be married, quarrelled over a trivial matter during which Fortune struck James with his whip. A week later, Fortune received a challenge to meet him in a field near Cartlett where James's second, Duvan, handed him a pistol and placed him at twelve paces. Fortune fired in the air, but James took aim and shot him in his side and he died the following day at his mother's house in Quay Street. James fled abroad and returned ten years later to inherit the estate of Pantsaeson, in north Pembrokeshire.

27. Admiral Sir John Borlase Warren (1753-1822) captured the French squadron that brought Wolfe Tone back to Ireland in Lough Swilly in 1798. In 1799 he was off Brest with Lord Bridport and, the following year, was with Lord Keith off Cadiz. In 1813 he was appointed commander-in-chief on the North American station.

28. The Duke of York, commanding the British army in Holland, ignominiously surrendered to the French at Alkmaar.

29. Mr Green presumably refers to John Green who was to become Mary's husband.

30. The reference to Davies the Jew is interesting. The only known Jewish connection with Haverfordwest at this time was provided by the two brothers Samuel and Moses Levi, immigrants from Frankfurt-am-Main. They were befriended by a man named Phillips whose surname, and religion, they adopted. An entry in the parish register at St Mary's Church, Haverfordwest, dated June 23rd 1755, reveals that 'Moses, a Jew, called Moses Phillips, aged about two and twenty years', had been baptised, and that he had married Anne Morgan the previous year. His brother, Samuel, became a Christian about the same time, and married Dorothy Hood by whom he had six children, one of whom, Sarah, married the Rev David Charles, the Welsh Calvinistic minister and hymn-writer. Their daughter Eliza married Robert Davies and became the founder of a family that made a significant contribution to Welsh life. Samuel and Moses set up as jewellers in the town and later they established the Haverfordwest Bank. Samuel's son, Nathaniel, was taken into partnership and succeeded his father as principal in 1812, and remained so until the bank, like many other country banks, crashed in 1826.

31. George Jenkins was a family friend. He was at the Admiral's office and able to assist in the conveyance of mail.

32. Slops were the sailor's clothes and bedding, kept in the ship's store, or slop-shop, on board ship. Sailors and pressed men coming aboard destitute were allowed to purchase to the value of two months' pay, after which they could spend 7 shillings (35p) a month on slops, if they really needed them.

33. Admiral Sir Alan Gardner (1742-1809) was made Admiral of the Blue in 1799 and raised to the peerage as Lord Gardner in 1800. He was appointed commander-in-chief of the coast of Ireland in 1801 and of the Channel Fleet in 1806.

34. HMS *Warrior*, a predecessor of the first iron-clad steam frigate launched on the Thames in 1860 and which remained a hulk on the Daugleddau, near Pembroke Dock, from 1929 until 1979 when it was restored and placed on display at Portsmouth.

35. The Pembrokeshire Militia, first embodied in 1759, entered its third embodiment in 1793 with the outbreak of the French Revolutionary war, under the command of Lieut. Col. John Colby of Ffynnone, and was stationed at Romford and at Yarmouth before proceeding to Languard Fort near Harwich. In 1797 the regiment moved to Bristol and, in April 1799, it embarked for Ireland where it was stationed for six months before returning to Plymouth and then to Cornwall. Colby resigned over a disagreement with his officers and he was succeeded by Lieutenant-Colonel Wm. Henry Scourfield. In June the regiment marched back to west Wales and spent the winter in quarters in Carmarthen and, in March 1801, following the Peace of Amiens, it returned to Haverfordwest to be disembodied. With the resumption of hostilities in 1803 the regiment was again embodied under Major John Mathias and marched to Chelmsford where it was joined by its commanding officer, Lieut. Col. Owen Philipps. It established a headquarters at Colchester and did not return to Haverfordwest until 1813 and it was disembodied once more in the following year, by which time it had become the Royal Pembrokeshire Rifle Corps. George may have heard a misinterpretation of the Colby affair: that he had been 'broke of his commission' (48) rather than that he had resigned.

36. Belle Isle, off the coast of Brittany had been captured by the English in 1759 and returned to France at the end of the Seven Years' War, in 1763. Following Napoleon's victory at Marengo, six thousand men sent to capture *Belle Île* and five thousand sent to Minorca, had to be recalled and put together to go to the aid of the Austrians. George appears to have misread the situation.

37. The question whether it would be 'agreeable to Lord K.' for George to address letters to his sister 'under cover to him' is difficult to explain, but it indicates a connection of sorts between the two families as near neighbours. In his letter of February 13th 1799, he told his sister that he would send his bill for clothes for her to see 'under cover to Lord K.' and, in a postscript to his next letter, he stated that he 'should have put a cover on this to Lord K' but that he was out of paper. There is no further reference to the matter until September 29th 1800 when, in a post script to a letter addressed to his parents, he asked: 'Should be glad to know if it is agreeable to Lord K. for me to address your letters under cover to him yet' and on March 10th 1801, he wrote to Mary stating that he had written to her on the 6th 'under cover to Lord K.' and hoped that she had received it. After the first Lord Kensington had been dead for almost a year, George wrote to say 'I miss Lord K. very much now as I am inclined to write by every post if it was not for the postage.' (76)

38. Ramascastle is Romans' Castle, originally Reymer's Castle, a farm in the parish of Walwyn's Castle.

39. Hannah Green married Jacob Attwood of Bristol.

40. Presumably the same Mr Powell who had persuaded George by his 'discourse that a mere trifle would fit one out' (2).

41. Admiral Sir Hyde Parker (1739-1807), the son of Vice-Admiral Sir Hyde Parker (1714-82), was appointed to command the fleet sent to the Baltic to act against Denmark as one of the Armed Neutrality.

42. Prince Augustus Frederick (1773-1843), sixth son of George III, was made Duke of Sussex in 1801.

43. The Act of Union of Great Britain and Ireland became effective on 1 January 1801.

44. Isle de Barry is a reference to Barry Island farm in the parish of Llanrhian.

45. Nelson had taken part in the battle of Cape St Vincent, where he captured two great Spanish battleships, and was promoted Rear-Admiral but suffered at Santa Cruz, in the Canaries, the following July, when he lost his arm. He was sent to blockade the French squadron at Toulon, but it escaped in thick weather and took Malta and landed Napoleon in Egypt. A week later, in August 1798, Nelson annihilated the squadron at the battle of the Nile, in Aboukir Bay. He was made Vice-Admiral in 1801 and fought at Copenhagen. In 1803 he became commander-in-chief Mediterranean and spent some time with Sir William and Lady Hamilton at Naples, where Sir William was the Envoy Extraordinary. He fell at the battle of Trafalgar in 1805.

46. The yards are the spars slung across the mast to support sail, either horizontal (square yard) or slantwise (lateen yard). Sailors stand along the yards as a form of salute.

47. George refers to the Preliminaries of London whereby Britain agreed to return to their former owners Elba, Malta, Minorca, Tobago, Santa Lucia, Martinique and the Cape of Good Hope, which were substantially reproduced in the Treaty of Amiens.

48. Sir James de Saumarez (1757-1836) was actively involved in the blockade of Brest (1795-96), Cape St Vincent (1797) and the Nile (1798). In 1801, with six ships, he defeated 14 French and Spanish ships off Cadiz. He later commanded the Baltic fleet and was sent to assist the Swedes in 1809. He was raised to the peerage as Lord de Saumarez in 1831.

49. Thomas and Cecil Picton of Poyston had eleven children, the seventh of whom, born in 1758, became General Sir Thomas Picton, and was killed at Waterloo. There were five daughters.

50. Admiral Sir John Thomas Duckworth (1748-1817) took possession of the Danish and Swedish West Indies in 1801. He was commander-in-chief at Jamaica 1803-05 and in 1806 he defeated a French squadron off Santo Domingo. In 1807 he forced the passage of the Dardanelles.

51. John Green, sheriff of Haverfordwest in 1781, died in December 1801.

52. Admiral Sir Thomas Foley, GCB, was born at Ridgeway, Llawhaden, in 1757 and he entered the Navy in 1770.

    He saw action at Finisterre and Gibraltar in 1780, off Toulon in 1793, and at the battle of Cape St Vincent in 1797. In 1798 he led the British fleet into the attack at the Battle of the Nile, and he was Nelson's Flag Captain at Copenhagen in 1801, but illness kept him from the battle of Trafalgar. He was promoted Rear-Admiral in 1808, and admiral in 1825. He was knighted in 1815. He was commander-in-chief of The Downs, and later of Portsmouth where he died in 1833. He received the Freedom of Haverfordwest in July 1802 at the same time as Lord Nelson, at his brother's house, Foley House, Haverfordwest. He married Lucy Anne FitzGerald, youngest daughter of the Duke of Leinster, in 1802, and settled at Abermarlais, Llansadwrn, Carmarthenshire, which he had purchased with his prize money.

53. Admiral Sir George Montagu (1750-1829) saw action at the Leeward Islands and later at Jamaica. He was commander-in-chief Portsmouth in 1803.

54. Pierre Dominique Toussaint L'Ouverture (1746-1803), the Negro revolutionary leader, born a slave, led the slave rising in Haiti and drove out the French and the British and declared independence. Bonaparte, however, proclaimed the re-establishment of slavery, which Toussaint ignored. He was arrested and ended his days in prison in France.

55. The Marines, originally the Duke of York and Albany's Maritime Regiment of Foot established in 1664, became a permanent part of the naval establishment in 1755. The Marines manned part of a ship's armament, as well as providing landing forces. They messed and had quarters apart from the sailors. They were carried in all ships of war and their numbers varied from about 170 officers and men in a First Rate ship, with about 100 guns, to a dozen in command of a sergeant in a 10-gun brig.

56. Colonel Edwardes succeeded his father on his death on 13 December 1801 as second Baron Kensington. As a boy at Haverfordwest, he had been tutored by the Reverend John Tasker Nash before being sent to a private school near Watford. He married Dorothy Patricia, daughter of Richard Thomas, by whom he had six sons and four daughters. He was mayor of Haverfordwest in 1805 and in 1809, and steward of the manor of Fishguard. He succeeded his father as Member of Parliament for the borough of Haverfordwest and appeared to have been an active, though volatile, politician. He was a Lord of the Admiralty in 1806-07 and then he joined the Whigs, but turned again and unsuccessfully endeavoured to regain a place on the Board. By 1818, he was living in Italy and lost his seat to William Henry Scourfield. Fenton commented that Johnston Hall had been let to a tenant since the death of the first baron and regretted that the present nobleman was 'obliged to seek a residence in a neighbouring county', and was of opinion that it was 'a material loss to the Pembrokeshire and a great drawback to his rising popularity'. He had moved to Westmead, Laugharne, where he was known for his philanthropy, particularly to Irish travellers. George enquired whether 'he has been with you yet', presumably wondering whether his lordship now called at the Blue Boar'.

57. The Royal Bucks – the Royal Buckinghamshire Regiment.

58. Cross-writing was written at right-angles to the previous writing in order to make maximum use of the space available. It provided at best an enigma and, with the passage of time, became indecipherable.

59. Stephen George had a farm, presumably in the vicinity of Haverfordwest. George comments on the quality of crops in England, where he is stationed and, in November 1802, he asked whether his father had sown his wheat yet (77). His father ran a chaise in connection with the inn and George enquires whether good use is being made of it (7).

60. Robert Bateman Prust was mayor of Haverfordwest on no less than six occasions between 1790 and 1802. The family had a long association with Haverfordwest and was said to have entertained Cromwell on his visit to the town in July 1648 at their house at the bottom of Barn Street. In 1886 John Higgon reported that 'a grenadier in Cromwell's army, named Prust, grabbed the ruins [of the castle] which being of no value he was allowed to retain and one of his descendants sold the old walls to the County for £300 to turn into a prison.'

61. The colonisation of New South Wales as a penal settlement began in January 1788 under Governor Arthur Philip. In 1790 a second fleet brought a special corps, called the New South Wales Corps, and in 1792 its commandant, Francis Grose, was appointed Lieutenant Governor.

62. A Gauger was an excise-man.

63. The captain of a man-of-war, once he took charge of his ship, had to use his best endeavours to get it manned. When all other means had failed, a press-gang would be sent ashore after dark to raid the dock-side taverns and brothels, or seize any men they could lay their hands on, and take them back to the ship and push them below deck for examination by the captain and the surgeon as to their fitness. Merchant seaman were much sought-after. This method of recruitment was used until the 1830s when pay and conditions improved.

64. Henry Addington (1757-1844) opposed Pitt's Irish policy and, in 1801, he resigned the Speakership to form his own government. He concluded the Peace of Amiens in March 1802. Following the resumption of hostilities in 1804 he resigned in 1804 and the following year he was elevated to the peerage as Viscount Sidmouth and was appointed Lord President of the Council.

65. Anthracite coal mined in the vicinity was transported by cart to Coppet Hall where up to thirty vessels were beached simultaneously, before the harbour was built at Saundersfoot. The quality of the coal was such that it was exported to European countries and even to Hong Kong. George was saving money by crossing the Bristol Channel on a collier but was delayed by the tide. Passengers crossing by the usual Bristol traders were sometimes windbound and delayed in out of the way places, causing anxiety to members of families.

66. A member of the Mends family of Haverfordwest. It is said that Mends, a weaver of Merlin's Bridge, had fourteen sons in the services, several of whom were killed during the French wars. Commodore Robert Mends died of cholera in 1823, while commanding HMS *Owen Glendower*. His brother, Admiral Sir William Bowen Mends (1781-1863), who served under Nelson at Boulogne was the father of Admiral Sir William Robert Mends, GCB, (1812-97) who commanded the Pembrokeshire built frigate HMS *Arethusa*.

67. Haverfordwest Racecourse was laid out in 1727 and race meetings were followed by grand balls held at the Assembly Rooms, later St Mary's Hall, to which ladies were carried in sedan chairs.

68. George, in his statement: 'I shall make you great by addressing this [letter] "Kensingtion Place" agreeable to promise' (94) reveals a little collusion: they must have felt that such an address would be superior to that of the inn. Lord Kensington had a house on Tower Hill, known later, if not then, as Kensington House, near, if not next to, the Blue Boar There is no record of such a street but James addressed a letter to his father on December 10th 1806 at 'Blue Boar Inn, Kensington Place.'

69. Colonel Lord Kensington commanded the Royal Pembrokeshire Corps of Volunteer Infantry, which George may have confused with the Pembrokeshire Militia commanded by Major John Mathias.

70. HMS *Fisgard* was formerly the French frigate *Le Résistance*, one of four ships that landed a force of 1400 French troops at Carreg Wastad, near Fishguard, on February 22nd 1797, an event that George remembered as a seventeen year old boy, and he may have witnessed the troops being mobilised on Castle Square at Haverfordwest, ready to march against the enemy. She was captured on March 9th on her return journey to Brest and renamed *Fisgard*, and joined the Channel fleet under the command of Captain, later Admiral, Sir Byam Martin, in December. She was off Brest in 1798, off Morbihan in 1800 and in Corunna harbour in 1801. Having been paid off in September 1802, a survey suggested that she was not worth repairing but, nevertheless, she was given an extensive refit and came out in September 1803, when George joined her. She left Plymouth on the 20th, under Captain Lord Kerr and sailed with a convoy, arriving at Spithead the next morning. In December she, and *Orpheus*, escorted the Quebec fleet from Oporto to the Downs. She went ashore near Jack-in-the-Basket, off Lymington, where she lay for a couple of days before being released, with little damage. In December she was informed that French troops had embarked along the coast and, with other vessels in Portsmouth harbour, she was ordered to drop down to St Helen's on the Isle of Wight (99). On October 15th 1804 when she was stationed off Cape St Maria, seventy miles east of Cape St Vincent, Kerr received news of the declaration of war with Spain and *Fisgard* captured a number of Spanish vessels valued at £14,000. In April 1805, while cruising off the coast of Gibraltar, she discovered that the French fleet at Toulon, which was being sought by Nelson, had passed through the Straits. (115) Kerr passed the news to Sir John Orde who sent a schooner to England. Later that year, *Fisgard* sailed with convoy from Cork to the West Indies. By 1808 she was commanded by Captain William Boulton and on 1 January in the following year, she took part in the attack on Curaçao, and in July she was one of the an advanced frigates of a fleet that proceeded up the Scheldt estuary. She was paid off in July 1812, completely worn out. In 1814 she was sold out of the service and, five years later, a second *Fisgard*, a 42-gun frigate, was launched at Pembroke. The present HMS *Fisgard*, is a shore establishment for training boy artificers at Torpoint, Cornwall.

71. St Helens, Isle of Wight.

72. The Texel, one of the West Friesian Islands lying between the North Sea and Waddenzee.

73. In 1804, in view of the threat of invasion by the French, Pembrokeshire, like other coastal counties, was additionally defended. Among the 3,000 men reviewed by General Gascoyne on Portfield Racecourse, apart from the Pembroke Yeomanry and ten companies of Lord Kensington's Corps of Volunteers, were the Royal Cornish Miners who had been quartered in Haverfordwest for five months.

74. Admiral Sir John Orde (1751-1824) was commander-in-chief Finisterre, and then Cadiz, and was made Admiral of the Blue in 1805.

75. Lieutenant William Davies, was now serving on HMS *Spartiate*, a French ship taken at Aboukir Bay by Nelosn, that had just come out of dock after a complete repair. Davies had lost George's respect but had managed to retain that of Mary George who sent him stockings. She appears to have agreed to buy 'a gown and gloves against Easter Sunday' – one assumes, as a present for his estranged wife.

76. George had been following his brother's movements as he was aware that the *Britannia* had arrived at Lisbon.

77. Letters of Marque were issued to a privateer authorised to levy war and to be armed and employed in the capture of hostile ships and to seize and sell their property as prize. *Fisgard* captured the *Tigre*, formerly the *Angola* of Liverpool, armed with twelve 18-pounder carronades and two brass guns, on her passage from Cayenne to Cadiz and found the master and crew of an English brig she had captured on board.

78. Droits of Admiralty were the proceeds from the seizure of enemy shipping, formerly belonging to the Court of Admiralty, but now paid into the Exchequer.

79. George was in Madeira, presumably on his way to the West Indies where HMS *Fisgard* may have remained until the following year.

80. George's fears were realised when his brother, James, was pressed in The Downs at Plymouth from the *Britannia* by the boats of HMS *Ariadne*. He wrote to 'a Brother Officer' on that ship seeking his help, but the result is unknown. James was serving on board HMS *Lucifer* by the end of the year.

81. Marloes Court, a farm in the parish of Marloes, Pembrokeshire.

82. The obligation that George laboured under was the financial one, from which, short of capturing a capital prize, he had little hope of finding relief.

83. As holder of 'the honourable post of Caterer', George had great delight in visiting Kingston market, as he had always shown a keen interest in the price of various commodities and in comparing them with those at home.

84. Apart from the one dated January 9th 1806, no letters from John George have survived for that year and therefore his movements are not known. HMS *Surveilllante* captured at Cape Francois, in the West Indies, in 1803, was brought to this country in 1806 and paid off at Deptford. It would appear that George may have served on her for a short time during this period, after he had left *Fisgard* and returned from the West Indies.

85. B. L. Taylor, was a former fellow officer on HMS *Fisgard* who appears to have had a remarkable escape. (121) He was writing off Cape Maisi, on the eastern tip of Cuba, in the Forward Passage..

86. Mona Passage lies between the Dominican Republic and Puerto Rico.

87. Mary George was married at St Martin's Church, Haverfordwest, on February 4th 1806, to John Green, son of John Green, admitted burgess in 1764 and sheriff of 1781 and first named of the nine trustees of the Wesleyan church. He is celebrated as the man who turned away from on John Wesley, when preaching in the street at Haverfordwest, so that Wesley could use his back as a lectern. Wesley's last visit is commemorated on a plaque affixed outside the County Library, close to the site of the Blue Boar Inn. John and Mary had eight children, three of whom died in infancy. Mary (1806-98) married Alfred Jones, Bristol; Anne, born in 1808, appears to have died unmarried; John (1815-78), sheriff 1848, mayor 1876, married Elizabeth Powell; George Morgan (1817-93), and Stephen (1821-99), mayor in 1888 and 1893, both of whom died unmarried. John Green died after a short illness in 1832 and Mary carried on his business as maltster and currier.

88. John Green had purchased a house in Bridge Street, opposite Skinners Lane, in 1806, where he lived with his wife and family. He had taken over his father's business as maltster which was conducted from the house next door.

89. Short Row, a group of eight 15th century houses that stood in the middle of High Street, Haverfordwest.

90. Sir Richard Philipps, Picton Castle (1765-1823) was granted an Irish peerage, as Lord Milford, in 1776. He defeated Lord Kensington, who had also been raised to an Irish peerage in the same year, as Member of Parliament for Haverfordwest in 1784, and in 1786 he obtained the county seat and Kensington was returned to the Haverfordwest seat which he held until his death in 1801.

91. Greenhill was a farm at Merlin's Bridge

92. Limestone quarried in south Pembrokeshire was taken by ship across the Channel to Bideford and George obtained passage on such vessels.

93. S.M. – Sally Mathias.

94. A number of prints were published following the French landing at Fishguard, among them 'A Plan of that part of the County of Pembroke called Pencaer' by Thomas Propert, Land Surveyor.

95. Cove, now spelt Cobh but pronounced 'Cove' and meaning 'haven', was formerly known as the Cove of Cork. It was renamed Queenstown to commemorate Queen Victoria's visit in 1849 but the Irish designation was re-adopted in 1922.

96. Evans of Mabws were farmers in the Mathry area. Farmers along the north Pembrokeshire coast had shares in coastal vessels, which were usually held in 64 shares. Some of the more prosperous farmers owned their own, which were used particularly to carry limestone and anthracite coal from south Pembrokeshire to feed the limekilns and produce lime to fertilise the land.

97. Attwood's, no doubt, was the business in Bristol of Hannah Green's husband (see 39 above).

98. This was the last extant letter written by John George. He was killed in action on board a prize of HMS *Garland* off Jamaica on October 3rd 1808.

99. Admiral Sir William Sydney Smith (1764-1840) aided Admiral Hood in burning the ships and arsenal at Toulon in 1793. He captured Acre in 1799, destroyed the Turkish fleet off Abydos in 1807, and blockaded the Tagus in 1810. The men of the Legion Noire captured at Fishguard were offered as a part of the four thousand prisoners in exchange for the release of Sydney Smith, held by the French in solitary confinement in the Prison du Temple in Paris.

100. Admiral Sir Samuel Hood (1724-1816), raised to the peerage as Viscount Hood, was a brother of Admiral Viscount Bridport. He distinguished himself in the West Indies and directed the occupation of Toulon in 1793.

*

The editor wishes to thank the following for their contributions towards the publication of this book: The Gild of Freemen of Haverfordwest, the Trustees of Sir John Perrot's Charity, the Haverfordwest Town Council, the Haverfordwest Civic Society, Elf Oil Uk Ltd., the Pembrokeshire County Council, Messrs Greens Motors, Mr Malcolm Green, Colonel John Green OBE, DL, Mr J. M. Green, CB, Mrs Richard Horrex; and also to thank Mr Malcolm Green for providing a copy of a manuscript history of the Green family by his father, Mr Stephen Green; to acknowledge the assistance he received from the officers of the National Library of Wales, the Public Record Office, the British Library, the Royal Commission on Historical Manuscripts, the National Register of Archives, the National Maritime Museum, the Royal Naval Museum, the Pembrokeshire Record Office, the Glamorgan Record Office, the Gwent Record Office, the Newport Library and Information Service, the Cardiff Library where Mr J. Brynmor John provided copies of three letters, and the Royal Marines Museum where the Archivist, Mr M. G. Little, went out of his way to prepare copies of 124 letters deposited at his Museum; and to express his gratitude to Gerald Oliver, Anthony James, Lynn Hughes and Anthony Miles for their help; to Judith for her care and, finally, to His Honour Judge Charles Neville Pitchford for his advice and, above all, for having saved the letters.

Index